VEILBORNE

Book One of The Holloway Chronicles

By
Mark Peters

Mark Peters

Copyright © 2025 Mark Peters

All rights reserved.

No part of this publication may be reproduced, stored in a retrieval system, or transmitted in any form or by any means, electronic, mechanical, photocopying, recording, or otherwise, without prior written permission of the copyright owner, except in the case of brief quotations used in reviews or articles.

This is a work of fiction. Names, characters, places, events, and incidents are either products of the author's imagination or are used fictitiously. Any resemblance to actual persons, living or dead, or actual events is purely coincidental.

The author has made every effort to respect the privacy of individuals and to avoid offence. No part of this book is intended to defame, malign, or harm any person, group, organisation, or entity.

Veilborne

Dedication

For Tash, who got me into it—

and then allowed me to follow through with it.

Mark Peters

Table of content

Dedication.. iii
Prologue The Storm 6
Chapter 1 The Thirteenth Winter 11
Chapter 2 Heartbeat in the Hollow 25
Chapter 3 Through the Hollow 38
Chapter 4 Watcher in the Rain 46
Chapter 5 Through the Veil 58
Chapter 6 Awakening at Calendor 68
Chapter 7 A New Dawn in Starfire 87
Chapter 8 The Locket Remembers 103
Chapter 9 Of Echoes and Awakenings 119
Chapter 10 Embers and Echoes 150
Chapter 11 Gilded Horizons 190
Chapter 12 Silent Divides 217
Chapter 13 Between Reflections 230
Chapter 14 Hidden in Plain Sight 237
Chapter 15 Threshold 253
Chapter 16 Veilbreak 265
Chapter 17 The Unraveling Thread 282
Chapter 18 The Council 293
Chapter 19 The Gathering of Houses 302
Chapter 20 Lanterns for the Lost 329
Chapter 21 The Watcher 340
Chapter 22 The Exchange 349

Veilborne

Chapter 23 The Pale Edge 361
Chapter 24 The Price of Loyalty 366
Chapter 25 The Weight of What Remains 381
About the Author 388

Mark Peters

Prologue
The Storm

It was a night to be feared.

The storm rolled over Blackthorn Hollow like a great and restless beast, clawing at the rooftops and howling through the alleyways as if hunting something long denied. Its winds rattled windows and slammed shutters, pressing against the stones of the town as though testing the strength of every wall. Lightning cracked across the sky, casting fractured shadows over chimneys and crooked spires. Thunder followed, the grinding growl of some ancient thing stirred from slumber.

Rain fell in curtains, not drops, sheets that blurred the outlines of buildings and turned the cobbled streets into dark rivers. The salty sting of sea air mingled with the earthy tang of rain-slick slate and moss. Below the cliffs, the ocean surged with fury, hammering the stone like a creature demanding entry, casting white spray high into the swirling clouds above.

Through the twisting veins of the old town moved a solitary figure.

A long, hooded cloak wrapped them entirely, the fabric soaked through and clinging to their frame. Each step was swift, deliberate. They cradled a satchel close to their chest, shielding it from the wind with their body, the way one might guard something precious, or fragile.

Lightning threw their shadow against the walls in sharp bursts. The town's buildings leaned into the lanes as though eavesdropping, their crooked chimneys and steep-pitched roofs looming like watchers in the dark. Many were half-timbered, slathered in pale plaster now streaked with rain, their warped windows glowing faintly from within like half-lidded eyes.

The figure paused beneath a rusted gas lamp that hissed and sputtered in protest. The lamp's dull orange light flickered across old bricks stained black with age. The figure turned slowly, breath fogging in the

Veilborne

cold, eyes scanning the alley behind them. Raindrops drummed on the gutters above and trickled down sloped tiles in narrow streams.

For a heartbeat, the shadows seemed to shift, unnaturally fluid, unnaturally aware.

Were they being followed? Or was it only the storm playing cruel tricks?

Another flash of lightning. Another moment of stillness.

The figure adjusted their grip on the satchel and pressed forward, weaving through the maze of side streets. They passed shuttered windows and sealed cellar doors, through the skeletal iron gate of a crumbling courtyard, until finally,

A crooked wooden sign creaked in the wind.

Morrowmere Orphanage.

The sign was faded, its gold-leaf lettering flaking away, barely legible in the rain. The building itself loomed like a forgotten chapel, tall and narrow, its grey stone façade pocked with lichen and worn by time and weather. Ivy clawed its way up one side of the frame, strangling an old wrought-iron lantern long since broken.

A slate-tiled roof pitched steeply above, its eaves sagging under the weight of storm and age. Most of the windows were shuttered. One glowed faintly through drawn curtains, a lone flicker of warmth in the chill of the night.

The figure stepped beneath the overhang and looked down.

Raindrops clattered against the stone doorstep. The satchel shifted gently in their arms. A tiny sigh escaped from within.

The figure raised a hand, gloved, trembling, and knocked. Once.

Twice.

Nothing.

The third knock was louder. Desperate. A sound that echoed like a challenge hurled at the storm itself.

Still, no answer.

The figure stood in silence a moment longer, staring at the door.

****

Within the orphanage, a dim oil lamp flickered to life, casting a sickly orange glow down a narrow corridor lined with dark wood panelling and old paintings dulled by dust and age. Footsteps approached, practical, slow, and irritated.

The woman who emerged wore a deep navy shawl that didn't quite conceal her sharp frame or sharper frown. Her greying hair was coiled tightly into a no-nonsense bun, every strand in place, her face carved with the kind of perpetual scowl that sent children scurrying before she spoke a word.

Miss Wren.

Warden of Morrowmere for nearly three decades.

She muttered as she reached the latch. "No one knocks this late 'less they want something… or they're bringing trouble with 'em."

With a grunt, she unlatched the door and cracked it open.

The wind surged in immediately, carrying the scent of sea, smoke, and storm.

On the step sat a soaked satchel. No note. No name. No sign of whoever had knocked.

Miss Wren squinted out into the street. Empty.

She bent down, lifted the satchel, and froze.

It was heavy. And warm.

Her expression flickered.

She shut the door quickly, bolted it with a practised twist, and carried the bundle down a side corridor into a dim parlour. The furniture was old but clean, the hearth dark, the shelves sparse save for a few tins of tea and a cracked clock that hadn't chimed in years.

Veilborne

Miss Wren placed the bundle gently on the worn sofa, beside a ragged stuffed bear abandoned by some long-departed child, the cushions still shaped by a forgotten guest. She began to unwrap it, layer by layer.

Rain-slick cloth gave way to wool, then to soft, silken swaddling. Finally,

A sleeping infant.

Tiny. Pale. Peaceful. Her cheeks were flushed with warmth, not cold. Wisps of dark hair clung to her forehead, curling at the temples like half-formed question marks.

And nestled in her impossibly small hand was a silver locket.

Miss Wren leaned closer, breath catching in her throat. Her eyes narrowed at the sight of it.

The locket was oval, no larger than a thumbprint, but shimmered with a soft, unnatural sheen. Fine engravings curled across its edges: spiral lines, starbursts, constellations. Runes. Older than ink. Older than memory. Symbols Miss Wren had seen only once, long ago, in the margins of a book she should never have opened.

At its centre sat a pale-blue gem, milky, opalescent. Like a frozen teardrop.

She reached out, fingers trembling now, not from cold, but from something older, deeper, as she moved to pry it gently from the child's grasp.

The moment her fingers brushed the chain, a crack split the air.

The locket recoiled, snapping back into the baby's fist with a sudden, unnatural force. Not reflex. Not instinct. Something else.

Something guarding.

Miss Wren jerked her hand back, heart hammering.

The baby stirred but didn't wake.

The locket settled once more against her chest, its gem pulsing faintly. Once. Then again. A soft, steady rhythm. Like a heartbeat in metal.

Wren's breath shook. She studied the child for a long moment, her gaze tracing the familiar line of the brow, the sharp cheekbones still softened by infancy.

"My god…" she whispered, memories long buried rising painfully to the surface. "You look just like her."

A beat passed.

Then, lower, softer, less a question than a memory returning:

"…Clara."

She drew the swaddling tighter, cradled the baby in her arms, and turned towards the parlour window, where the storm still beat against the glass with wild insistence.

Behind her, the lamp flickered.

And outside, far beyond the gate at the edge of the street, a pair of pale, watchful eyes stared through the storm, patient and unblinking, before vanishing into the darkness with a final flash of lightning.

Then disappeared with the thunder.

Veilborne

Chapter 1
The Thirteenth Winter

Thirteen was supposed to feel different.

Clara Holloway lay wide-eyed beneath a threadbare blanket, her breath misting in the cold morning air. The ceiling above was cracked and mottled with stains, watermarks that spread like bruises across old plaster. Pale light crept through the warped windowpane beside her cot, casting a faint silver glow across the dormitory. Outside, the first whispers of dawn stirred in the sky, but the warmth of day had yet to arrive.

Her body ached from the chill seeping through the stone walls of Morrowmere Orphanage, and still, she hadn't slept. She'd counted the cracks in the ceiling. Traced the shapes of shadows. Wondered, again and again, whether this birthday would feel any different from the twelve that had come before.

It didn't.

She turned her head, but the room was already empty. The other cots stood in quiet disarray, blankets thrown back, pillows dented, the scent of sleep still lingering in the air. Breakfast had already started. She was alone. And late.

The dormitory smelled of old wood, damp stone, and soot. A single iron stove in the corner stood cold and empty, long since burned out in the night.

Clara reached beneath the collar of her nightdress and closed her fingers around the one thing that had never left her side.

The locket.

Smooth, silver, and warm from her skin. She traced the spirals etched into its surface, tiny swirls that looped like curling vines and stars. A pale-blue gem was set into the centre, faintly milky in the gloom. She had never seen it open. Never found a clasp, or seam, or mechanism. It simply… was.

Mark Peters

Her earliest memories were of holding it. Clutching it when she was frightened or lonely. Miss Wren had tried to take it once, long ago. The chain had pulled taut, then snapped back into her fist like it had a will of its own.

Clara had never let anyone touch it since.

She sat up slowly, brushing strands of dark hair from her face. The cold bit at her legs through the thin cotton of her nightdress. Her hair, long, black, and usually untamed, hung past her shoulders in soft waves, framing a face made of sharp angles and steady eyes. Her pale skin stood out starkly in the dim light.

They always said she had a fox's face, clever, pointed, always watching.

She didn't mind the comparison.

Swinging her legs over the side of the cot, she placed her bare feet on the icy floorboards, flinching as the cold bit in.

Clara crossed to the window and peered through the warped glass.

Below, Blackthorn Hollow sloped toward the harbour, its crooked rooftops just beginning to catch the dawn. Mist clung to buildings like cobwebs, curling between chimneys and drifting across narrow lanes. Fishing boats bobbed in the tide, moored tightly to the wharf. Gulls wheeled above, their cries muffled by the glass.

A typical morning. Bleak. Grey. Still.

Clara rested her forehead against the pane.

Another birthday in the Hollow.

Another year without answers.

She dressed quickly in the half-light, pulling on the uniform every girl in Morrowmere wore, an ash-grey dress with a frayed collar, the elbows patched more times than she could count. Over it, she laced a worn bodice the colour of old slate, the fabric stiff from years of washing and repairs. Her fingers worked fast, though the cold made them clumsy.

Veilborne

Her shoes, scuffed and peeling at the heels, waited beneath the cot. She slipped them on with practiced care, wiggling her toes to find where the lining had come loose. One sole flapped when she walked, no matter how often she tried to fix it. Miss Wren never replaced anything unless it was completely beyond saving.

As she knelt to tuck the laces in, the dormitory door creaked.

Clara froze.

Three figures blocked the entry, silhouetted in the glow of a guttering hallway lantern. The lead girl stepped forward, a smirk tugging at her lips.

Elsie.

She always looked too polished for the Hollow, long flaxen braid, pressed bodice, chin tilted like she'd been born to better things. Her eyes glittered with cold amusement. Behind her were Mina and Ruth, always present, always quiet unless prompted to laugh.

"You're up early," Elsie said, her voice syrupy and mocking. "Couldn't sleep through the sound of rats in your sheets?"

Clara straightened without answering.

Mina and Ruth snickered behind their hands.

Elsie sauntered closer, arms folded. "Or maybe… it's a special day." She drew the words out like a game, her gaze narrowing. "Thirteen now, aren't you?"

Clara's stomach dropped.

"Orphanage girls don't get birthdays, Holloway," Elsie added, tapping Clara's chin lightly with one finger. "Nobody's lighting candles for you."

Clara flinched but held her ground.

"I wasn't bothering anyone," she muttered.

"You exist. That's usually enough."

Clara stepped sideways, slipping past Elsie's shoulder with her head down. The hallway beyond was cold, the lanterns barely lit. She didn't look back.

Their laughter followed her like footsteps.

The hallway outside was colder than the room she'd left. The stone walls, slick with the Hollow's constant sea mist, leached warmth from her skin. Candle sconces flickered along the corridor, their weak flames casting gold and shadow across iron pipework that clung to the ceiling like veins.

The scent of old wax, damp stone, and something faintly metallic filled the air, coppery, like rust or dried blood.

Morrowmere always smelled like that.

No matter the season. No matter how hard the girls scrubbed.

Clara's footsteps echoed softly as she descended the narrow stairwell.

She didn't rush. She never did.

The dining hall was already full when she entered. Dozens of children hunched over long wooden benches, their heads low, spoons clinking dully against tin bowls. The hearth at the far end coughed up more smoke than heat, the flames barely alive beneath a heap of blackened logs.

Clara joined the back of the breakfast line.

From the front of the room, Miss Wren watched like a hawk carved from stone. She stood tall despite her age, draped in a shawl so dark it seemed to swallow the candlelight. Her iron-grey hair was coiled tight, not a strand out of place. Her lips were fixed in a permanent scowl. Her eyes missed nothing.

"Late," she said coolly as Clara passed.

"I," Clara began, but Miss Wren turned away before she could finish.

She took her bowl in silence.

The porridge was grey. Always grey. Slightly burnt, always thin.

Veilborne

She carried it to the farthest table and sat alone.

Spoons scraped. Voices murmured.

At the other end of the hall, Elsie and her shadows giggled behind cupped hands. Clara didn't need to look. She could feel their eyes on her, sharp, amused, waiting.

Just like always.

She kept her gaze on the bowl, forcing herself to eat slowly. The porridge tasted like boiled dust, but it was warm, and warmth was rare here.

Above the clatter of breakfast, the hearth crackled and spat. Bits of ash drifted lazily into the air like snowflakes, catching the firelight in brief flickers before vanishing.

Clara's hand drifted unconsciously to her chest, to the locket hidden beneath the fabric of her bodice. Her fingers found its familiar shape through the cloth.

Still closed. Still silent.

But today... something about it felt different.

Like a sound just beyond hearing.

A breath before thunder.

A pull beneath her skin.

After breakfast, routine returned like clockwork.

Clara was assigned to scrub the main stairwell, a chore as thankless as it was exhausting. The steps, worn smooth by years of boots and buckets, were slick with grime and cold to the touch. Kneeling on the stone chilled her through the knees of her dress. She dipped her rag into a battered pail and began the slow, silent work of scrubbing each riser one by one.

The water turned grey almost instantly.

The scent of soap and wet wool filled her nose, sharp, bitter. Her fingers, already cracked from the cold, stung as they worked over rough stone. Still, she said nothing. Just kept her head down. Let the rhythm of the task carry her forward.

She tried not to think about the day. Or the year that had passed. Or the locket, still warm against her skin.

A loud footstep made her pause.

Elsie.

She descended the stairs with deliberate grace, her boots clicking louder than necessary on the freshly cleaned stone. Her eyes never left Clara. That smirk played again at the corners of her mouth.

Then,

A kick.

Her heel caught the pail and sent it tumbling. Soapy water sloshed across the steps, soaking Clara's knees and undoing all her work in seconds.

"Oh no," Elsie cooed, her voice thick with mock concern. "Clumsy you."

Clara's jaw clenched. The icy water seeped through her skirt, stealing her breath.

Above, Mina and Ruth giggled from the landing. A moment later, their laughter echoed down the hall as they slipped away like ghosts.

Clara sat still for a long moment, hands curled into fists, the rag dripping in her lap.

It wasn't just the spilled water. Or the ruined work. Or even the sting of humiliation.

It was the way this always happened.

No matter how quiet she stayed.

No matter how much she kept to herself.

Her fingers brushed the locket again. It pulsed faintly now, like a heartbeat buried deep in metal.

Veilborne

Or maybe she was only imagining it.

Maybe it was just the cold.

Maybe it was her own pulse, echoing in her chest.

By midday, the storm outside had thickened into a dull drizzle, streaking the orphanage windows with grey. Indoors, the cold had sunk deeper into the bones of the building.

Clara's next task took her to the portrait gallery on the second floor, a long, creaking corridor lined with frames that seemed older than the orphanage itself.

She hated this hallway.

Not because it was drafty. Or dark.

Or haunted by the groans of old wood.

But because the paintings never blinked.

Why would they?

Gilded frames lined both walls, each holding the yellowed likeness of some long-dead benefactor or former headmaster. Their oil-painted eyes followed her with unnatural stillness as she moved down the corridor, feather duster clutched in reddened hands.

The children whispered about these portraits after lights-out.

How some were cursed.

How one boy had once gone missing near them.

How, if you stared too long, you might see them move.

Clara didn't believe any of that.

But today... she paused beneath the largest one.

A severe-looking woman with iron-grey hair sat stiff-backed in a velvet chair, her hands folded atop a ledger in her lap. Her painted eyes were sunken and hard.

Clara stared up at her.

"Do you know who I am?" she whispered.

Her voice barely carried in the hush.

The portrait said nothing, of course.

Clara looked away quickly and brushed dust from the nearby frame. Her throat felt tight.

None of them knew. Not the staff. Not the children.

Maybe not even Miss Wren.

She was just a girl with a locket and a name that didn't come with answers, left on the doorstep like a secret no one claimed.

But someone had.

Once.

Maybe.

Her hand drifted to the locket again.

Still pulsing. Still warm. Still silent.

Late in the afternoon, Clara was sent to the cellar, tasked with hauling buckets of black fuel to the kitchen's tired hearth.

The stairs groaned as she descended, and the air grew colder with each step. Down here, the walls sweated moisture, and old tools lined the shelves like forgotten bones.

The cellar floor was uneven, made of packed earth and cracked stone. The lanterns on the walls sputtered with dying flames, their light barely reaching the corners. Cobwebs dangled like lace from the exposed beams.

The coal heap waited in a rusted bin near the back wall, piled high and glittering faintly in the dim.

Clara grabbed a dented bucket and began shoveling.

Dust filled her throat. Her arms ached.

But she worked quickly, eager to escape the weight of the dark.

Veilborne

Halfway through her second trip, she paused, bucket in hand, and glanced around.

Something was... off.

The cellar was always quiet. Dead quiet.

But now, she could feel something.

A tremor. A flutter just beneath her skin.

Her free hand flew to her chest.

The locket was vibrating.

Not much. Just a tiny tremble. But it was there, faint and rhythmic, like the flutter of a bird's wing trapped beneath her ribs.

She froze.

Then, just as quickly as it began, the vibration stopped.

Clara stood still for a long moment, surrounded by shadow and dust, the bucket heavy in her hand.

She looked down at her chest, then shook her head.

Maybe it was just the cold.

Maybe it was nothing.

But her breath came faster, and the hairs on her arms stood up.

She finished loading the coal in silence, her mind racing.

When she returned to the kitchen, her fingers were black with soot and trembling slightly.

No one noticed.

Evening fell like a heavy curtain, slow and suffocating.

The wind off the sea howled louder now, rattling the orphanage windows and sighing through the cracks in the old stone walls. Candlelight flickered in iron sconces, throwing restless shadows across the corridors.

Clara sat alone on a wooden bench in the narrow hallway outside the common room.

The others had gone inside, to read, to play, to crowd near the struggling hearth, where flames danced low over blackened logs.

No one invited her to join.

Not that she expected them to.

She pulled her coat tighter around herself. The rough wool did little to keep the chill from settling into her bones. Her knees ached from scrubbing, her shoulders from hauling coal. Her stomach grumbled, though dinner had long passed.

Another birthday come and gone, without a single word.

No nod. No smile. No moment spared.

She hadn't expected more.

But that didn't make it hurt any less.

Clara wiped at her eyes with the back of her sleeve, quick and rough. No one was looking. But still, just in case.

Above her, the old walls creaked with the restless shift of wind and settling wood. The building groaned like something half-asleep, tired from bearing the weight of so many forgotten children.

Clara glanced toward the hallway window. Beyond the warped glass, the mist had thickened. The town below was gone from view. Only the sea remained, endless and dark and unknowable.

She sat there a long time, watching candlelight flicker across stone, trying not to feel too much.

Clara had nearly dozed off sitting upright when she heard the soft creak of the hallway door.

A long shadow stretched across the stone floor.

Miss Wren.

Veilborne

The matron's silhouette stood motionless for a moment. Then her voice, quieter than usual, broke the silence.

"Get up, Holloway."

Clara blinked and stood quickly, startled.

Had someone said something? Was this about the locket?

She followed without question, bare feet whispering against the cold floor as Miss Wren led her down the corridor. The orphanage was quieter than usual, only the distant wind and the occasional groan of old beams overhead.

They stopped at the door to the matron's office.

It was a room Clara had entered only a handful of times, never under good circumstances.

Miss Wren opened it and stepped aside.

The room was dimly lit by a single oil lamp on the desk.

Ledgers and ink bottles were stacked neatly along the shelves.

The window behind the desk was silvered with frost.

A small, slightly threadbare rug covered the floor, and a ticking clock marked the seconds in slow rhythm.

Wren gestured to the chair opposite her desk.

Clara sat, stiff-backed, uncertain.

Without a word, Miss Wren opened a drawer and pulled out a small object wrapped in wax paper.

A cupcake.

It was slightly lopsided, the frosting smudged, and the single candle jammed in the top leaned as if it didn't want to stay upright.

Clara's mouth parted, but no sound came out.

From the other drawer, Miss Wren retrieved a matchbox. With a brisk flick, she struck a match and lit the candle.

The tiny flame flared, casting a soft glow that felt strangely out of place in the cold, grey office.

Wren's mouth pressed into its usual stern line, but her eyes, just for a flicker, softened.

"Blow out the candle," she said. "Make a wish."

Clara stared at it. The warmth of it. The sheer absurdity and beauty of it.

No one had ever given her anything like this. Not ever.

She knew what to wish for.

She'd always known.

Leaning forward, she closed her eyes, and blew.

The flame vanished in a twist of smoke.

Miss Wren stood, already brushing past the moment.

"Don't leave crumbs in the bedding," she said briskly.

"And don't go getting used to this."

Clara nodded quickly, cradling the cupcake like it might dissolve if she breathed too hard.

Wren opened the office door and stepped aside.

"Go on."

Clara stepped into the hallway, the candle still faintly warm between her fingers.

Back beneath her blanket, Clara sat upright in bed, the covers pulled over her lap to shield what she held.

The cupcake.

The candle had long since gone out, leaving behind a blackened wick and a curl of wax hardened into the frosting. The paper wrap crinkled beneath her fingers, soft with steam, still faintly warm from the office.

She stared at it as if it might vanish.

Veilborne

It was small. A little lopsided. The icing had slid slightly to one side. But it was real. Tangible. Hers.

Clara's stomach clenched.

She wanted to eat it. Every crumb.

But another part of her wanted to hide it. To keep it, just to prove something good had once been given to her.

What if Elsie found it tomorrow? Or Ruth? Or Mina?

They'd mock it. Or steal it. Or worse, laugh at the idea that Clara Holloway had a birthday anything at all.

She hesitated.

Then, slowly, with reverent care, she peeled away the paper wrapping.

She took the tiniest bite.

The sweetness bloomed across her tongue like sunlight through fog, rich and buttery, unlike anything the kitchens ever served. It tasted like something meant for someone else. Someone wanted.

She ate slowly. Thoughtfully. Each bite smaller than the last.

And then, she felt it.

A warmth beneath her collar. Steady. Rhythmic.

The locket.

It pulsed again, faintly, just once. Then again.

Like a heartbeat. Like someone knocking softly from the inside.

Clara pressed a hand to it, startled. The gem at its center felt almost alive, as though catching the echo of something just out of reach.

She stared down at it, the final crumbs of cupcake resting on her skirt.

"I don't understand you," she whispered.

But something in her chest... loosened. Just a little.

She lay back slowly, pulling the blanket up to her chin, her fingers curled lightly around the chain.

Mark Peters

The wind battered the window again, howling against the glass like a restless spirit.

But Clara felt a quiet warmth, something small and steady she hadn't known she was missing.

She closed her eyes.

And slept.

Chapter 2
Heartbeat in the Hollow

The rain had returned in the early hours—soft, steady, cold.

Outside the frost-rimmed dormitory windows, Blackthorn Hollow lay quiet beneath a veil of mist. The sea beyond was hidden, swallowed by low clouds. Grey light crept through the warped glass panes, casting pale ribbons across cracked stone walls.

Clara Holloway stirred beneath her blanket, blinking at the ceiling above her cot. The chill was familiar, but today something else prickled at the edges of her thoughts—something quiet and strange.

She sat up slowly.

Her fingers found the chain at her neck and traced it beneath her nightdress to the locket resting against her skin.

It was warm.

Not hot. Not glowing. Just… warm. Like someone had held it for a long time.

Then she felt it—a gentle thrum, faint but steady, like a second heartbeat ticking beneath her own.

Clara clutched the locket, her heart fluttering.

It wasn't humming. It wasn't glowing.

But it felt alive.

For a long moment she sat in silence, watching the fog stretch its fingers across the windowpanes. She didn't dare move. The dormitory remained still—breaths soft, beds undisturbed. The other girls had yet to wake.

It's happening again, she thought. First last night… now this.

She didn't know what it meant. Only that it wasn't nothing.

The locket's rhythm stayed soft and consistent—too steady, too real to be imagined.

Clara swallowed and pulled her blanket tighter, shifting toward the edge of the bed.

She didn't feel different. Not really. But today, the world felt like it was tilting—just a little, just enough.

And she was starting to notice.

She dressed in silence.

Her hands moved through the motions out of habit—threading her arms into the same faded woollen dress, tightening the worn bodice, pulling her hair into a low braid that always came loose before noon. Her shoes, softened by years of wear, slipped on with ease. The flapping heel still hadn't been fixed.

The locket never left her neck. She tucked it carefully beneath her collar, the warmth still there, subtle but steady. Each time she moved, she felt its rhythm brush against her skin like a whisper.

She didn't know why, but it made her nervous. Not afraid exactly, but wary—like something inside her was waiting for the other shoe to drop.

The corridors were quieter than usual as she descended the creaking stairs toward the dining hall. Candles flickered low in iron sconces, wax pooling in lazy drips down the stems. Damp clung to the plaster walls like it had no intention of leaving.

In the dining hall, the usual clatter of bowls and chatter was muted.

Clara took her tray and sat in her usual corner—a seat the others rarely bothered with. The bench was colder there, near the cracked window that never quite shut.

She ate slowly. The porridge was thinner than usual, almost translucent. She barely tasted it anyway.

Across the room, no one looked at her.

Elsie's usual table was missing its queen bee. Mina and Ruth sat stiffly, whispering about something that made them glance toward the door

Veilborne

more than once. But Clara kept her eyes down. No Elsie meant a temporary peace—though it didn't feel right.

She glanced toward the high windows. The grey light had barely shifted. Another dreary morning in a world that hadn't changed... except for her.

The locket pulsed faintly beneath her layers, steady as the ticking of the grandfather clock in Miss Wren's office.

Clara pushed her spoon through the last of the porridge, then stood, tray in hand, already dreading the day ahead.

She could feel it in her bones—something was coming.

And the locket knew it too.

The stairs to the coal cellar groaned beneath Clara's steps.

She held the coarse burlap sack close to her chest, the rough weave scratching her arms as she descended into the dimness below. Cold air curled up from the floor like breath from a sleeping giant—damp and heavy with the bitter scent of coal dust and wet stone.

A single lantern hung near the door, its flame wavering with each draft slipping in from above. It cast long, twitching shadows across the cellar's arched ceiling and the heaped piles of coal rising like black dunes.

Clara didn't mind the cellar. It was quiet. Forgotten.

She crouched near the pile, scooping coal into the sack, her fingers already smudged with soot. Each clink of coal sounded sharper in the silence.

And then—footsteps.

A slow scuffing on the stairs.

She froze.

Three shadows stretched across the wall. Familiar shapes.

Elsie. Mina. Ruth.

"Thought you could hide down here all day?" Elsie's voice curled through the air, smug and mean.

Clara stood, brushing coal dust from her knees. "Can't I get just one day without you annoying me? Just let me do my work in peace."

Mina stepped into the lantern light, arms crossed. "You've been acting even weirder since yesterday."

"She's still got that locket," Ruth said, nodding toward Clara's collar. "No one's ever gotten it off her. Not Wren. Not us. Not even Elsie that one time with the scissors."

"That was different," Mina muttered. "We thought it was just stuck."

"Well, maybe it isn't," Ruth said, eyes narrowing. "Maybe she's the one keeping it there."

Clara instinctively brought a hand to her chest. "Leave it alone."

Elsie descended the last step, her boots crunching into stray pieces of coal. "Funny how no one's ever been able to take it off you, isn't it? Not even Wren."

"Maybe it's cursed," Mina whispered, eyes wide in mock fright.

"Maybe she is," Elsie sneered.

Clara backed away, bumping into the coal bin behind her. The locket thudded against her sternum—its pulse quickening.

"I said leave it," she warned, voice firmer this time.

"Oh, please. It's just a necklace."

Elsie stepped closer. "If it won't come off… maybe we break it instead."

Clara twisted away, but Ruth grabbed her wrist.

"Stop it!" Clara yelled, struggling. "Leave me alone!"

Mina grabbed at her arm.

Then Elsie's hand curled around the locket's chain.

Veilborne

And the locket reacted.

With a sound like a stone dropping into deep water, the silver pendant flared hot against Clara's skin—white light bursting outward in a sudden pulse of raw energy.

BOOM.

The wave of energy slammed into all three girls like rag dolls, sending them sprawling backward into the coal bins. Black dust exploded into the air, thick and choking. The lantern swung wildly, casting frantic, trembling shadows that danced like spirits desperate to escape the gloom.

Clara dropped to her knees, clutching the locket. It throbbed fiercely beneath her palm—fast, urgent, impossibly alive.

A deep hum echoed low in her bones, a distant bell tolling far beneath the earth's crust. For a fleeting moment, her vision blurred, a pale glow flickering faintly behind her eyelids like moonlight caught in glass. The air rippled with a whisper of silver smoke—ethereal, fleeting. Then—silence.

Stillness.

The cellar was thick with swirling coal dust, the air heavy and stale. Clara coughed, blinking through the haze.

Elsie, Mina, and Ruth scrambled to their feet, faces smeared with soot, eyes wide with shock and fear.

"You're a freak," Elsie spat, voice trembling with venom. "A freak!"

Without looking back, they bolted—racing up the stairs and into the daylight, their footsteps echoing sharp and hurried.

Clara remained kneeling in the soot, heart hammering, hands trembling.

The locket's furious pulse slowed, settling back into its gentle rhythm—like the dying echoes of a storm's roar.

She was alone.

But not the same.

The dust clung stubbornly to her sleeves for the rest of the day. No matter how hard Clara scrubbed, it settled in the folds of her dress, beneath her fingernails, lingering in the silence that followed her every step.

By midday, the whispers began.

Not the usual snickers or sneers from Elsie's circle. This was something colder—avoidance, edged with fear.

In the chapel wing, as Clara passed the windows with her dustpan and rag, the other children shrank away, like shadows recoiling from flame. No one met her eyes. No one handed her the soap when she reached out. No one spoke.

Even the little ones—who once tugged at her sleeves or asked for help tying boots—turned their faces down, staring at the floor.

As if she'd sprouted fangs overnight.

Clara forced herself to focus on her chores—the rhythm of scrubbing, wiping, polishing—but the world felt askew. Her ears strained for every hushed word trailing behind her.

"…light, I swear…"

"…it knocked them across the room…"

"…dangerous…"

But the word that scraped beneath her skin like a hidden splinter, repeated again and again, was one she couldn't escape:

Freak.

She heard it hissed in the laundry room. Felt it crawl behind her in the hallway. Even Ruth flinched when their shoulders nearly brushed.

And Elsie?

She said nothing.

No glare. No insult.

Veilborne

Just distance.

Clara might have preferred cruelty.

At supper, she ate silently. Alone. A bowl of thin, cooling stew sat before her, untouched on either side by company. The hall was crowded—voices humming low and suspicious.

"…shouldn't be here…"

"…unnatural…"

"…witch…"

Her spoon scraped the wooden bowl, the only sound she made.

The locket pulsed faintly at her chest—steady but subdued—like it, too, was withdrawing, watching and waiting.

She barely tasted the broth. Her stomach churned with unease.

Miss Wren said nothing. No reprimands, no warnings to the others. Just tired eyes that watched from the front, unreadable and distant.

That night, the storm returned.

Rain tapped at the dormitory windows—soft, persistent, like fingers drumming glass. But the rhythm grew heavier as darkness deepened, until it was relentless, alive.

The wind howled low and mournful, curling around the orphanage walls and sneaking through every crack.

The dormitory felt colder.

Clara curled beneath her blanket, lying on her side, knees drawn tight. The others were asleep, breathing soft and even. Some muttered in dreams.

No one had spoken to her since supper.

She blinked at the cracked ceiling above her cot, tracing its familiar web of fractures.

Thirteen had come and gone with the storm. It was meant to mean something. Instead, it left her lonelier than before.

The locket pressed warm and rhythmic against her collarbone. Its pulse faint, softer than before—but still there. Still watching.

She laid a hand over it and closed her eyes.

At least it didn't feel wrong. Just alert.

She fought the rising tide of thoughts—the cellar, the stares, Miss Wren's silence. Surely the girls had run straight to her—crying, shouting, coated in coal dust. Why hadn't Clara been called in? Not for cake this time... but for questions, for punishment, for something.

Still, the questions churned loudly in the quiet.

Somewhere deep in the building, a door creaked.

The wind rose again—louder now. Thunder rolled, distant and low, over the cliffs.

Clara tucked the blanket tighter around her chin.

Then she heard it.

A sound that did not belong.

A scream.

High, panicked, tearing through the walls like a nightmare's ragged cry.

She sat bolt upright.

Another scream—closer.

The dormitory stirred—girls shifted in their beds, blinking awake.

"What was that?" a whisper.

"From the west wing," another guessed.

Then—a crash.

Wood splintering. Glass shattering.

The air changed.

Beneath the chaos, Clara caught another sound.

Veilborne

Chittering.

Faint at first—a dry rasping, like insect legs scraping wood.

Then footsteps—slow, deliberate—moving down the hallway beyond the dormitory door.

Heavy. Dragging.

Her stomach dropped icy cold.

Without thinking, she slipped from her bed and crawled beneath it, heart pounding fiercely.

She folded herself into the tightest space she could find, hands pressed over her mouth. The locket thumped against her ribs like a war drum.

Screams shattered the night again—shrill, scattered.

Something sharp scraped across the timber floor—slow, deliberate.

Then the door creaked.

Soft. Long. Wrong.

The dormitory door opened.

And something stepped inside.

From her hiding place, Clara saw only shadows.

But even shadows told stories.

The lantern flickered weakly in the hallway, casting trembling fingers of gold.

And there—silhouetted against the light—a shape.

Slender. Wrong.

Its arms hung too long.

Its legs jerked with an unnatural rhythm, joints clicking like bones grinding in empty sockets.

It twitched as it stepped inside, then paused.

Listening.

The chittering returned—louder now—echoing sharp and brittle against the wood. It wasn't speech. Too jagged. Too wrong. It scraped through Clara's mind like claws scratching glass.

The creature's feet slid silently across the dormitory floor. Each clawed toe clicked softly, a sinister metronome. Its skin was pale—almost translucent—like candle wax left to melt beneath the unforgiving sun. And its eyes... gods, its eyes.

Sunken. Hollow. Burning with a sickly white-blue light that pierced the darkness like lanterns turned inward, scanning the room with cold, merciless hunger.

Clara held her breath.

The girls around her stirred—whimpering in sleep, shifting—but none yet aware of the thing gliding silently between their beds.

The creature moved toward the center of the room.

It stopped beside her cot.

Her heart slammed against her ribs as if trying to escape. She pressed herself flat against the floor, fingers trembling, the locket searing hot against her chest.

The creature's skeletal hand reached out—and gripped the bedframe.

The wood groaned under its grip.

The chittering rose, harsher now, like a thousand nails scraping stone.

It leaned forward. Clara glimpsed its head—tilted, upside down just beyond the mattress slats—sniffing, listening. Its mouth was a jagged rift of uneven teeth, lips pulled back in a grotesque mask somewhere between hunger and curiosity.

It knew.

Then the hand slid from the bedframe.

And gripped the floor beneath her.

Clara squeezed her eyes shut.

Veilborne

Crash!

The bed was hurled across the dormitory, splintering into shards as it slammed against the far wall.

Girls screamed—wide awake now—as others scrambled from their cots, panic flooding the room.

But Clara was already moving.

The locket surged.

A burst of white light exploded from her chest—blinding, raw—flaring outward in a sudden halo of brilliance.

The creature shrieked—a piercing, keening wail like iron scraping iron—and staggered back, claws raised to shield its glowing eyes.

Clara didn't wait.

She ran.

Barefoot, breath ragged, heart hammering like war drums.

She fled from the room into the corridor beyond—just as more screams erupted down the hall.

Behind her, beds overturned. Lanterns shattered. Children scattered like startled birds.

But Clara didn't dare look back.

The corridor was unrecognizable.

Doors swung wildly on broken hinges. Shards of glass crunched beneath her feet. Somewhere behind her, a creature howled—a long, hollow sound, like wind moaning through a crypt.

The storm outside had fully arrived. Rain lashed the windows in furious sheets. Thunder boomed overhead, shaking the walls.

Clara rounded a corner and nearly collided with another orphan—Tessa, barely seven—frozen in the hall, sobbing quietly.

Before Clara could reach her, one of the creatures lurched out of the shadows.

"Run!" Clara screamed.

But the girl stayed rooted, trembling.

The creature paused, sniffed the air, searching.

Clara's locket pulsed fiercely.

The creature snapped its head toward her.

It wasn't after the girl.

It was hunting *her*.

Clara backed away slowly, then spun and bolted, breath ragged, heart threatening to burst.

She passed the dormitory again—now chaos incarnate. Beds overturned, blankets smoldering with magical backlash. Girls screamed, hiding beneath furniture or clutching each other.

She heard Elsie sobbing somewhere. Mina praying.

Then the thunderous crash of another door buckling inward.

The creatures were spreading.

Clara raced for the main stairwell. Every step grew heavier, the air thicker, her legs burning. Bare feet numb and bruised from the cold and running.

Down the steps.

Through shadows.

Into the front hall.

There, sprawled like a broken marionette at the base of the staircase, lay Miss Wren.

Clara skidded to a halt.

The matron's eyes stared blankly at the ceiling. Hair clung wet to her cheeks. Her shawl slipped to the side, one pale hand outstretched toward the front door.

Veilborne

A frost had begun to crawl from her skin—delicate patterns of ice spreading across the stone like lace woven from winter itself.

Clara's throat tightened.

"I'm sorry," she whispered.

Behind her, a chittering growl snapped her back to the moment.

She sprinted to the door, threw the latch, and pushed.

The door groaned—and gave way.

Rain slammed into her like a wall.

It soaked through her dress instantly, chilling her to the bone. The wind whipped her braid as she stumbled onto the steps.

Behind her, shadows stirred.

Glowing eyes blinked from the darkness.

And then she ran—down the path, through the garden gate, and into the winding alleys of Blackthorn Hollow.

The storm had swallowed the town whole.

Lightning forked across the sky, illuminating crooked rooftops, twisted iron lampposts, and slick cobblestones gleaming wet with rain.

She didn't know where she was going.

Only that she had to go.

Chapter 3
Through the Hollow

The streets of Blackthorn Hollow twisted beneath Clara's frantic steps like tangled veins.

Rain sluiced from gabled rooftops, streaking uneven tiles before pouring into rusted gutters, which overflowed in the storm's fury. Gutters gurgled, spilling onto the cobblestones, turning every alley into a winding stream. The storm had swallowed the town whole—its roar a wild symphony of wind, water, and the distant crash of waves slamming against cliffs beyond.

Clara ran without direction, breath ragged and uneven. Her soaked nightdress tangled around her knees, dragging with every stride. Rough stone bit into her bare feet—cold, slick, unforgiving. Every step stung, and every alley seemed to twist back on itself, as if the town itself conspired to trap her. Rain lashed her skin, invisible hands pulling her backward, slowing her.

She ducked beneath a sagging awning, gasping, water dripping from her braid.

The locket pulsed hot and steady against her chest.

The sensation wasn't painful. It felt alive. Not just reacting to storm or cold—but responding to something unseen.

Behind her, she still heard it: that high, insect-like chittering threading through the wind. Maybe it was real. Maybe not. Maybe only her imagination.

But she couldn't stop running.

She glanced back once—just once—and then plunged deeper into the hollow's heart.

Doors were shut tight. Windows shuttered. Curtains drawn. No voices. No flickering lights. No figures calling to her.

Veilborne

Only the groan of wind, the rattle of iron hinges, and the relentless rain.

Blackthorn Hollow felt emptied while she slept.

Clara pressed on, weaving through backstreets and passageways she barely knew. Cracked cobblestones jutted up, slick with moss and rain. Ivy curled along crumbling building edges that leaned too far into the street, whispering secrets across the way. Rusted ironwork and soot-stained chimneys loomed overhead like skeletal arms.

Her legs ached. Her breath came in sharp gasps. Her only compass was the burning pulse in her chest where the locket beat—steady, insistent.

Then, ahead, the air shifted.

She stumbled to a halt at the mouth of an alley.

For a brief second, the rain shimmered strangely in the air—like heat rising from sunbaked stone. But the air was freezing.

The cobblestones blurred, their edges melting. Beyond them—layered atop her world—was something else.

Towering trees with black bark stretched into a grey sky. Their trunks bore unfamiliar markings, etched deep and glowing faintly with pale blue light. Strange foliage shimmered in the gaps—too wide, too still.

The vision lasted less than a second.

Then it vanished.

Just a dark, rain-slick alley again.

Clara stumbled back, heartbeat quickening. She blinked hard, turning sharply into the next passageway, unwilling to linger.

Further on, her pace slowed.

The rush of fear gave way to exhaustion. Lungs burned, feet raw from unrelenting cobblestones. Her soaked nightdress clung heavy, weighted by the storm.

Mark Peters

She ducked beneath a crooked archway into a lane barely wider than her outstretched arms. Wind howled overhead, tearing through chimneys like a chorus of wolves.

And then she saw them.

Perched along guttering rooftops above—motionless—crows.

A dozen, maybe more. Black as oil. Feathers slick with rain, eyes like glass beads.

They didn't shift, caw, or shake water from wings.

They simply watched.

Heads tilted, beaks pointed at her.

Clara slowed, gaze flicking between them.

She kept walking.

They didn't follow.

They didn't move.

But their presence clung like smoke.

She quickened her pace and turned into another street—breath catching.

The fog rolled in fast—too fast.

It spilled from alleys like smoke, curling low along cobblestones, creeping between her ankles, lapping at doors and shutters.

In moments, it thickened—a white wall swallowing the path behind, muting even her footsteps.

The air grew colder with every step.

Frost bloomed in delicate spirals across windowpanes. Crystals dusted iron railings and spread across ivy-choked brick like the breath of winter itself.

Behind Clara, her footprints left trails in frost—vanishing moments after she passed.

Veilborne

The hollow was icing over behind her.

She turned toward the old market square—anywhere open, anywhere she could see—but the fog deepened, swallowing alleys that should've led there.

Familiar routes disappeared, replaced by streets she didn't know.

The locket pulsed harder. Her pulse quickened with it.

"No, no, no…" she whispered, voice swallowed by whiteness.

A narrow passage opened left.

She bolted blindly into it.

Fog thickened like a shroud, muffling the world.

Then—she heard them.

At first, just a rustle. Leaves disturbed by wind. But there were no trees nearby.

Then voices.

Soft at first. Murmurs. Slippery, fragmented. Threads of half-heard lullabies carried on the air.

Then a word cut through the mist—sharp, unmistakable.

"Clara…"

She froze mid-step, breath catching.

She spun, eyes straining through fog.

Nothing.

Another voice followed—different this time. Lower. Uneven. As if echoing from some unreachable distance.

Then more. Whispered fragments in words she didn't understand. Tones twisting, turning—spoken backward. Foreign. Ancient. Wrong.

Her hands trembled.

Footsteps echoed behind her.

Mark Peters

She whirled—but no one was there.

Only her own footsteps, traced briefly in frost… then gone.

The locket's pulse was frantic now—thudding like a second heartbeat.

Clara ran.

She burst from the alley into an open courtyard—though it felt anything but open.

Buildings leaned too close, windows shuttered, stone stained by age and weather.

A rusted fountain stood alone and full from the storm. Water pouring out through the many cracks along its rim.

The sky boiled overhead—dark clouds rolling, lightning flickering like fire behind curtains.

And then… she saw him.

Beneath a swaying iron lantern at the courtyard's far end stood a man.

Still. Silent. Drenched.

His long coat lost details to rain; his face—if it was a face—hidden beneath a water-darkened hat brim.

Clara halted, heart tight in her throat.

The figure didn't move.

The lantern flickered.

And he was gone.

She spun—nothing.

Another alley opened to her right.

She darted in—and stopped short.

A second figure stood there.

Not the same as before. Not dressed the same. Not shaped the same.

But watching.

Veilborne

Just like the last.

She blinked—and it vanished too.

They're watching me.

The locket trembled against her skin.

Panic surged, and she bolted deeper into the city's maze—chased not by footsteps, but by unseen eyes.

The twisting alleys narrowed, walls pressing closer. The storm above reached its peak—rain hammered rooftops, splashing onto cobbles in endless sheets.

Thunder rolled, shaking shutters loose and sending water pouring from broken gutters.

Clara's breath tore through her lungs.

Feet ached on rough stone—toes numb, legs trembling.

But she didn't stop.

Not until she turned sharply into a narrow lane—and froze.

Voices.

Low. Slurred. Male.

Four shapes emerged from the rain and fog, blocking the far end of the alley. They moved with a swagger that wasn't confidence—it was menace. Long coats. Scarves. Muffled silhouettes beneath the storm.

The tallest grinned. "Well now," he said, stepping forward, "what's a girl like you doing out in this part of the Hollow?"

Clara backed up a step, eyes darting behind her—but the alley ended in a crumbling wall of brick and ivy.

Trapped.

Another man chuckled, teeth crooked and yellow. "Lost, are we?"

One pulled a battered flask from his coat and took a swig. "Little thing like you? Could get snatched up. Lucky we found you first."

"Unlucky," muttered another, and they all laughed.

Clara's shoulders pressed against the damp stone. The locket burned fierce and alive against her chest—but gave no light. No flash. No help.

"Stay back," she said, voice hoarse.

One of the men laughed, low and cruel.

Her eyes flicked down—near the wall, half-buried in a puddle, a fist-sized shard of broken brick.

She lunged for it.

"Hey—!"

She hurled the stone with everything left in her.

It sailed wide, smashing into the alley wall with a crack and a cloud of dust.

The men flinched.

Clara straightened, breath ragged, and the motion tugged her soaked collar open.

The locket slipped free.

It gleamed in the half-light—pale silver, slick with rain, pulsing once, as if it had its own heartbeat.

"Well now…" the tallest said, grin returning. "What have we here?"

"Oh-ho," the crooked-toothed one jeered. "She's got fight."

The tallest advanced slowly. "You look like you've got something valuable there," he said, eyes flicking to her locket. "Let's have a look."

He reached out—

And then—

A hand settled firmly on Clara's shoulder.

She froze.

Veilborne

Breath caught.

Slowly, heart pounding, she turned her head to see who—stood behind her, calm against the storm.

Clara froze.

Chapter 4
Watcher in the Rain

The hand on her shoulder was steady, grounding—neither harsh nor gentle, but unmistakably there. She turned slowly, heart hammering, and found herself face to face with a cloaked figure standing against the storm.

Rain poured in rivulets from the man's hooded coat, shadows clinging to the sharp lines of his face. His eyes—clear and pale—locked onto hers with unsettling stillness, unreadable yet oddly calm, like deep water hiding something just beneath the surface.

Before she could speak, he stepped past her, placing himself between Clara and the men closing in.

She took a shaky breath—then caught it.

Just behind him, for the briefest heartbeat, the rain bent the wrong way.

A shimmer.

Like heat rising off stone, or glass catching sunlight where there was no light.

It vanished as quickly as it came, leaving only falling rain and her own uncertainty.

She blinked hard. Soaked, freezing, exhausted—maybe she was seeing things.

But something whispered inside her—no, you saw it.

"Well now," the tallest thug sneered, flicking his knife from hand to hand, "who's this then? Come to collect the stray?"

The others gave dry, low chuckles—but hesitation flickered in their eyes. Something about the stranger unsettled them. He stood too still. Too sure.

Clara took a step back, barely breathing.

The tall one lunged, blade flashing in the rainlight.

Veilborne

The stranger moved like smoke—silent and impossibly fast. He caught the man's wrist mid-strike with one hand, twisted hard with a crunch of bone, and sent him reeling with a blow to the ribs that cracked like timber.

Another thug charged, brandishing a rusted pipe. The stranger ducked low, swept his feet out, and drove the man back into a stack of crates. Wood shattered. The man didn't rise.

Clara's breath caught in her throat.

Two remained.

The stranger extended a hand. A faint pulse of golden light shimmered beneath his coat sleeve—and then a sigil burst to life beneath the next thug's boots. Bands of glowing light lashed up his legs, locking him in place like iron shackles.

The man screamed, tugging wildly. "What—what is this?!"

The stranger stepped forward without hurry. He placed a hand against the thug's chest.

The glyph pulsed once—

And the stranger's eyes flashed with light. Not bright, not blinding—but sharp, like metal gleaming in moonlight. For a breath, silver smoke curled faintly from the corners of his eyes, dissipating into the rain.

Then the air cracked.

The man was hurled backward like a broken doll, crashing into overturned barrels. The light shattered and vanished.

The last man bolted, slipping in the rain, vanishing into the fog without a word.

Only silence remained, thick and humming.

Clara stared at the stranger, wide-eyed. His chest rose and fell steadily, unmoved. Sigils still glowed faintly along a bracer hidden beneath his coat, fading as the rain hissed against them.

He turned just enough to glance back at her.

"Stay close," he said, calm and edged with quiet command.

Clara didn't hesitate. She nodded and followed him into the storm.

They moved like shadows.

The stranger's footsteps were swift but sure, silent on slick cobblestones. Clara struggled to keep up, her soaked nightdress dragging against her legs, cold biting deep into her skin. Rain hammered above, turning every alley into a stream and every roof into a drum.

"Who are you?" Clara called after him, breath catching. "How did you do that? With the light—and those symbols?"

No answer. He didn't even turn.

They slipped through a narrow passage between leaning stone buildings, their rooftops nearly touching. A broken sign creaked above, paint worn unreadable.

Clara stumbled over a loose cobble. "Why were those men after me?" Her voice wavered. "And how did you even find me in time?"

Still nothing. Only the scrape of wind and the rush of rain down crooked walls.

Frustration flared. "Do you always ignore people when you swoop in out of nowhere and save them?"

The stranger didn't break stride. But at the next turn, beneath a crooked awning dripping stormwater, he finally stopped.

He looked back over his shoulder.

"You've just turned thirteen, yes?"

Clara blinked at the sudden shift. "Yes."

"You've worn an heirloom since you were a baby?"

She instinctively placed her hand over the locket. "Yes. My... necklace."

Veilborne

He turned fully now. Rain clung to his coat folds. "It's never been removed. Not by anyone."

Clara nodded slowly, heart thudding. "No one's ever been able to."

His eyes drifted toward the alley behind them, scanning the fog.

"One more," he said. "Have you felt anything before tonight? Warmth? Movement? Dreams?"

She hesitated. "Sometimes it feels warm. Or like… like it's alive. But only recently."

He gave a short, tight nod—more to himself than her.

Clara crossed her arms. "Hey. I've answered all your questions. Maybe now you can answer some of mine?"

For a beat, only the storm dripping from rooftops.

Then he sighed. "All in good time. We need shelter first."

Clara stepped forward, grabbing his wrist, slick with rain. "No! Not until I get something. Who even are you?"

The stranger turned, hood slipping back just enough for her to see his face.

His eyes were grey, steady. His features worn but strong. A man shaped by hardship—but not broken by it.

"I am Eldric Ducart," he said. "And for now… you are safe. But not if we remain here."

Clara's grip loosened, but she didn't back away.

Eldric held her gaze. "We need to move. I'll explain what I can—once we're truly safe."

She hesitated, chest heaving from cold and fear.

He did save me. And he hasn't run, or left, or hurt me.

"…Fine," she said, voice barely above the wind.

Eldric turned again and stepped back into the storm. Clara followed close, the locket still pulsing faintly against her chest.

The storm drove them toward the edge of Blackthorn Hollow, where buildings thinned and stone streets gave way to creeping weeds and cracked earth. Trees bent in the wind, branches scraping like claws against rooftops.

Clara's legs ached, breath steaming in ragged clouds as she stumbled after Eldric. The town behind them felt like a different world now—swallowed by rain, fear, and unanswered questions.

They turned down a forgotten path choked with ivy and overgrown thorns. Nestled between two towering oaks stood a crumbling chapel, nearly lost to time. Ivy claimed most of its stone walls, and shattered stained-glass windows scattered colored shards that glittered faintly in the wet grass.

The roof sagged under the weight of rain and moss, and the wooden door hung crooked on rusted hinges.

Eldric approached without hesitation, resting a hand against the weathered wood. It groaned as he pushed it open.

"Inside," he said, glancing over his shoulder.

Clara stepped over the threshold into the gloom.

The chapel was cold and damp, cracked stone walls hunched beneath sagging beams. Faded carvings lined the walls, and tattered hymnals rotted in warped pews. The scent of mildew, ash, and something long forgotten clung to the air like a film.

Clara stayed near the doorway, shivering, arms wrapped tightly around herself. Her soaked dress clung like a second skin, and her bare feet left smears of mud and blood across the cracked stone floor with every tentative step.

Eldric knelt near a crumbling hearth, producing scraps of parchment and splinters from beneath his cloak. With swift, practiced motions, he

Veilborne

conjured a small flame that caught instantly, coaxing it to life with a flick of his hand.

Clara eyed him warily. "Are you going to explain any of this now?"

Eldric said nothing at first, feeding damp kindling into the fire. The flames crackled hesitantly, casting flickers of orange across the pews and the ruinous stained glass above.

Frustrated, Clara stepped closer. "I saw things—at the orphanage. Creatures. They weren't… they weren't human." Her breath hitched. "One of them—it… it threw my bed across the room like it weighed nothing. There were others, everywhere. And Miss Wren—" Her voice cracked. "She was just lying there. Like a doll someone dropped. And the frost—there was frost crawling over the floor, like it was alive."

She blinked hard, as if trying to hold the memory back. "They weren't human. Tall and bone-thin, like their bodies had been stretched too far. And they… they looked at me like they'd found what they were looking for."

Eldric finally looked up, calm but solemn.

"Pale Revenants," he said softly. "Born from the tears in the Veil, the fabric between here and elsewhere."

Clara furrowed her brow. "The Veil?"

"The barrier between this world and another. Most people live their whole lives without ever glimpsing it. But it's weakening."

"Why were they after me?" she asked, glancing instinctively down at her chest. The locket's warmth still pulsed softly beneath the damp fabric.

"They weren't after you," Eldric replied. "They were drawn to the relic you wear."

Clara's fingers curled protectively around the locket. "Relic? But… it's just a locket."

Eldric's eyes darkened. "Not just a locket. It's ancient, powerful, and very much not lost by accident."

Clara stepped back. "So what is it, then?"

His gaze held hers for a long beat. "An answer for another time. For now, what matters is that the Auricals know how to protect you—and how to help you understand what's coming."

"The Auricals?" Clara repeated cautiously.

Eldric nodded. "Guardians of the Veil. Keepers of our realm's balance. You'll be safe with them. They'll explain everything in time."

Clara crossed her arms tightly. "You keep saying that. 'In time.' 'Later.' What about now?"

Eldric returned to the fire, adding a final sliver of wood. "Now... we survive the night."

The rain slowed to a drizzle as they slipped past an old abandoned house. Its crumbling walls resembled more a skeleton than a dwelling at all. The path then gave way to tangled hedgerows and old woodland tracks, carved out by whatever animals still roamed here.

The last gas lamps flickered behind them, swallowed by thick mist clinging to the outskirts. Eldric pressed forward in silence, boots sure on the slippery trail.

Clara followed barefoot, toes numb and raw from wet stone and bramble-strewn ground. She tried not to wince with each step, but cold bit deep, and her legs ached from the night's ordeal.

The trees grew denser, branches gnarled like ancient hands reaching across the path. Rain dripped steadily from the canopy above; the forest smelled of wet earth, bark, and moss. The world here felt hushed—too still, as if holding its breath.

Finally, the woods opened into a small grove.

A circle of ancient oaks loomed high above, their roots coiled thickly through the earth like sleeping serpents. Mist wound between them, and the clearing shimmered faintly with a kind of invisible pressure, as though the ground itself hummed with quiet memory.

Veilborne

Eldric moved to the center of the grove and knelt. From beneath his cloak, he withdrew a worn brass disc engraved with layered glyphs. It clicked softly as he twisted it, each glowing rune sliding into place.

Clara lingered at the edge, arms wrapped tightly around herself. Her dress clung like a second skin, hair plastered to her neck. The locket thudded faintly at her chest—quiet now, but present.

She took a hesitant step closer. "What were those things called again?... back at the orphanage?"

"Pale Revenants," Eldric said without looking up.

The name sent a chill deeper through her than the rain ever could.

"They weren't human," she murmured. "They were... like skeletons. But wrong. Like they'd forgotten what being alive meant."

"They're drawn to relics," Eldric replied calmly, fingers moving over the brass device. "Especially when those relics start to stir."

Clara pressed her hand against the locket beneath her soaked bodice. "Why now? Why me?"

"You've always been important," he said. "But the Veil is weakening. And now, others will come."

Clara hesitated, shifting her weight from one aching foot to the other. "You said earlier... you prepare people. What does that mean? You train them?"

Eldric's eyes lifted to hers, rain tracing lines down his face. "Yes. When needed."

"What happens if they... fail the training?"

"They try again," he said simply, as if it were the only option.

Clara sank onto a mossy root, her body finally giving in. She winced, curling her frozen toes beneath her. "I've spent my whole life in that place. Scrubbing steps. Hauling coal. Getting pushed around by girls like Elsie."

She glanced at him, eyes narrowing. "Why would anything about me matter?"

"You've been through more than any child should," Eldric said, voice low but steady. "And yet here you are. That courage... that resilience... it's rare. It's what sets you apart. Hold onto it, Clara. Because what comes next will ask even more of you."

Clara swallowed hard. "You keep saying that—like you know me. Like you've been watching me."

Eldric didn't flinch. "I've known your name far longer than you've known mine."

She frowned. "Then how? How did you find me in that alley? How did you even know where I'd be?"

The rain filled the silence between them—a soft, steady rhythm.

Then Eldric spoke, quieter now. "Because something changed. When you turned thirteen, the locket began to stir. Ancient magic like that doesn't wake for nothing. It leaves a trace... if you know how to listen."

"A trace?" she asked, uncertain.

"Ripples," he said. "Echoes. Whatever you want to call them. It's not perfect science—but when something long dormant begins to beat again, it doesn't go unnoticed. Not by those who know what to look for."

Clara looked away, rain dripping from her lashes. Her voice came smaller now, rough around the edges. "Like those creatures knew where to come..."

She paused, throat tightening. "Is it my fault?" she whispered. "Miss Wren... the others... did they die because of me?"

Eldric was silent for a moment. When he finally spoke, his words were deliberate—measured and warm.

"No, Clara. What happened at the orphanage wasn't your doing—it was theirs. You didn't call them. You survived them."

Veilborne

"But they were looking for something," she said quietly. "And they found me."

"They found the locket," Eldric corrected gently. "They didn't understand what it meant. Not fully. And neither do you. Not yet."

She hesitated, fingers curling protectively around the silver chain. "So it's not just... a keepsake."

"No," Eldric said, gaze steady. "It never was."

Clara exhaled slowly, breath fogging the air.

"I never even knew my parents," she said quietly. "No one ever told me anything—not Miss Wren, not anyone. I've spent my whole life not knowing who they were... just this locket. That's all I've ever had. That's all they left me."

Eldric didn't speak at first, but his gaze lingered on her longer than before. "That locket will lead you to more answers than you know. But for now, we must move again. This place... is not safe for long."

Clara looked up, startled. "Even here?"

"The Veil is thinner in places like this. Beautiful, yes. But watched."

She shivered.

Eldric stood, the device in his hands beginning to glow faintly. "Come. There's one more step before the journey truly begins."

He knelt again, placing the brass device gently on the damp earth at the center of the grove. Glyphs along its surface shimmered brighter now, as if awakened by something in the air—or in Clara herself.

He rotated the outer ring once clockwise.

The grove answered.

With a low, harmonic hum, concentric circles of golden light rose from the device, spinning slowly into the air. They hovered just above the forest floor—perfectly still, perfectly silent—each ring inscribed with symbols Clara had never seen before. They drifted outward like ripples on a pond, then locked together with a soft, magnetic click.

The space between the rings warped—light bending inward like the fabric of the world was being gently pulled apart.

Clara gasped.

Inside the spinning circle, the air swirled and deepened into a vortex of color and mist. Stars blinked in and out of view. Shapes like trees—taller than any she'd ever seen—moved behind the veil of fog within. There was a sky in there… a forest in there… a whole world, impossibly folded into the space between heartbeats.

It was like stepping up to the edge of a dream.

The grove shimmered with quiet tension, as though even the earth held its breath.

Clara took a half-step forward, barefoot on the moss, every sense alight. The locket at her chest pulsed—not with fear, but something else. Recognition. Like it had always been waiting for this.

Her throat tightened. "Is that…?"

Eldric stood beside her, rain plastering his cloak to his shoulders. "A doorway."

"To where?"

He looked down at her, eyes calm. "To the answers you seek. To the life you were always meant for."

Clara stared into the swirling light. It was so much. Too much. Her legs wanted to move forward, but her heart clutched the last familiar thread of the world she knew.

"What if I don't belong there?" she asked quietly.

Eldric didn't smile, but there was something gentler in his voice. "The world you came from never gave you the chance to find out. This one will."

Clara swallowed hard. Her toes curled against the damp earth.

Then, without speaking, Eldric stepped back.

Veilborne

"You go first," he said, nodding toward the portal. "I'll follow. I need to make sure the way holds until you're through."

Clara hesitated.

The glowing rings spun slower now, as if waiting for her.

She glanced over her shoulder—back toward the hollow, the ruined orphanage, the empty life behind her.

Then forward.

She took a breath.

And stepped into the light.

The portal shimmered around her, and for an instant, the cold vanished. She felt warmth. Wind. The scent of wildflowers and woodsmoke. She felt seen—by something ancient and vast and kind.

Then she was gone.

Eldric watched until the glow around her form vanished fully into the portal.

Then, drawing in a breath of his own, he stepped in after her.

Behind them, the rings dissolved into golden dust, and the grove fell silent once more.

Mark Peters

Chapter 5
Through the Veil

Crossing the Veil was like falling through a breath held too long—light, sound, and weight collapsing inward before rushing back all at once.

Clara stumbled as she emerged from the portal, the sensation of weightlessness still clinging to her limbs like mist. For a heartbeat, she felt suspended—untethered, like her body hadn't quite caught up with her soul. Then her bare feet found moss-covered earth, cool and damp beneath her toes, and the world settled.

She gasped.

The air here was different. Warm, but not heavy—rich and crisp, like it had passed through sunlit leaves and mountain springs. It smelled of rain and blooming things, of pine and something faintly sweet, like crushed petals. The chill of Blackthorn Hollow was gone, shed like a second skin the moment she stepped through.

Above her, a twilight sky stretched in hues of indigo and soft lavender. Wisps of cloud curled lazily across the expanse, and twin moons—one full, one barely a sliver—hung low and luminous near the horizon. Even in daylight, stars peeked through the haze-like watching eyes.

All around, the forest whispered with light and movement.

The trees towered impossibly tall, their dark trunks smooth as polished stone. Their branches arched like vaults, canopies woven with silver-veined leaves that shimmered as they shifted. Some trees pulsed faintly from within as if light flowed through their roots and into every leaf, alive with a quiet rhythm. High above, blossoms the colour of moonlight bloomed at unreachable heights, dropping glowing petals that spiralled slowly to the ground and vanished like mist.

Vines coiled through the underbrush, humming softly when brushed, while patches of moss released gentle puffs of golden dust beneath her steps. Strange, long-tailed birds with jewel-toned feathers fluttered silently between the branches, their wings trailing glowing streaks in the air.

Clara didn't move.

Her heart pounded as her wide eyes took in the dreamlike forest. Every sense buzzed—sight, sound, scent. Even the earth beneath her felt alive, as though the world itself was breathing beneath her.

Behind her, the air shimmered again as Eldric stepped through the portal.

Clara turned toward him, her voice soft, breathless. "This... isn't Earth."

Eldric's expression was calm as he nodded. "No," he said. "Welcome to Eryndor."

They walked in silence, the forest parting like a dream around them.

Every step Clara took felt like trespassing in a world not meant for her. The moss underfoot was soft, and springy—so unlike the rough floorboards of the orphanage. Even the air seemed to sing faintly, as though the forest was humming a tune only the trees understood.

Twice, she slowed to observe strange creatures she didn't dare name—once, a fox-like animal with feathered ears and antlers that watched her unblinking from the shadows. Another time, she passed a patch of mushrooms glowing pale blue, their light swaying gently as if stirred by some unseen tide.

Eldric didn't speak, but Clara noticed how the trees shifted ever so slightly as he passed—vines recoiling from his boots, branches arching overhead as if in silent recognition. She stayed close behind, keeping her eyes on the sway of his cloak.

Soon, the trees thinned.

They stepped out onto a rocky ledge—and Clara's breath caught.

Before them, carved into the far cliffs across a yawning valley, stood Calendor Keep.

Mark Peters

It rose from the stone like it had always been there—part fortress, part forest. The walls were ancient and thick, but ivy cascaded down in green waterfalls, dotted with violet and gold star-shaped blossoms. Trees rose through the very architecture—great oaks whose roots wove through the foundations like veins, as if the keep and the forest had grown into each other over centuries.

Bridges of living wood stretched between the spires, their broad arches formed by entwined branches and roots. Floating lanterns—glass spheres filled with drifting, glowing light—moved gently between towers, casting light like captured starlight.

From here, Clara could see courtyards nestled among trees, rooftops shaped like the petals of vast flowers. The stone shimmered faintly with runes—delicate etchings that pulsed with a soft, silvery glow, alive with magic.

Her mouth parted. She had no words.

"It's…" she finally managed, "…it's alive."

Eldric's voice was quiet beside her. "This is where your answers begin."

Clara stepped closer to the edge, eyes wide, heart thudding with awe. The wind tugged at her dress and hair, but she barely noticed. Below, the valley shimmered with rivers that glowed faintly blue under the twin moons. Beyond, the forest stretched on into forever—an ocean of twilight and silver mist.

The scent of moss and wildflowers mingled with something sharper—an iron tang that made her skin prickle. Magic, she realised. She could smell it. Taste it. The air was thick with it, humming beneath her skin like the pulse of the locket against her chest.

She turned slowly to Eldric. "I don't understand any of this."

"You will," he said.

Then, without another word, he started down a narrow, winding path carved into the cliffside.

Veilborne

Clara hesitated a moment longer, then followed—each step taking her closer to the impossible.

The descent was steep but quiet.

Clara moved carefully, one hand brushing the cliff wall for balance. The path twisted through tall silver grasses that swayed without wind, their tips glowing faintly. White motes drifted lazily through the air—pollen, perhaps, or something stranger. Now and then, a distant sound echoed through the valley, soft and musical, like a flute played by the forest itself.

Below, the great keep grew larger with every turn. It wasn't just one structure—it was many, woven together by trees, bridges, and light. Some towers were carved from the stone itself; others looked as though they'd been grown from living wood. The tallest spire stretched skyward, crowned with a ring of lanterns orbiting slowly, like a halo.

Clara hardly noticed the cold seeping into her bare feet. The stone beneath her was warm to the touch, pulsing faintly like a heartbeat. She looked down and saw that the path shimmered now and then, adjusting ever so slightly with each step.

"The land moves here," Eldric said over his shoulder, "for those it recognises."

Clara frowned. "The land recognises people?"

Eldric didn't answer directly. Instead, he gestured ahead to a wide, arched bridge made of interwoven roots and branches. It rose like a natural sculpture, curving elegantly toward one of the keep's outer gates. Moss and tiny white flowers sprouted along the railings.

Clara paused at the edge of the bridge. It was clearly alive. She could feel the gentle shifting beneath her feet, like the bridge itself was breathing.

Eldric stepped onto it without hesitation.

Clara followed, and the surface adjusted to her weight—firm, warm, and subtly flexing beneath each step. It was unlike anything she'd ever known.

As they crossed, she took it all in—the keep's architecture carved around the forms of ancient trees, the glow of runes in the stone, and the soft murmur of water from channels flowing beneath the bridge. High above, robed figures moved slowly across upper terraces, some pausing to touch glowing glyphs carved into the walls. One conjured a trail of floating leaves with the wave of a hand, guiding a group of younger Auricals into a chamber shaped like a hollowed-out tree trunk.

Clara's heart was racing. Not from fear but from something else—something close to wonder.

"Who are they?" she asked softly.

"Guardians," Eldric said. "You'll meet many of them soon."

They passed beneath a tall archway into the first courtyard, where trees grew directly through the stone, their roots shaped into benches, staircases, and even columns. Floating orbs of light bobbed gently overhead, casting a soft golden hue across the mossy stone floor.

Magic drifted through the air like pollen.

The keep was alive in every sense—growing, moving, glowing. But not chaotically. There was purpose in its design, harmony in its wildness. Clara had never seen anything so strange. Or so beautiful.

She swallowed hard. "This is… nothing like home."

Eldric glanced at her, his expression gentler than before.

"No," he said quietly. "It isn't. But it will keep you safe."

Clara looked up at the towers, the walkways, the open-air balconies laced with vines. She wasn't sure if she was comforted… or just more overwhelmed.

But she didn't look away.

As Clara and Eldric stepped deeper into the winding heart of the Keep, the pathways narrowed into a corridor formed entirely from knotted roots and stone. The scent of wild herbs and damp bark filled the air. Here and there, tiny lizards with iridescent scales darted across the walls, vanishing into mossy crevices.

Veilborne

The corridor tightened as they walked, folding inward like the forest itself had grown around it. Vines dangled from the ceiling in looping braids, and the walls, though stone, bore the faint impression of bark—etched as though grown, not carved.

Clara stayed close to Eldric, her steps quiet. For the first time since crossing the Veil, a thread of unease crept beneath her awe. It wasn't the beauty of the place—it was how much it seemed to notice her. The moss held the shape of her feet longer than it should have. The lanterns above her flickered brighter as she passed beneath them. Leaves on nearby vines rustled faintly in her direction, even with no breeze.

Eldric, as ever, said nothing. But Clara could tell—he noticed, too.

They rounded a bend.

A man sat sprawled on a root-formed bench ahead, whittling something small from a stick of silverbark. He looked older than Eldric, or perhaps just more weathered—his hair wild, streaked with mossy green and copper, his patchwork coat stuffed with oddments and sprigs of who-knew-what. A pipe, unlit, hung from one corner of his mouth. When he looked up, his eyes gleamed like amber glass in the lamplight.

"Well, there's a look," he said, squinting at them.

Clara blinked.

Eldric gave a rare exhale—something between a sigh and a laugh. "Fennrick."

"Present," the man replied cheerfully, rising in one smooth motion. He tucked the carved figure—some kind of miniature owl—into one of his many pockets and turned toward Clara.

"You're Clara, then."

She hesitated. "How do you know my name?"

Fennrick's eyes sparkled, though his tone softened. "Word travels fast around here. Especially when the Council starts whispering."

He gave a small, off-kilter bow. "The Keep's been expecting you. The how and why—that's their story to tell, not mine."

Clara tilted her head slightly. "So you don't know?"

Fennrick gave a lopsided grin. "Oh, I know plenty. I just enjoy watching people find things out for themselves."

Eldric gave him a flat look. Fennrick ignored it.

"Come on then," he said, turning down the path. "Let's walk while they're still waiting on the ceremony."

The trail opened beneath arching trees and braided roots, forming a living corridor of moss and dappled light. Birds trilled softly overhead, their wings painting faint streaks of gold as they passed.

"They're sending you to the Council, I assume?" Fennrick called back to Clara. "All robes and riddles, those ones. Don't let the silence fool you—they talk in circles when they don't want to give a straight answer."

"Why do I need to meet them?" Clara asked, stepping around a root that curled like a question mark across the path.

Fennrick didn't look back. "Because something ancient just stirred. Not just in you—in that." He gestured toward the locket beneath her collar. "And when relics start waking up, the Keep listens. The Keep remembers."

They reached a small fountain nestled among a cluster of roots. Its waters glowed softly, casting silvery ripples across the mossy stones.

Fennrick dipped his fingers into the pool. "You'll want answers. Of course, you will. But what matters more than answers," he said, glancing up at her, "is knowing the right questions to ask."

Eldric stepped up beside him. "She's ready."

Fennrick arched a brow. "She's thirteen. Nobody's ready at thirteen."

He looked at Clara. "But some don't get the luxury of waiting."

Veilborne

Clara studied him, uncertain. "Why won't you just say what you mean?"

Fennrick gave a small shrug and smiled—less playful this time, more worn. "Because the truth's heavier than you'd expect. And it tends to stick."

He stepped aside as another set of robed Auricals approached from the hall ahead. They said nothing, but their presence was undeniable—calm and exacting, as if they'd been carved from the very stone of the Keep.

One inclined his head toward Clara. "The Council is waiting."

Fennrick gave her a small bow. "Don't let them pin you down, girl. You're not a question to be solved. You're a story still being written."

And with that, he turned and wandered off the way they'd come, humming to himself, a cluster of firefly-like lights trailing behind his boots.

The Council chamber rose like a hollowed tree cathedral—wide and echoing, with roots spiralling up into a vaulted ceiling. Glyphs shimmered in the air like constellations frozen mid-breath. Clara stepped lightly, trying not to make a sound as she crossed the moss-carpeted floor.

At the chamber's centre stood a ring of five high-backed chairs, each distinct—one of etched stone, one of gnarled wood, one woven from golden reeds, one pale as bonewood, and a final chair that shimmered like shadow held in shape. In them sat the Aurical Council.

The air buzzed faintly.

"You are Clara Holloway," said one—a woman cloaked in slate-blue robes, her face half-shadowed by a deep hood.

Clara blinked. "Yes... but how do you know that?"

The woman gestured faintly toward the locket at Clara's chest. "Your name is bound to the relic. When it stirred... it spoke it back to us."

Clara's hand rose instinctively to the chain.

Another Councilor spoke, voice low and smooth. "Do you know where it came from? Who gave it to you?"

She shook her head. "No. I've had it as long as I can remember. I grew up in an orphanage—Blackthorn Hollow. I never knew my parents."

Silence settled briefly. Then another Aurical leaned forward—his chair of etched stone groaning softly beneath him.

"The locket disappeared from our sight many years ago," he said. "Its signature faded. Hidden."

"Until three days ago," the woman added. "It awoke again—beyond the Veil. And with it, a name."

Eldric stepped forward. "Once we confirmed its resonance, I was sent to find her."

"And now," said the lead Aurical, "you are here."

Clara looked down at the locket as it pulsed softly in her palm. Not cold. Not hot. Just… alive. Like it was listening. Or waiting.

"Why now?" she asked quietly. "Why would it wake up at all?"

The woman's voice was soft but certain. "Because some magic waits until it's needed. And sometimes… until the one meant to carry it is ready."

"There are things we can tell you," she continued, "and things you must learn for yourself. But this much you should know: something has noticed you. And it will not stop."

A beat.

"Do you know the name MalVaran?"

Clara shook her head.

"Be glad," murmured the stone-seated elder. "His name alone has toppled kingdoms."

"And be wary. His name is older than dust and deeper than death. He is the reason the Veil exists. And he is the one who would tear it open."

Veilborne

"And the locket?" Clara asked, her voice barely above a whisper.

Another Councilor spoke. "It is part of the lock. Or the key. Sometimes both. Its nature depends on who carries it."

Clara swallowed hard.

Eldric stepped forward at last. "She's tired. Cold. Let her rest. Let her ask her questions when she's strong enough to carry the answers."

A long pause. Then the robed figures nodded, one by one.

"She will be placed with the others," said the lead woman. "Watched. But welcomed."

The chamber dimmed as they withdrew into the walls like shadows dissolving.

Only Eldric remained.

He turned to Clara, his voice softer now. "You did well."

"I don't understand any of it," she said.

"You're not meant to. Not yet."

An attendant arrived, leading her through the winding halls to a quiet room nestled in the roots of the Keep. She barely noticed the carved door the lanterns shaped like sleeping birds, or the faint runes humming above the bed.

She lay down. Held the locket.

The last thing she felt before sleep took her was a single, steady pulse.

Not hers.

The locket's.

Chapter 6
Awakening at Calendor

Clara woke to the soft hush of dawn curling through the narrow window, its pale gold light tracing patterns on the stone wall beside her bed. For a long moment, she lay still, listening to the faint creak of branches shifting in the wind, the distant call of a bird that didn't belong to any world she'd known.

Her room was quiet—too quiet.

Gone were the whispered cruelties of Elsie and her shadows—snide remarks about being strange, about the locket, about never belonging. No more cold buckets and coal dust, or the sting of cracked knuckles from endless scrubbing. The stink of burnt porridge was a memory now, as distant as the chill of those grey stone walls.

And Miss Wren... stern, silent Miss Wren. Clara had spent years flinching beneath her stare—yet now, with everything changed, it wasn't the harshness she remembered most. It was a quiet moment by candlelight. The cupcake. The look in her eyes that hadn't quite been cold.

Instead, Calendor Keep greeted her with silence and stillness, wrapped in soft tapestries and the scent of woodsmoke and rain-damp stone.

She sat up slowly, fingers instinctively finding the locket on her chest. It was warm again, its slow, steady pulse thrumming beneath her fingertips like a second heartbeat. Not urgent. Not afraid. Just... alive.

Clara swung her legs over the edge of the bed, the stone floor cool beneath her bare feet. A neatly folded tunic and trousers sat at the foot of her bed—simple but finely made, in forest grey and moss green hues. She dressed quickly, her fingers clumsy from the chill, then ran a hand through her sleep-tangled hair.

A quiet knock startled her.

Veilborne

When she opened the door, a boy no older than herself stood in the hallway—an acolyte, judging by his silver-trimmed robes. He said nothing, merely inclined his head and gestured for her to follow.

Clara hesitated only briefly before stepping into the corridor. The stone beneath her feet was smooth, worn by centuries, and the walls were etched with faintly glowing runes that pulsed with a slow rhythm, as though the Keep itself were breathing.

The acolyte silently led her through gently curving corridors woven with roots and vine-draped archways. Light spilled from crystals overhead—some floating lazily in place, others embedded in the walls like stars caught in stone. The scent of moss and ancient parchment filled the air, mingling with the faint aroma of roasted herbs drifting from somewhere deeper in the Keep.

Clara followed the others through a high-arched doorway and into what could only be described as a feast hall—though it felt more like a forest grove that had decided to become a dining room.

The ceiling was a canopy of living branches arching high overhead and woven through with soft, glowing light threads. Clusters of lantern blooms hung like suspended fireflies, casting golden hues over long wooden tables carved from single, seamless trees. At the far end, a hearth roared with flickering violet flame, its heat gentle but constant, and the walls shimmered faintly, as if whispering with unseen magic.

Clara's stomach growled the moment the scent hit her.

It was nothing like the sour porridge of Morrowmere. This was warm bread crusted with salt and rosemary, honey-glazed roots that smelled of cinnamon and smoke, and something tangy and rich that made her eyes sting with hunger. Platters floated between tables, gliding gently to a stop before students with a hum of magic.

Roasted sky-fruit, caramelised and blistered, peeled itself as it drifted. Creamy soups ladled themselves into bowls, steam curling like spellwork from the surface. Baskets overflowed with stuffed bread shaped like twisted vines, their centres glowing faintly with melted butter and enchanted herbs. Golden pastries cracked open to reveal drifting wisps of cheese and bright green moss-leaf chutney.

And amid it all—familiar comforts.

Sliced apples. Soft-boiled eggs. Biscuits spread with clotted cream. A silver tray of roasted chicken legs that looked startlingly normal. Even a bowl of porridge—thick and golden, topped with shaved sugar root and something that might've been sliced pear, drizzled with syrup Clara could've sworn smelled like maple.

She hesitated as she approached, staring at the selection like it might vanish if she blinked.

"Outta the way, books," a voice said nearby.

Clara turned just in time to see a girl weaving expertly around two taller students, balancing a tray piled high with bread, fruit, and something skewered and steaming with spice. She dropped the tray unceremoniously onto a bench and flopped beside it like she owned the table.

She was taller than Clara, with wild auburn curls and sharp green eyes that didn't seem to miss a thing. Her sleeves were rolled to her elbows, ink smudges along the cuffs, and she spoke like someone who'd never been afraid to say exactly what was on her mind.

"You're new," the girl said bluntly, pointing a crusty roll at Clara.

"I—yeah," Clara managed, still overwhelmed by the colours, the scents, the sheer strangeness of it all.

The girl shoved a basket of glowing fruits to one side and patted the bench beside her. "Well, new's better than boring. Sit."

Clara blinked. For a moment, she hesitated. Then, as though her legs decided, she slid onto the bench. Jasper followed with a resigned sigh and settled on her other side.

"You'll get used to her," he muttered. "I'm Jasper." and gently shook her hand.

Veilborne

"Spoilsport," the girl shot back cheerfully, biting into the roll she'd been brandishing. "Name's Sadie. Don't worry, I bite less than I growl."

Clara gave a small, uncertain laugh. The scent of roasted root vegetables, warm cinnamon bread, and sweet, honeyed tea filled the air, grounding her. A pastry shaped like a flower and dusted with powdered gold steamed invitingly on a nearby tray.

"I'm Clara," she offered at last.

Sadie nodded. "Nice to meet you, Clara-not-from-here." Then, with a mouth half-full of food, she added, "So—Hollow-side or Keep-born?"

Clara blinked. "What?"

"She means," Jasper clarified, adjusting his glasses, "are you from this side of the Veil? Or the other?"

Clara hesitated. "Oh. Hollow-side. I'm from Blackthorn Hollow."

Sadie gave a low whistle. "Well, aren't you rare?" She eyed Clara with new interest. "You're the first one of those we've had in years. Used to be more common, but lately... not so much."

"Expect stares," Jasper added, his tone gentler. "People aren't always subtle."

"Especially the Dawnspire lot," Sadie muttered darkly. "Elitists, the lot of them."

Before Clara could ask more, a hush swept through the hall like a gust of wind.

It was initially subtle—the quiet that prickles the back of your neck. Then voices dropped. Cutlery slowed. Heads turned, one by one, towards the far end of the hall.

Clara followed their gaze.

A group of older students had entered through a tall set of carved doors. Four in total, their robes darker than the others—midnight blue trimmed in silver, sharp and immaculate. Their steps were coordinated and deliberate, like shadows with purpose.

Leading them was a boy who looked older than the rest—maybe fifteen, sixteen. His hair was dark, tied neatly at the nape of his neck, and his features were pale and angular. Cold. Beautiful, in a way that looked sculpted rather than born. His eyes were grey—storm grey. Distant and unreadable.

An insignia gleamed in silver thread on his shoulder: a curved blade wrapped in obsidian flame.

He didn't look at anyone—until his gaze landed on Clara.

The corner of his mouth curled. Not in amusement. Not in kindness. A smirk, sharp as a blade.

"Well," he said, his voice silk over frost, "didn't think they'd start letting Veilborne stray this far from their gutters."

Clara's stomach twisted. The word struck like a slap.

"Excuse me?" she asked, trying to keep her voice level.

"You heard me, Veilborne. Try not to stink up the Keep while you're here."

Sadie stood so fast her chair scraped back with a screech. "Back off, Draven."

Jasper grabbed her sleeve. "Sadie—don't."

The boy's smirk deepened, eyes flicking over Jasper with dismissive contempt before returning to Clara.

"How quaint."

Then he turned and walked away, his entourage trailing behind him like shadows untouched by light.

Clara watched them go, her chest tight.

"What… what does that mean?" she asked at last.

Veilborne

Jasper sighed. "It's what they call people from your side of the Veil. Veilborne. It's... not a compliment."

"It's a slur," Sadie snapped, returning to the bench. "Means you're not 'pure' Eryndorian. As if bloodlines matter more than actual skill or sense."

Clara looked down, her fingers tightening around the edge of her tray.

"But for what it's worth," Jasper added gently, "you're not the first. There've been others before you—Veilborne who came through, learned the craft, fought for Eryndor when it counted."

"Some even died for it," Sadie said. "Proper legends, a few of them. The Council doesn't like to talk about it much, but their names are still carved into the stone halls. So don't let someone like Varek make you think you don't belong here."

Clara glanced between them, something warm flickering just beneath her ribs.

"They had to start somewhere too," Jasper nodded.

Sadie elbowed her gently. "And who knows—maybe you'll be the next legend. Wouldn't that be something?"

Clara's hand tightened in her lap. Old memories stirred—whispers in dormitory corners, the snide smiles of girls like Elsie, the way Miss Wren's eyes always lingered a second too long when Clara asked about her parents. Different world, the same rules.

But then Sadie's shoulder bumped gently against hers.

"Hey. Forget him," Sadie said. "You've got us now."

Clara glanced between them—Jasper, with his quiet steadiness, and Sadie, all wildfire and certainty. They weren't from her world. But something about them felt solid. Real.

"Thanks," she said, voice quiet but genuine.

Sadie stood again, grabbing her tray. "C'mon. Let's give you the tour before they toss us into runes and lectures."

She winked. "Might as well get lost somewhere pretty."

Clara stood slowly, though her eyes lingered on the hall around her.

Students talked and laughed and clinked their mugs. A girl across the table popped a floating berry into her drink, and it burst into fragrant smoke that shaped itself into a tiny bird before vanishing with a soft flutter.

Clara stared, wide-eyed.

Maybe this wasn't home.

But it was something else.

Something better.

****

The trio stepped into the open air again, emerging through an arched stone doorway framed by flowering vines. The morning mist had lifted just enough for the golden light of dawn to pour over Calendor Keep, catching on the leaves and rooftops and setting the courtyard aglow.

Clara stopped short.

The training grounds stretched before them in a wide expanse of terraced platforms, soft mossy lawns, and low stone circles etched with runes that pulsed faintly beneath students' feet. Beyond that, the forest loomed—tamed in places, wild in others—cradling the Keep like a protective ring.

High above, bridges of root and rope spanned between towers. Floating glyphs hovered mid-air as students practised casting spells. Some duelled with wooden staves. Others summoned glowing runes, shaping them into barriers or tools before they dissolved into the breeze like falling stars.

Clara's breath caught in her throat.

It was alive. Unfolding. Like stepping into a story still being written. Magic wasn't hidden here—it was worn openly, like sunlight caught in every leaf.

Veilborne

Sadie stretched lazily. "Welcome to the proving grounds."

Jasper adjusted his satchel as they wove between the platforms. "They call it that because we all spend our first few weeks here proving we're not going to blow ourselves up."

"Or each other," Sadie added cheerfully.

They passed a pair of students mid-duel. Sparks burst from their outstretched hands as luminous glyphs clashed like blades. An Aurical instructor watched nearby, murmuring corrections that rippled through the air like smoke.

"Is all of this... normal?" Clara asked, ducking instinctively as a glowing sphere sailed overhead and burst like a bubble.

"For here?" Sadie said. "Pretty much."

"They won't let us near the fancy stuff until we've got control," Jasper added. "There's a reason the upper towers are forbidden to first-years."

Clara turned slowly, trying to take it all in—the runes, the training, the strange harmony between nature and structure. Vines grew across balconies without damaging them. Trees bent gently away from paths. Even the light seemed to know where it was needed most.

They crossed a polished stone bridge spanning a gently curving stream, its waters so clear the stones at the bottom looked like polished gems. Clara slowed, her steps faltering as something moved beneath the surface—ripples of colour, impossible to miss.

Dozens of fish drifted through the water like living brushstrokes. Their bodies were slender and fluid, but their fins trailed behind them in long, silken strands, shimmering like woven ribbons. Some bore streaks of deep indigo and fiery orange; others rippled with gold and violet, like stained glass come to life. They turned and twirled in slow, elegant spirals, their movements too graceful to be anything but deliberate. Even the water seemed to hum faintly where they passed.

Clara leaned against the edge of the bridge, entranced. "What are those?" she asked, voice barely above a whisper.

Sadie paused, glancing down. "Those?" She grinned. "Riverlace. They're harmless. Unless you count stealing attention as dangerous."

The forest opened up ahead into a wide, circular platform—raised slightly from the earth, as though the land had lifted it into being. At its centre stood an immense, ancient tree whose gnarled trunk twisted skyward like a spiral of time. Its sprawling canopy unfurled in layered tiers of silver-dappled leaves, casting soft light patterns across the stone below. The roots curled outward in great arches, thick as pillars, wrapping protectively around the platform's edge—like the tree held the space in a quiet embrace.

Vines adorned with glowing seedpods dangled from the lowest branches, swaying gently in the breeze, and faint glyphs shimmered beneath the moss-laced stone—marking it unmistakably as a place of learning. Of challenge. Of power.

Dozens of students were already gathering.

Sadie gestured with a piece of fruit she'd stolen from breakfast. "This is where they dump the first-years."

Clara's pulse quickened.

She could feel eyes drifting toward her—some curious, some sceptical. Whispers passed in pockets, and though no one spoke directly to her, Clara recognised the weight of being the outsider. Of being watched.

But Sadie and Jasper stayed close.

The three of them settled near the platform's edge beneath the tree's sprawling limbs. Clara leaned against the smooth bark, the rune-marked surface warm beneath her fingertips.

Sadie crossed her arms, gaze sweeping the other students. "So," she asked, "first impressions?"

Clara hesitated, then exhaled. "Overwhelming."

Sadie grinned. "Good. Means your brain's working."

Veilborne

Jasper settled onto a moss-covered stone beside them, already flipping open a small leather notebook. "It gets easier. Most things here aren't designed to make sense straight away."

Clara gave a half-smile. "How long have you both been here?"

"Two weeks," Sadie said, casually rolling an apple under her boot. "He reads everything. I break things. It's a system."

Jasper didn't look up from his scribbles. "Not everything. Just the relevant things."

Sadie grinned. "He's modest. Last night he read three chapters on warding glyphs and then explained them using fruit. Actual fruit."

"Because someone," Jasper said, glancing sideways at her, "thought a 'runic melon shield' was a real spell."

"It should be," Sadie muttered.

Clara laughed.

Sadie leaned back on her elbows, eyes scanning the sky between the trees. "I came from the Western Crags. Not much out there but wind, wild goats, and endless mountains. My parents are traders, always chasing the next caravan, so I got dropped off here when the letters started arriving."

Clara tilted her head. "Letters?"

"Yeah," Sadie said. "The letter bloomed out of one of the lantern-flowers near our camp—just peeled back its petals and unfurled like it had grown there. Said I'd been chosen for early Aurical assessment. My old foster mum cried. My foster dad told me to be back in time for planting season."

Jasper smiled faintly. "Mine was much quieter. I'm from Farrosh. Small place. Lots of bookshops. When my test scores spiked, someone from the Keep showed up at our door. I think my parents were relieved, honestly. I nearly set the library on fire trying to decode an illusion script."

"Twice," Sadie added helpfully. "He nearly set it on fire twice."

Jasper pushed his glasses up the bridge of his nose. "The second time was deliberate."

Clara blinked. "Wait—there are tests? People apply to come here?"

"Well, not everyone," Sadie said, tapping the apple again. "Some kids are born into it. Keep-born, like I said. Others get tested by scouts, usually when weird stuff happens around them."

"And then there's you," Jasper added. "Your arrival wasn't exactly… standard."

Clara looked down, fingers brushing the locket beneath her tunic.

"Not that that's a bad thing," Sadie said quickly. "Just… rare. The Veil doesn't send many of you our way anymore."

"And never without reason," Jasper added, his voice quieter now.

Clara didn't respond—not straight away. But the warmth of their words settled something in her chest. A quiet place that hadn't known what to call itself until now.

Clara chuckled softly, the tension in her shoulders loosening by degrees.

She found herself touching the locket again without thinking. Beneath her tunic, it pulsed faintly—steady, like a heartbeat. A quiet reminder that whatever this place was, she was meant to be here.

A distant horn echoed—low, deep, and ancient.

All around the courtyard, students fell still.

Two Aurical stewards appeared on the stone path, their robes edged with silver and gold. They raised their arms in unison.

"New initiates," one called, his voice resonating without the need for magic. "Form ranks and follow. Orientation begins now."

Sadie popped the rest of her apple into her mouth and stood. "Well. So much for taking the morning off."

"Come on," Jasper said, rising beside her.

Veilborne

Clara nodded and followed.

They joined the flow of students climbing the winding path that led towards a wide colonnade above the courtyard. The pillars were carved with ancient glyphs and wrapped in flowering vines, and from the open sides, the entire valley of Eryndor stretched out in panoramic splendour.

It felt sacred.

Sacred—and strangely final.

Clara stood near the back of the gathered crowd as the Auricals assembled at the stone dais ahead. Their robes flowed like water, their presence commanding. And then—one figure stepped forward.

She was taller than the others, her posture effortless yet imposing, like someone who had never once doubted where she stood. Her skin was a warm bronze tone, weathered by age but radiant with vitality. Silver streaks ran through her thick braid, which spilled over one shoulder in a precise pattern that looked woven by spellcraft. Her deep green cloak hung heavy with stitched glyphs that shimmered faintly—lines of light that moved like constellations across a night sky. Beneath it, layered leathers and barkweave armour hinted at a past spent far beyond the safety of the Keep's walls.

Her gaze swept the students—not cold, but sharp enough to carve truth from stone. Eyes like polished obsidian caught the early light and seemed to reflect more than just what they saw.

When she spoke, her voice carried like a bell through still water—clear, calm, unshakable.

"I am Master Vaelryn," she said. "Welcome to Calendor Keep."

Clara's breath caught. The locket pulsed once against her chest.

Vaelryn's gaze swept the assembled students. "You will be tested—mind, body, and spirit. You will learn what it means to walk between worlds. Some of you will rise. Others may fall. But no one will walk this path alone."

A hush fell over the group. Even Sadie—normally all winks and wisecracks—stood straight, eyes locked forward.

Vaelryn gestured behind her, where four other Auricals stood in a quiet line of authority.

"This is Master Kell," she said first, nodding toward a broad-shouldered man with weathered skin and iron-grey hair tied back in a short braid. His cloak was deep forest green, clasped with a polished rune-stone, and a sword hilt jutted from the strap slung across his back. "Head of Physical and Survival Training."

Master Kell gave a short, pragmatic nod—no smile, no flourish. His stance was that of a soldier, feet planted, arms folded, eyes scanning the students as if measuring them for battle.

"Archivist Heren," Vaelryn continued, gesturing to the next. He was tall and reed-thin, with long limbs and parchment-pale skin. His robes were midnight blue, lined with pale gold script that shimmered faintly with moving text. Ink stains darkened his fingertips, and his sharp eyes—wide and glassy like an owl's—took in the crowd with uncanny stillness. "He oversees History, Lore, and Veil Studies."

Heren inclined his head the barest degree, his gaze pausing briefly on Clara—unreadable.

Vaelryn turned to the next. "Professor Lirah Valen," she said, her tone more formal now. "Instructor of Advanced Magical Application and Veil Theory."

Lirah stepped forward lightly, her presence elegant but contained. She wore robes of deep violet threaded with silver glyphs, the cuffs glimmering faintly with residual spellwork. Her black hair was pulled into a tight braid wrapped in copper wire, and her expression was almost too calm. Controlled. Measured.

Her eyes swept the gathered students and briefly landed on Clara. She offered a smile that didn't quite reach her eyes, then stepped back without a word.

Veilborne

"And finally," Vaelryn said, turning slightly toward the last figure, "Master Eldric Ducart. Senior Aurical. Head of Relic Retrieval and Veil Operations."

Eldric didn't step forward so much as straighten, his long coat cinched with Aurical cords, the scabbard at his hip worn but well-kept. His silver-streaked hair was tied at the nape, and his expression was as familiar to Clara as it was unreadable to the others—sharp, protective, and reserved. His cloak was charcoal grey, clasped with a triangular rune that pulsed faintly.

He gave no bow, no smile—only a slow, deliberate nod. There was something in it that said: I'm still watching.

"These four will guide your training," Vaelryn said. "Each in their way. Each from a path you may one day walk yourselves."

She lifted her chin. "Together, we will shape your training. But first—your placement."

From the side of the dais, a steward stepped forward carrying a long scroll sealed with a sun-and-spiral crest. He unrolled it with ceremonial slowness.

As he did, two great banners unfurled behind the Auricals—one bearing a spiral of starlight against deep navy, the other a golden sun pierced with a blade of light.

"From this day forward," Vaelryn said, "you will be assigned to one of four Houses—Starfire, Dawnspire, Mistveil or Stoneward. These are not mere dormitories. They are your cohorts, kin, and first anchors within Calendor Keep."

She turned, her silver-threaded cloak catching the light. One by one, the Auricals each stepped forward—not just as instructors, but as living embodiments of what lay ahead.

Master Kell stood with arms folded, his voice as solid as stone.

"You'll earn your footing where it counts—out there. Cold nights, steep climbs, and magic that doesn't ask nicely. Get ready to bleed for your strength."

Archivist Heren spoke next, his tone soft, patient, and utterly without condescension.

"Knowledge is a blade finer than steel and sharper than pride. You'll wield it—or you'll falter."

Professor Lirah Valen offered a polite nod, her voice smooth and composed, like ink flowing across parchment.

"Magic is not chaos. It is discipline. Precision. If you lose focus, it will not hesitate to remind you."

Eldric stepped forward last, his grey eyes sweeping the students.

"You are not here to be told who you are," he said quietly. "You're here to uncover it. And once you do, the world will not look the same."

Clara felt a chill ripple down her spine. It wasn't fear. It was weight. Truth. Like something vast had just begun to shift.

A soft murmur spread through the crowd as the steward began to read.

Names echoed across the colonnade, one by one, students peeling off to stand beneath their assigned banner.

Clara's heart pounded.

When her name came, it almost didn't register.

"Clara Holloway—House Starfire."

She stiffened, then moved on instinct toward the spiral banner, passing other first-years who whispered as she walked by. Her skin prickled.

She glanced up once and saw Varek Draven watching her from the crowd, his grey eyes unreadable. A faint smirk played at his lips.

She looked away.

A moment later—

"Sadie Thorne—House Starfire."

Sadie pumped a fist. "Ha!" She trotted over and slung an arm across Clara's shoulders. "Meant to be."

Veilborne

Then—"Jasper Quell—House Starfire."

Clara couldn't help the grin that broke across her face as he joined them, already adjusting his satchel like he was preparing for a lecture.

"Perfect balance," Sadie said proudly. "The chaos, the calm, and whatever you are."

"Still deciding," Clara murmured.

One by one, more names followed. A few familiar faces, others she didn't recognise. Then—

"Varek Draven—House Dawnspire."

Clara stiffened. So did Sadie.

Varek moved with that same unnerving grace, his entourage flanking him like shadows. He didn't spare them a glance as he took his place beneath the sun-marked banner.

When the sorting ended, the two cohorts stood opposite across the colonnade—twenty students apiece. A quiet tension shimmered in the air.

Vaelryn stepped forward again.

"Balance is not found in sameness," she said. "It is forged in opposition. Your Houses will grow together, clash, and, in time, depend on one another."

The silence that followed felt ceremonial.

"Your dormitories await," she said finally. "Rest well. Tomorrow, your path begins."

The path to the Starfire dormitory wove through a corridor of stone and root, where pale glyphs shimmered softly along the walls like constellations guiding their way. The air was warm, tinged with the scent of cedar and old parchment.

At the corridor's end, an arched doorway of living wood unfurled like petals as they approached, revealing a wide chamber carved into the heart of one of the Keep's great trees.

Clara stepped inside and stopped.

The dormitory was nothing like the bare stone halls of Blackthorn Hollow. Here, everything felt alive.

The chamber rose several storeys high, its walls shaped from polished bark and smooth stone laced with veins of glowing moss. Dozens of alcoves lined the inner curve, each framed by thick vines and hung with light fabric curtains. Beds, writing desks, and shelves had been carved directly into the tree's heartwood, all glowing faintly with magic woven into the grain.

A spiral staircase led to a lofted reading nook, where floating lanterns drifted lazily between tall shelves. A small hearth crackled near the base, its fire a gentle blue.

And opposite the entrance, a wide archway opened onto a balcony that looked out across the valley. The twin moons hung low above the distant hills, casting silver light over the treetops.

"This is ours?" Clara whispered.

Jasper adjusted his satchel and nodded slowly. "Apparently."

"Dibs on the top bunk," Sadie said automatically—then paused, scanned the room, and snorted. "Right. No bunks."

She pointed toward a vine-draped alcove with a wide window overlooking the treetops. "In that case… that one's mine. Prime moonlight. Decent breeze. And close enough to the balcony for a dramatic escape, should the need arise."

She dashed off to investigate.

Clara wandered toward the window instead, her hand brushing against the wood as it responded with a soft shimmer of warmth. The magic here wasn't loud. It was quiet—woven into every breath of air, every floorboard. It wasn't showing off. It simply was.

She sat on the edge of her chosen bed—a curved recess beneath a flowering vine—and drew her knees up to her chest.

Veilborne

Jasper dropped into the seat at the nearby writing desk and began sorting his satchel with practised precision.

"Not a bad first day."

"Not the worst," Sadie agreed, flopping backwards onto her mattress and folding her arms behind her head. "Still not thrilled about sharing dorms with Varek, even if he's on the other side."

"He won't bother us here," Jasper said. "Too many eyes."

Sadie gave a noncommittal grunt.

Clara remained quiet, staring out at the moonlit valley.

So this was it.

A new world. A new beginning. And already, it felt heavier than she'd expected. Enchanted forests. Living stone. Guardians of the Veil. A locket that pulsed like a second heartbeat. And enemies—like Varek—who seemed to hate her without even knowing her name.

She reached beneath her tunic and pulled out the locket. It rested in her palm, warm and steady, glowing faintly like a coal left just long enough in the hearth.

She turned it over in her fingers.

"You okay?" Jasper asked gently.

Clara nodded. "Yeah. Just... thinking."

Sadie sat up. "Well don't think too hard. I heard orientation's nothing compared to what comes next."

Jasper muttered something about bone-cracking sparring matches and week-long hike simulations.

Sadie laughed. "Sounds like fun."

Clara smiled softly. For the first time in what felt like years, the weight pressing against her chest had started to ease—not gone, but not as suffocating.

She stood and moved to the balcony, hands resting on the wooden railing as the breeze played gently through her hair.

The stars over Eryndor were brighter than any she had seen before—like the sky was trying to make up for all the nights she'd gone without wonder.

Behind her, the voices of her new friends faded as they settled into their spaces, laughter and quiet rustling marking the end of their long day.

Clara touched the locket one last time and whispered into the night:

"Wherever you've brought me... I'm ready."

Chapter 7
A New Dawn in Starfire

The soft chime of bells stirred Clara from sleep.

For a moment, she lay still, blinking up at the wooden beams arched above her, each carved with gentle curves and knotwork patterns that shimmered faintly in the rising light. The canopy above her bed glowed with a dappled blush of dawn, soft and pale, as though the world itself was stretching, yawning, and beginning again.

Then memory returned, not all at once, but like sunlight filtering through tree branches: warm, scattered, and real.

The storm.

The portal.

The strange, pulsing locket beneath her collar.

The world beyond the Veil.

Eryndor.

A place of glowing forests and floating lanterns, of living architecture and whispered legends. A world of magic that had felt like a dream, until it wasn't. Until she was here, heart pounding in a dorm carved from the heartwood of a tree, surrounded by strangers who wielded spells as naturally as breathing.

She wasn't in Blackthorn Hollow anymore.

This wasn't some fairy tale. It was real. All of it.

Clara sat up slowly in the round alcove of her bed, brushing a strand of hair from her face. The stone walls of the dorm glowed with the soft light of early morning, and through the tall windows, the valley below was painted in silver mist. Twin suns hung just above the horizon, one pale gold, the other a soft bluish-white, casting long streaks of colour through the waking forest.

Across the room, Jasper sat cross-legged on his bed, already dressed, nose buried in a small green-bound book. His brow was furrowed in concentration, lips moving silently as he read.

Sadie, by contrast, remained thoroughly asleep.

She sprawled across her mattress in a crooked tangle of limbs, one leg dangling off the side, a half-eaten slice of glowfruit rind stuck to her cheek. She snored softly, steady, content, and completely unaware of the world waking around her.

Clara smiled faintly and swung her legs over the edge of her bed. The smooth wood beneath her feet radiated a gentle warmth, as if the room itself was welcoming her into the day.

For a moment, she simply sat there, toes curling against the polished floor, breathing in the scent of morning moss and distant firesmoke. No bells clanged. No icy buckets slammed against stone. No sharp whispers from Elsie or the others. Just the soft rustle of vines, the faint murmur of wind through leaves, and the quiet breath of a place that felt… safe.

It was strange, how easily her body expected hardship. Expected cold. Hunger. Cruelty. She reached for none of those things now. Her clothes were warm and clean, not scratchy hand-me-downs. Her bed hadn't sagged or creaked beneath her. No one had tried to shove her aside or steal her breakfast.

Instead, she had Sadie's smirk and Jasper's quiet steadiness. She had magic in the air and stars she didn't have to wish on, because here, maybe she didn't have to wish anymore.

Clara closed her eyes briefly.

She didn't know what the day would bring. But for the first time in a long time, she wasn't afraid.

She dressed quickly, tugging on a simple tunic and trousers set beside the bed from the night before, both soft and subtly embroidered with swirling thread patterns that seemed to shift slightly if she looked too long. Her boots fit better than anything she'd worn before, sturdy, flexible, and warm around the ankles.

The air in the room was fresh and fragrant, carrying the faint scent of moss, something floral and sweet, like petals unfurling just out of sight, and the distant tang of forest rain.

Her fingers slipped beneath her collar, brushing the smooth silver surface of the locket resting at her chest.

Still warm. Still silent.

But undeniably... there.

Clara exhaled, shoulders rising and falling.

Whatever today brought... she would be ready.

****

The courtyard beyond the dormitories was soaked in morning light.

Misted gold filtered through towering trees that arched overhead like cathedral spires. Dew clung to every leaf and vine, turning the forest's edge into a shimmering curtain of silver threads. The cobbled path beneath Clara's boots was warm and dappled, stones nestled among thick roots that pulsed faintly with life.

Somewhere above, birds sang, not quite like those she'd known in Blackthorn Hollow, but stranger creatures, with trilling, layered calls that echoed like flutes played underwater.

Jasper strolled beside her, his book now tucked under one arm. Sadie trailed just behind, rubbing at her eyes with one sleeve and yawning as though recovering from a century's sleep.

They rounded a bend past a hedge of broad-leaved plants that folded closed as they passed, and a familiar mossy voice called out from ahead.

"Up and about already, are we?"

Clara turned.

Fennrick Bramble stood at the base of a twisting tree whose bark shimmered faintly with patches of lichen glowing like moonlight. He crouched in the shade, tugging gently at the edge of a tangled vine with what looked like a tiny, winged creature perched on his shoulder. The creature gave an indignant chirp and dove into his satchel, which squeaked in protest.

"Morning, you little forestlings," Fennrick said, patting the satchel affectionately. Then he looked up at the trio, eyes twinkling beneath wild brows. "Ah, Miss Holloway. You're looking more at ease this morning. Less like a squirrel in a thunderstorm."

He nodded, almost to himself. "Starting to look like you belong."

Clara smiled, still not quite used to how this strange man always seemed to appear just when the world felt like it was tilting sideways. "I think so."

Sadie padded forward, grinning. "Fennrick. Did the woods spit you out again, or are you just collecting twigs for your ever-growing beard?"

Fennrick stroked his tangled hair thoughtfully. "Ah, Sadie," he said with a twinkle in his eye. "Wit before breakfast. Always a promising sign."

"What do you know about the cohorts?" Jasper asked, ever the practical one.

Fennrick straightened and leaned on his walking stick, a gnarled branch that looked suspiciously like it had sprouted a new leaf since yesterday.

"Ah yes. Starfire and Dawnspire," he said with mock grandeur. "Names older than the Keep itself. Some say they were once constellations. Others claim they're metaphors. Personally, I think someone just liked how they sounded."

Jasper waited patiently, though Clara caught a flicker of curiosity in his eyes.

Veilborne

"But what's the point of splitting us up?"

"Balance," Fennrick replied simply. "Temperament. It's not about magic or merit. It's about learning from tension. Harmony through friction. Growth through challenge."

Sadie stretched with a groan. "So much for switching Houses. Guess we're stuck with the same banners."

Fennrick leaned on his staff, a half-smile tugging at his lips as he regarded her.

"Some banners shine brighter than others, Sadie. You lot might just surprise them."

Sadie smirked. "Good. I like surprising people."

"That's the part I'm worried about," Jasper muttered.

Fennrick chuckled. "Worry less, Master Quell. Some trouble's worth the mess."

With that, he tipped an imaginary hat. The vine curling around his staff coiled lazily as he turned away. The satchel at his side squeaked again, and Fennrick shot it a stern glance.

"Yes, yes, I know. No more climbing the herb wall without permission."

He wandered off into the sun-dappled forest, humming tunelessly as tiny motes of light stirred in his wake.

Clara stood still for a moment, listening to the breeze shift through the canopy above.

She didn't fully understand what he meant, about balance, about tension, but something in his voice made her believe it mattered.

****

The dining hall of Calendor Keep had transformed with the morning.

Golden sunlight streamed through high stained-glass windows, casting rippling patterns across the long oak tables and polished stone floor. Overhead, enchanted lanterns floated lazily, adjusting their glow to match the warmth of dawn. Thick wooden beams stretched above like the branches of a vast, inverted tree.

Clara entered slowly, flanked by Sadie and Jasper, her gaze drinking in every detail.

The air was rich with the scent of toasted spicebread, woodsmoke, and something faintly floral, lavender and lemon balm mingling softly. Platters and pitchers hovered gently above the tables, gliding along invisible tracks. When someone reached for a dish, it paused patiently, then continued once they'd taken what they wanted.

Steam curled from bowls of golden-root stew, flecked with emerald herbs and tiny pearl-like grains that shimmered faintly under the light. Loaves of honeycrust bread crackled softly as they sliced themselves, revealing swirls of cinnamon and dried forestberries baked into the dough. There were soft wedges of moon-milk cheese resting on greenleaf crackers, charred slices of flamefruit drizzled with sticky, spiced syrup, and delicate petal dumplings that changed colour slightly with each bite.

Among the wonders, there were comforts Clara recognised, sliced apples dusted with sugar, hard-boiled eggs tinged faintly blue from herb brine, little mugs of hot chocolate thick enough to coat a spoon, and porridge, yes, actual porridge, rich and golden, heaped with roasted nuts, jewel-red jam, and a drizzle of syrup that smelled almost exactly like maple.

Clara's eyes danced across the floating dishes, unsure whether to reach out or just keep staring.

Sadie leaned closer, eyes narrowing at a platter of something gelatinous and lilac-hued, shaped like tiny domes.

"Okay, I've lived in Eryndor my whole life, and I've never seen that before."

"It's wobbling," Jasper said, fascinated. "Why's it wobbling like that?"

The dish gave a gentle shimmer, then released a tiny, cheerful whistle like a flute.

Veilborne

Sadie recoiled. "Nope. Not food. That's a creature pretending to be food."

Jasper, entirely unbothered, reached out and tapped one gently with the tip of his fork.

"Still warm. Possibly sentient."

Clara giggled, surprised by the sound herself.

Sadie grinned at her. "Welcome to breakfast in the Keep. Equal parts delicious and vaguely threatening."

Jasper plucked something that looked like a cross between a baked fig and a rosebud.

"Some of these dishes are from the lower valleys," he murmured, "but others... I think they're conjured. Not cooked. Like the ingredients don't even grow anymore."

Sadie arched a brow. "You mean we're eating extinct vegetables?"

"I mean we're recreating them," he said, already scribbling notes in his ever-present journal.

"Someone's been digging deep into Eryndorian culinary archives."

Clara watched a bowl of violet-glazed mushrooms steam beside a floating tray of sugar-glass petals folded like pastries. She reached slowly, carefully, selecting a slice of warm, crusty bread studded with glowing golden raisins.

She bit in, and for a moment, everything else stopped.

It was soft and sweet, with just a hint of something... wild. Like sunlight had a flavour.

Maybe this wasn't home.

But whatever it was... it had breakfast sorted.

A coiled pastry shaped like a spiral galaxy hovered before Clara and dipped delicately into her bowl. As it unraveled, warm golden nectar filled the hollow centre, steaming faintly.

"What is this?" Clara whispered, wide-eyed.

"Starvine swirl," Jasper replied without looking up. He was already halfway through his own, crumbs dusting the page of his latest book.

"Tastes like spiced pear and sunlight."

Clara blinked. "What does sunlight taste like?"

Jasper paused, then adjusted his glasses slightly.

"Like warmth after a storm. Sweet, but not sugary. Kind of like… the feeling when you first step outside and everything smells clean."

Clara took a bite. The flavour bloomed across her tongue, rich, golden, and unexpectedly soft. Like fruit warmed by sun and memory.

"Oh," she said quietly. "That's actually… right."

Sadie, sitting cross-legged beside them, bit into a shimmering blue fruit.

"Try the shimmerfruit. Fizzes on your tongue. Like lightning lemonade."

Clara took a cautious bite, and nearly laughed aloud as a rush of tiny bubbles danced across her tongue like starlight caught in a rainstorm.

She glanced around. The tables were full of Starfire students, chattering, laughing, some hunched over their trays, others already trading enchanted utensils like rare treasures.

Across the hall, the Dawnspire students sat in neat, straight-backed rows. Their table was quieter, more formal. Plates were arranged precisely. No one laughed.

At the centre sat Varek Draven, sipping something dark from a cut-crystal cup. He didn't glance their way, but Clara had the strange feeling he didn't need to. Like he always knew exactly who was in the room.

Clara quickly looked away.

Sadie noticed.

Veilborne

"Don't waste your energy," she muttered, popping another slice of shimmerfruit into her mouth.

"He drinks swampwater and pretends it's tea."

Clara smiled faintly, but the knot in her stomach lingered.

A few seats down, someone summoned a pitcher of sweetroot tea with a whispered word and a flick of the wrist. The pitcher hovered politely, poured itself into the cup, then floated on.

Every part of this world still felt surreal, like stepping into a book mid-chapter. And yet, it was real. She was here.

She glanced at Sadie and Jasper, laughing about something she'd missed, and felt the warmth spread through her, soft as the glow of the lanterns above.

Not home, Clara thought, but maybe… something close.

****

Later that morning, the students were led down a wide spiral staircase that descended deep beneath the Keep. The walls shimmered faintly with inlaid runes, and a hush settled over the group as the air grew cooler with every step.

At the bottom stood a great oaken door, slightly ajar. Its surface was carved with swirling glyphs and ancient markings that shifted subtly, like ripples across water. Beyond it, the air pulsed with quiet knowledge.

Inside lay the Lorehall, a vast circular chamber with tiered seating carved from smooth stone, each level ringed with floating lanterns casting a soft golden light. Above, a breathtaking dome painted with constellations, stars that actually moved, tracing their paths across a night sky impossibly deep.

At the chamber's centre, a crystalline map hovered above a wide dais, slowly rotating. Two worlds spun in perfect balance, their edges rimmed with shimmering light.

Beside the map stood a tall, rail-thin man draped in deep midnight-blue robes, lined with pale gold script that shimmered faintly like crawling ink. His long limbs folded neatly behind his back, posture impeccable, too still to be casual. His pale skin bore the waxen hue of one who spent more time with books than sunlight, and his owl-like eyes, enlarged behind curved spectacles, seemed to take in the entire room at once. A faint scent of old parchment and fresh ink clung to him like an aura.

"I am Archivist Heren," he said, voice resonant and low. Each word measured, weighted, as if chosen with surgical precision. "Today, we begin not with spells, but with stories. Not magic, but memory."

With a flick of two long, ink-stained fingers, the map flared to life. The floating worlds glowed brighter, their surfaces swirling with faint currents of light and shadow. A soft hum filled the room as the constellation-dappled dome above flickered like a living sky.

"This," he said, motioning to the first world, "is Eryndor. And this", he gestured to the second, "is the world some of you came from."

Clara leaned forward instinctively, heart quickening.

"The Veil between them has existed for as long as records allow us to remember," Heren continued. "But it is not a wall. It is a scar, a wound left by a fracture that should never have occurred."

As he spoke, a ripple of shadow passed across the floating map. A hooded figure emerged between the two glowing worlds, indistinct, formed of swirling smoke and arcane mist.

"He is called the Divider of Worlds," Heren said, voice dropping like the opening of a crypt. "Known to some as MalVaran."

Clara's breath caught. Her hand drifted to the locket at her chest without thinking, fingertips brushing its warm curve.

"His motives are debated," Heren went on, pacing slowly along the dais's edge. "His legacy, less so. He disrupted the natural order, not with brute force alone, but with knowledge. Forbidden knowledge."

Veilborne

The shadowy figure dissolved, replaced by a grid of shimmering symbols, faction banners, magical rifts, fragments of crumbling citadels. Lines connected them in impossible patterns, like threads through a loom.

"There was a war," he said. "Not one most mortals noticed. But to those who walk between worlds, to the Auricals, the Obsidian Court, the Gilded, and others, it was a war of belief. A war of inheritance. A war over the very foundation of reality."

Jasper's pen scratched furiously across parchment. Sadie leaned toward Clara and whispered, "Bet we're tested on this next week."

Clara said nothing, eyes fixed on the space where MalVaran had stood, a place now empty, yet still pulsing with silent menace.

Archivist Heren's voice softened as he circled the map's edge. "Some of you may feel disturbed by this history. Good. That means your instincts are intact."

His robes whispered as he moved, the runes etched along their hem shifting like living script.

"This class will not teach you fire or force. It will teach you context. Without context, magic is chaos, an accelerant in untested hands."

Above them, the star-painted dome flickered again. The constellations twisted into a vast battlefield of golden light. Ethereal figures clashed, some clad in flowing Aurical robes, others wrapped in swirling darkness. Arcs of raw magic rent the sky, which cracked open with visible rifts. The illusion pulsed with such depth and sound Clara almost flinched.

"This," Heren said, voice barely more than breath, "was the Silent Rebellion. The last time MalVaran's influence rose."

The room fell silent.

Clara stared. The mural shifted again, to a lone tower, crumbling but ringed in protective light. Two shadowy figures stood at its heart, hands outstretched toward something flickering between them. A flash of silver. Then the image faded like mist.

"The records are incomplete," Heren said. "Some truths were lost. Others hidden. And some, deliberately buried."

He turned to face them once more, hands folding neatly behind his back.

"But remember this," he said, his voice rising with quiet gravity, "magic is memory. And memory, like magic, must be protected."

A soft bell rang high above them, clear and melodic, like wind chimes stirred by moonlight.

"Class dismissed."

Clara gathered her parchment slowly, though she hadn't written much. Her thoughts were scattered, frayed like loose threads. Something about MalVaran's figure, the tower, that silver glimmer between worlds, clung to her like breath on a cold window.

Around her, students filtered out in murmurs and pairs, some buzzing with excitement, others subdued. The crystalline map dimmed, its light folding inward like a flower closing at dusk.

At the front, Archivist Heren settled onto a carved stool and summoned a hovering scroll and quill. With faint flicks of his hand, the quill dipped and scratched mid-air, making silent annotations.

Sadie leaned close, whispering, "I like him. He's got that 'smile once and you'll never forget it' thing. Like a bedtime story that might strangle you."

Jasper adjusted his satchel and nodded. "He's one of the oldest Auricals. I read he was the last to speak with the previous Council head before the Rebellion."

Clara's gaze drifted back to the centre of the room, where the Veil had shimmered. It lingered in her mind's eye, like the ghost of a door once open.

She touched the locket again, gently, through her tunic.

It was still.

Veilborne

But not silent.

****

Their boots echoed softly along the polished stone floor as Clara, Jasper, and Sadie made their way through one of the lesser-used corridors on their way back to the dormitory. The passage was dimmer than the rest of the Keep, lined with tall arched windows of stained glass. They shimmered faintly with shifting patterns, runes and sigils hidden within the coloured panes that revealed themselves only under moonlight's touch.

"I'm pretty sure this isn't the way back," Clara murmured, glancing around. The floor tiles beneath their feet flickered subtly between green, gold, and silver.

"It's the scenic route," Sadie declared confidently, stepping up to a glimmering alcove framed with ivy. "Maybe we'll stumble on a hidden armory or a cursed mirror."

As if summoned by her words, one of the tall mirrors beside them let out a sharp, irritated sneeze.

The trio froze.

A squat, round-faced reflection appeared in the centre of the glass, rubbing its nose with an exaggerated snort. "Well, don't just stand there gaping. Say hello, would you? It's rude."

Clara blinked. "...Hello?"

The mirror harrumphed. "Much better. Honestly. Enchanted for two centuries, and still the only manners I get are from first-years."

Another nearby mirror rolled its eyes, yes, actually rolled its eyes, and muttered, "They never dust anymore either."

Sadie burst out laughing. "I love this place."

Jasper, already scribbling in a leather-bound notebook, muttered, "Self-aware enchantments. Probably residual soul fragments from a bound memory charm. Possibly ancient. Definitely annoying."

The grumpy mirror glared. "I heard that, lore-lover."

Clara smiled despite herself. The warmth of the moment sliced through the last of the day's tension.

"We'll come back and visit later," she said quickly, tugging Sadie gently by the sleeve before she could start arguing with the furniture.

"Before someone challenges us to a debate we can't win," Clara muttered, pulling Sadie along.

"I wouldn't mind being outwitted by a mirror," Sadie said, casting a playful glance over her shoulder. "Better than half the conversations I've had this week."

They broke into a run as they left the chamber behind, laughter bubbling before any of them could stop it. The halls of Calendor echoed with the sound, bright, unrestrained, and alive.

Jasper clutched his satchel to keep it from bouncing, breathless between chuckles. "We are absolutely going to get blamed for something again, aren't we?"

"Oh, definitely," Sadie grinned, her curls bouncing as she skipped ahead. "But at least it'll be for something interesting this time."

Clara couldn't help herself, she laughed too, her voice rising with theirs, the weight of the morning falling away with every step. For the first time in days, it felt like they were just kids again. Not chosen. Not hunted. Not different.

Just three friends, racing down ancient corridors beneath glowing lights, in a world full of magic and mischief.

And for that brief, golden stretch of hallway, it was enough.

****

Later, the three sprawled across the rug in the dormitory's reading nook. The sky outside the balcony was dark now, spangled with stars that drifted ever so slowly, constellations shifting like clockwork above Eryndor.

Veilborne

"Today was... a lot," Clara said softly.

"No kidding," Sadie replied, tossing a pillow upward and catching it with one hand. "I liked the breakfast. Ten out of ten. Would swirl again."

"I liked the library we passed on the way to the Lorehall," Jasper added quietly. "Did you see the ceiling? The star map moves in real time."

Sadie poked Clara's arm. "What about you?"

Clara hesitated, wrapping her arms around her knees. "I don't know. It all feels... big. Like I'm missing something everyone else already understands."

"You're not," Jasper said, adjusting his glasses. "You just got here. You're not behind, you're at the start."

A thoughtful pause fell, the flicker of crystal lanterns casting warm halos on the walls.

Then Jasper asked, "Do you know anything about your parents?"

Clara's breath caught. She shook her head slowly. "No names. No stories. Just the locket, really. I didn't even know it was magical until it started... doing stuff."

Sadie's usual smirk faded. She leaned back against the cushions, unusually quiet.

Jasper offered quietly, "Maybe there's something here, a spell, a relic, or a trace of magic, that could help you find out. You're in the right place to look."

"I hope so," Clara whispered, her fingers drifting once more to the locket. "I really do."

Later, curled beneath the softly glowing canopy of her bed, Clara listened to the faint rustle of leaves beyond the dormitory balcony. The night air in Eryndor was cooler than she'd expected, but not unfriendly, like the forest itself was breathing around her, whispering secrets it wasn't quite ready to speak aloud.

Sleep came slowly.

Her fingers curled loosely around the locket resting at her chest, as they had every night for as long as she could remember. Tonight, though, the weight of everything pressed down on her like a thick, heavy blanket: the orphanage, the storm, the creatures, the stranger, the portal, the Keep.

And now... questions. So many questions.

About her parents.

About herself.

About the locket.

In the hush of the dormitory, where the only sounds were faint creaks of ancient roots and the soft sighs of sleeping students, Clara finally drifted into dreams.

She didn't stir when the locket pulsed, not with warmth, but with something else.

A thread-thin arc of silver lightning flickered across its surface, tracing the engraved spirals with a faint crackle like distant static. It flared again, two slender arcs of light dancing briefly across the metal, then fell still.

As if the locket had... exhaled.

Beneath the canopy of stars beyond the window, the night in Eryndor deepened.

Veilborne

Chapter 8
The Locket Remembers

Some things are not forgotten. Only waiting.

Clara sat upright at her desk, shoulders tense, eyes wide. Around the circular chamber, relics floated in slow, deliberate orbits, each enclosed in a thin field of shimmering light that pulsed softly, as if the magic holding them aloft were breathing.

They moved along invisible tracks just above head height, rotating gently as they passed the rows of students. It was like sitting in the heart of a slow-moving constellation, each relic a star trailing its own quiet story.

A charred gauntlet turned slowly in place, its surface blackened and cracked, as if it had once burned from within. Beside it drifted a shard of mirrored glass, its reflection showing not Clara's face but flickers of something else, mountains, perhaps, or shadowed figures passing through fog. Then a small silvery music box floated by, no larger than a fist and sealed tight without hinges. It spun lazily on its axis, emitting a soft, breathy tune, like wind weaving through pine needles at dusk.

The chamber itself was unlike anything Clara had seen before, nothing like the cold stone classrooms of Blackthorn Hollow or the damp, coal-scented orphanage halls. Here, the walls curved seamlessly, carved from pale, veined stone glowing faintly with embedded glyphs. Dozens of arched windows pierced the upper walls, not glass but clear crystal shimmering with iridescent colour. The light filtering through shifted subtly as relics passed beneath, casting halos and dancing patterns onto the floor.

Tiered desks ringed the chamber in a sunken amphitheatre shape, each row lined with smooth wood polished to a soft sheen. The students sat in quiet wonder, whispering occasionally but mostly watching in reverent silence.

Clara's desk felt warm beneath her fingers, not from heat, but from the steady thrum of ambient magic woven through the room itself. Every so often, a subtle breeze stirred her hair, though no windows were open, no doors ajar. It was as if the room breathed alongside the relics.

At the chamber's centre stood a wide platform of dark stone, etched with concentric circles and ancient runes. A glowing crystal sphere hovered just above, emitting a soft hum that resonated deep in the chest, like distant thunder muffled by snowfall. From this orb, arcs of energy extended outward, branching like veins into the air, anchoring the relics in their orbits.

At the far end, a quiet Aurical stood sentinel near the containment dome, robes faintly shimmering, hands folded behind their back. They neither spoke nor moved much, merely observed. Their presence was more guardian than teacher, as if to ensure nothing… stirred.

Clara hadn't caught their name; she was too busy staring at the music box, the mirrored shard, the dozens of impossible objects moving with careful precision. Each whispered without words.

She didn't yet know what she was meant to learn.

But part of her, the part that had clung to the locket her entire life, already understood this room was important.

These weren't mere artifacts.

They were memories.

And memories, as she was rapidly learning, were the most dangerous kind of magic.

Beside her, Jasper's eyes sparkled behind his glasses. He scribbled furiously in his notebook.

"These are real," he whispered. "Pre-Veil era. Museum-grade."

Sadie leaned over Clara's desk, squinting at the music box.

"Bet something explodes before the hour's out."

Clara tried to laugh, but her chest felt tight. The locket beneath her uniform wasn't pulsing, but it was warm. Watchful. As if aware.

Veilborne

A side door clicked open softly, and a new figure entered the chamber, narrow-shouldered, hawk-eyed, composed with the sharpness of command. Her silver earrings shimmered like coiled runes, and the moment she stepped inside, the air seemed to straighten its spine.

"I am Professor Lirah Valen," she said, voice clipped and clear.

"This course is an introduction to relics, what they are, what they do, and why most of you should never touch one unsupervised until you are ready."

A few students laughed nervously.

Professor Valen's eyes swept the chamber. She lifted a thin brass glyph-pointer and tapped the glowing chain of a relic on display.

"Relics are not tools," she said. "They are echoes. Each item carries memory. Some benign. Others… less so. All of them are alive, not in mind, but in history. They remember what they were made for."

Clara's locket warmed slightly against her chest.

She shifted in her seat, fingers brushing the metal beneath her tunic as Professor Valen began a story about the first Relic War, an arcane conflict between factions who believed relics could predict fate.

Clara barely heard it.

The warmth in the locket deepened, not painful, not uncomfortable. Distinct. Intentional. Like the gentle pressure of a hand resting over her heart.

Her breath hitched.

It wasn't just reacting, it was remembering.

As if something in the room, in the relics themselves, had stirred an echo within it.

A flicker of a song long forgotten.

A whisper passing from one memory to another across time.

Not a sound or a vision, but a sensation, faint and flickering, like candlelight behind fogged glass.

The way one might feel returning to a place once known in another life.

She pressed her palm to the locket through her tunic.

The sensation lingered.

Not frantic. Not fearful.

Just... aware.

Attentive.

As though it had heard these stories before. As if the music box's soft tune, or the shimmer of the mirrored shard, had brushed against something once known, someone it had once belonged to.

Someone who had been here before.

Professor Valen moved like a drawn blade, precise, polished, dangerous in the right hands. Her reed-thin wand tapped against the obsidian plinth at the chamber's centre, and the relics slowly rotated beneath a shimmering containment dome.

"Each of these objects was forged before or during what we now call the Age of Fracture," she said. "They are remnants of an older craft, when enchantment was raw, ungoverned, and ambition often outpaced caution."

Clara felt the air shift, charged, like a gathering storm. The locket pressed warm against her collarbone, no longer a dull thrum but a low, electric hum. It was like standing near a leyline, or how she imagined standing near one would feel, charged and alert, as though the world itself had paused to listen.

Professor Valen paused beside a silver circlet suspended in a containment field, its surface traced with fine etchings that glowed faintly as light caught them.

"This is called a Whisperbind," she said, calm but deliberate. "Recovered from the ruins near the Tarlith Fold nearly seventy years ago. Its enchantments were never fully mapped. Some say it held prophetic visions; others believe it was used to bind oaths sealed by thought alone."

She let the silence linger.

"Relics are not simply old things. They are moments frozen. Echoes captured. Magic doesn't always fade, it embeds itself. In metal. In wood. In bone."

She moved down the line, her silver rune-shaped earrings catching the glow of containment fields.

"These artifacts remain here not because they are inert, but because they are unstable. We don't keep them to display; we protect them because they still listen. Still resonate. Still remember. Some were forged in the earliest days of the Age of Fracture. Others far older, salvaged from before the Veil split."

Her eyes swept the room, pausing a fraction longer on Clara.

"When you study a relic, you are not handling an object. You are confronting a memory. And memory," she added, voice low and weighted, "is the most unpredictable form of magic we have."

The Whisperbind shimmered faintly. A hum passed through the air, felt more than heard.

Clara barely heard her. The heat rose, not enough to burn, but enough to command attention.

Her hand slipped beneath her tunic, fingers brushing the locket's smooth shell.

Then, footsteps.

Measured. Unhurried.

The kind of stride that didn't need to demand attention, because it was used to having it.

The classroom door creaked open, and a figure stepped inside.

He wasn't dressed like a professor.

Travel-worn leather armour lay beneath a weather-streaked cloak, edges frayed and darkened by long days on the road. His boots bore dried mud, cracked and clinging, from places Clara couldn't name. Across one shoulder, a faded crest was stitched into the leather, a feather crossed with an arrow, circled by curling script she didn't recognise. Gold and storm-blue, the thread dulled by age and exposure.

Clara frowned, squinting. It wasn't an Aurical insignia.

She leaned toward Jasper. "What's that symbol?" she whispered.

Jasper didn't look up from his notes. "Courier Guild," he murmured. "High-tier. They carry enchanted messages, artifacts, even Veil-sealed deliveries. Most never meet one unless something big's happening."

Clara sat back, watching the man closely. His movement, shoulders loose but alert, gaze sweeping the room without seeming to, told her everything. He was a man who mapped every exit, listened before speaking, vanished the moment it was needed.

A thin scar carved one brow, a white arc like lightning. In one gloved hand, he held a scroll, sealed tight, wax deep forest green. A metallic sigil gleamed at its centre: complex, unfamiliar, unmistakably official.

Professor Valen turned as he approached. Her expression, usually tightly measured, shifted just enough to suggest she'd been waiting.

"Excellent," she said simply, as if expecting him for hours.

The courier nodded, reached beneath his cloak, and retrieved the scroll with practiced ease. He placed it into her outstretched hand with silent precision, then stepped back with a short, respectful bow.

He turned immediately and strode back toward the door, quiet, efficient, already halfway gone.

And that's when it happened.

As he passed the rows of students, his eyes swept the room.

They landed, just for a breath, on Clara.

The locket stirred.

Veilborne

Not a glow. Not a sound.

Just heat. Pressure.

A sudden surge beneath her collarbone, like breath caught in the throat of the world.

Clara gasped, sharp and silent.

It wasn't pain. Not discomfort.

Something deeper. Older.

Like standing too close to lightning.

Like recognition you can't place.

Her vision blurred at the edges. The classroom muffled, as if underwater.

The courier's gaze paused on her. Just for a moment.

Then it passed.

He dipped his head slightly, a nod that might have meant nothing at all, and vanished through the arched doorway, his cloak brushing stone like falling ash.

The warmth in the locket faded slowly, leaving something behind, a humming, echoing tension beneath her skin.

A static charge not physical at all.

More like a whisper without words.

A name hovering at memory's edge.

Clara sat perfectly still, fingers curled around her desk edge.

"Clara?" Jasper's voice was soft. Concerned.

She blinked. "I, yeah, I'm fine." she said, thin and breathless.

Sadie leaned over, brow furrowed. "You don't look it."

Clara didn't answer.

Not yet.

Something in her chest was still listening.

Meanwhile, Professor Valen broke the seal.

She held the scroll in one hand, eyes scanning the contents as the room slowly settled. Her expression revealed nothing, no frown, no flicker of surprise. Just the steady tick of her gaze across the parchment.

Then, as she reached the end, her eyes lifted.

They swept the room.

And paused, briefly but deliberately, on Sadie.

The moment passed as quickly as it came.

Clara's fingers curled tight around the edge of her desk.

She wasn't afraid of the relics.

But the locket… it had always felt personal. Part of her.

Something steady. Safe.

And yet, as Valen spoke, a new thought crept in, unwelcome, but impossible to ignore.

What if, without knowing it, she'd already brought a relic into the room?

Not one sealed behind glass.

But one pulsing quietly beneath her collar, remembering things she didn't yet understand.

The obsidian plinth sank slowly into the floor, the final hiss of arcane pressure releasing like a sigh. Professor Valen swept her wand through the air, dismissing the containment dome, and turned away without another word.

Students shuffled quietly, some murmuring about the relics, others rushing to their next lesson. But Clara remained frozen beside her desk.

Her hand pressed over the locket, her heartbeat echoing somewhere deeper than her chest.

Veilborne

Sadie looped her satchel over one shoulder and nudged her.

"Come on. You look like you just saw a ghost."

Clara gave a faint nod and rose to follow.

They stepped into the corridor, where stone arches gave way to open light and warm breezes drifting from the garden paths beyond.

Only then did Jasper speak.

"Okay," he said softly, "what happened?"

Clara exhaled slowly, searching for words.

"It was when that man came in. The moment he entered... the locket reacted. Like it knew him."

Sadie frowned.

"Reacted how?"

Clara touched the locket through her tunic.

"Not pain, not heat. More like... a jolt. Recognition. Like something clicked into place I couldn't see."

Jasper was already pulling a notebook from his satchel.

"That fits. If your locket's a relic, and I think it is, it might be aura-bound."

"Aura-bound?" Clara repeated.

"Yeah," Jasper said, flipping pages.

"Some relics tether to people, places, even bloodlines. If someone connected to its history passes close, it might respond. Recognition, warning, sometimes even,"

"defence," Sadie cut in.

"Like back at your old place, when those things broke into the orphanage. The Revenants. You said the locket did something... helped you get away, right?"

Clara blinked.

"Exactly."

Jasper's brow furrowed.

"But if the locket reacted when he looked at you… maybe there's some link. Not necessarily with him, but… something he was carrying. Or something about him."

Clara looked away down the corridor, recalling the man's eyes, sharp, calm, measuring.

"It didn't feel like he saw me. It felt like… something else saw him. Through me."

Sadie tilted her head, thoughtful.

"Or maybe it was the locket that recognised him," she said.

"Not the other way around. Like it… remembered something."

Jasper glanced at Clara's collar.

"You think it's that specific?"

Sadie shrugged.

"It's old. Older than any of us. Who knows what it's seen, or what it's still holding onto."

They walked in silence, footsteps echoing softly through the corridor.

The locket had gone quiet again beneath Clara's collar, its warmth faded to a faint hum she barely noticed now. And yet… she couldn't shake how it had surged. Not frightened. Not hostile.

Just… aware.

As if something in that moment had stirred it awake.

Sadie was first to speak.

"Well," she said, stretching overhead, "remind me never to take a class called Relics lightly again. I thought we'd just be polishing old forks and pretending they were magic."

Jasper raised an eyebrow.

Veilborne

"Polishing relics is how people lose fingers."

"Exactly," Sadie said brightly.

"Lesson learned."

Clara managed a small laugh, but it faded fast. Her eyes traced the edge of a stained-glass window, where golden light spilled across the stone floor like a river of colour.

In that light, the day felt gentler. Simpler.

But the locket beneath her tunic reminded her otherwise.

She didn't understand it. Not yet. But she was beginning to listen.

Jasper glanced over, eyes searching.

"You sure you're alright?"

Clara nodded.

"Yeah. Just... thinking."

Sadie bumped her lightly with her shoulder.

"That's allowed. But not too much thinking. That's his job," she added, nodding at Jasper.

Jasper looked mock-offended.

"It's a full-time burden."

Their laughter was quiet, but it felt good. Real. Like it belonged here.

Clara smiled. Not because everything made sense. Not because she wasn't scared.

But because, for the first time in a long while, she didn't feel alone.

And for now, that was enough.

****

The late afternoon sun slanted low across the courtyard, turning stone paths to gold and casting long shadows between Calendor Keep's tall arches.

Clara, Sadie, and Jasper moved slowly now, conversation fading into thoughtful silence as they passed quieter northern walkways. The buzz of training drills had died away, and the murmur of students in distant study halls gave the Keep a soft, dreaming quality.

Then Clara saw him.

Leaning with practiced stillness against the ivy-wrapped base of a sun-dappled colonnade stood Eldric Ducart.

He spoke in low tones with two other Auricals, one older, the other barely more than a boy, but even as he gestured calmly to a map scroll, his eyes flicked up and locked with Clara's.

He gave her a small, deliberate nod.

She returned it instinctively, though her steps slowed.

Sadie followed Clara's gaze and snorted softly.

"Eldric. Still looks like he's judging the hallway for crimes it hasn't committed yet."

Clara cracked a faint smile.

"He probably is."

"Yeah, well," Sadie added, brushing curls off her shoulder, "if I ever go missing, remind me to get someone less terrifying to come find me."

Clara's smile softened.

"He might be terrifying to you," she said, "but he saved me. He doesn't scare me."

There was no menace in Eldric's stare. But there was gravity, like he was waiting for something, and would wait until it revealed itself.

As the trio moved on, his gaze lingered on Clara a heartbeat longer before he turned back to his companions, his voice never rising.

****

Veilborne

Evening came gently, spilling gold and lilac light across the upper balconies of Calendor Keep.

In the heart of the Starfire dormitory, the reading nook glowed with quiet comfort, cushioned benches curved around a low hearth, where a pale blue fire crackled softly. Floating crystal lanterns drifted above, dimming with dusk like tired fireflies.

Clara sat curled in a deep chair, a thick blanket wrapped around her shoulders. The warmth of the elathrin brew seeped into her fingers, spiced root and citrus peel, sweet and earthy. It reminded her of something she couldn't name, only feel.

Sadie was upside-down in the armchair beside her again, legs tossed over the backrest, sipping noisily from her mug.

Jasper sat cross-legged on the rug, surrounded by an organised chaos of open books, scrolls, and parchment. His drink perched precariously atop a stack of tomes, steam curling in lazy spirals.

For a while, no one spoke. The fire cracked. Pages turned. A soft breeze stirred the gauzy curtains near the balcony, carrying the scent of nightflowers and distant pine.

Clara closed her eyes briefly, letting the warmth soak in. The locket lay quiet against her chest, no pulsing, no flare. Just present. Just hers.

"This place still feels unreal," she murmured finally.

Sadie flipped upright with the grace of someone who made chaos look natural.

"You mean the talking mirrors, magical pastries, or the bit where our dorm is a literal tree?"

Clara laughed softly.

"All of it, I guess. Some days, it feels like I dreamed the whole thing."

Jasper looked up from his notes.

"Dream or not, you're here. We all are."

"I keep waiting for someone to tell me it's a mistake," Clara said.

"That I'm not supposed to be here. That I was never meant to cross the Veil."

Sadie snorted.

"If anyone says that, I'll hex their eyebrows off."

Jasper added,

"Starfire wouldn't be half as interesting without you."

Clara's smile tugged at her lips. The fire cast shifting shadows on the walls, and the locket, warm and silent beneath her tunic, felt less like a question and more like a promise.

She leaned her head back, eyes half-lidded.

"Do you think it'll get easier?" she asked quietly.

Sadie was already half-asleep, her reply muffled by her oversized scarf.

"Probably not."

"But we'll get better," Jasper offered.

"That's how these things work."

And somehow, that was enough.

Outside, the twin moons began their rise, silver and pale gold.

Inside, laughter returned in small doses, sleepy and soft. Books rustled. Steam curled.

And for the first time that day, Clara didn't feel like she had to hold the world together.

She just had to hold on.

****

That Night

The stars over Eryndor wheeled slowly past the high dormitory windows, their constellations unfamiliar but strangely comforting, like songs heard through a dream.

Veilborne

The dormitory had quieted. The fire in the common nook had burned low to embers. Somewhere deeper in the Keep, a bell tolled once, long and low.

Clara lay beneath her canopy, curled on her side with thick blankets pulled up to her chin. The carved runes above glowed faintly, pulsing like distant fireflies.

But Clara wasn't asleep.

Her eyes remained half-open, watching the shifting light across the wooden ceiling. Her thoughts refused to quiet, not with the locket pressing against her skin like a question she didn't yet know how to ask.

She rolled onto her back, staring into the soft shadows.

Who was that man in class?

Why did the locket react so strongly?

What did it see in him that she didn't?

Her fingers slipped beneath her tunic, closing gently around the locket.

It didn't burn. Didn't pulse. It was just... there.

But it felt heavier now. Not in weight, but in meaning. As if the magic sleeping inside had begun to stir.

Clara exhaled slowly and closed her eyes.

She whispered into the stillness, barely louder than breath:

"What am I supposed to do with you?"

The locket stayed silent.

But just as her breath began to slow, drifting toward sleep, the air around her shifted.

A soft pressure. A vibration deep in her bones, like the world holding its breath.

Then, something split. Not with sound, but with feeling.

Mark Peters

A hairline flicker of silver light traced itself across the locket's surface, so fast she might have missed it. A shimmer. A pulse. Then, gone.

Clara's eyes flew open. Her fingers clenched tighter.

Another faint spark arced across the metal. This time she felt it through her skin, like static before a storm. But the warmth was gone. It wasn't comforting.

It was electric.

The locket fell still again, cold and silent as before.

But something had changed.

Clara didn't move. Didn't speak.

Outside, the stars kept shifting. Somewhere deep within the Keep, unseen gears turned.

Not of stone or iron, but of memory. Of purpose.

The past was waking.

Veilborne

Chapter 9
Of Echoes and Awakenings

Day One

The classroom was dim and circular, carved into the stone like a forgotten observatory buried deep beneath Calendor Keep. Its ceiling shimmered with a slow-moving swirl of mist and light, resembling a globe caught mid-turn. Faint golden lines arced and curved through the fog—shapes that might've been continents, constellations, or half-remembered dreams.

Clara sat upright at her desk, trying not to gape as her eyes followed the motion above. Her desk was carved from polished basalt, etched with ancient glyphs that pulsed softly in time with the magical currents in the air. The other students sat in descending rings, amphitheatre-style, watching the ceiling's silent dance.

At the base of the room stood Professor Lirah Valen, spine straight, robes cut with the severe lines of her station. Her silver rune earrings caught the dim light with every shift of her head. She spoke without a preamble.

"Today," she said crisply, "we begin our study of the Veil."

At her words, the mist above began to shift. Two orbs coalesced from the swirling fog—one glowing green with gentle light: Eryndor. The other, pale and dim, hovered opposite it in shadow.

Clara inhaled quietly. That one—her world.

"The Veil," said Lirah, her voice clear but cold, "is not a boundary. It is a fracture. A tear. A mistake. A wound in the weave of what is and what should never have been."

The room hushed further. Even the mist seemed to still.

"There was a time before the Veil. Before the sundering. Before the forgetting. And then one man—driven by brilliance, desperation, or arrogance—tore a hole through the fabric of two worlds."

She flicked her wand, and the burning script unfurled across the mist.

Nikolas Emberlain

The name hovered there, pulsing faintly.

Gasps rippled through the room. Jasper gripped the edge of his desk.

"An inventor," Lirah continued. "A theorist. A rogue. One of the Gilded, later… something else entirely. His name endures, whether we welcome it or not."

She let that hang in the air a beat longer than necessary. Clara felt the silence like a weight.

"Some claim he sought to return to a place glimpsed only in dreams. Others believe he fled something that chased him through the void. But what is known," Lirah said, turning slowly to regard the entire class, "is this: he opened a door. And reality has been fraying ever since."

Clara's gaze drifted back to the dim Earth orb overhead. She felt the echo of her first night here—the swirling portal, the cold wind, the pale creatures. And always, the locket. Heavy. Watching.

A student near the front raised a tentative hand. "Professor… did he vanish?"

Lirah's lip twitched—barely a smile.

"No one vanishes," she replied. "Some simply go where others dare not follow."

She turned to a velvet-lined case and lifted something small and crystalline into view.

"This," she said, raising it just enough for the room to see, "is the only verified fragment of Emberlain's original work. Recovered from the collapsed archive beneath Drosfen."

Inside the cube, delicate gears turned slowly around a glimmer of trapped light—something caught like a firefly under glass.

Veilborne

"It's inert now," Lirah said. "But once, it was part of a larger system. A gate, perhaps. A stabiliser. Or maybe... a key."

She returned it to the pedestal with a soft chime. Her voice grew quieter now—measured, careful.

"Emberlain had a workshop here at Calendor in his final years. The primary study was sealed and picked clean long ago. The artefacts were removed. The doors closed."

Her tone sharpened.

"But some believe he maintained a second space. A hidden chamber. An auxiliary lab, not catalogued, not mapped."

Lirah turned, her wand's tip lowering to her side. Her next words felt casual, but Clara didn't believe that for a moment.

"Of course, no such place has ever been found. And if it were, any student or researcher stumbling upon it would be expected to report it immediately—before triggering... unfortunate consequences."

Jasper shifted in his seat. Sadie leaned forward, brow furrowed.

"And if you ever do encounter relics or constructs from his final work—" Lirah paused, her eyes sweeping the rows until they landed—too deliberately—on Clara "—do not attempt to activate them."

Clara froze.

She hadn't moved, hadn't reacted—but still, it felt as though something sharp had passed just inches from her heart. She gripped the desk tighter, the locket warm beneath her collar.

Above, the mist began to thin. The twin orbs dissolved into vapour.

"That is all for today," said Lirah. "Your essays on Veil theory are due at week's end. Be precise. And remember—curiosity has consequences."

With that, she turned sharply and walked from the room.

Chairs scraped. Cloaks rustled. Students began to rise.

But Clara remained still.

Mark Peters

Because whether Lirah had meant to or not—and Clara suspected she very much had—she had just placed something dangerous into motion.

And part of Clara already knew: they weren't meant to let it go.

****

They didn't speak of it straight away.

Not in the corridor, not in the dining hall.

Clara barely touched her plate. Her thoughts churned like stormwater behind glass, replaying Lirah Valen's voice again and again. The way she'd said "if such a place exists"—calm, deliberate, like she already knew it did.

It wasn't until they found themselves along a winding trail behind the Keep—beneath copper-leaf trees and fern-choked stonework—that Sadie finally broke the silence.

"So," she said, pushing aside a branch, "is it just me, or did Professor Valen basically invite someone to go looking for that hidden study?"

Jasper let out a slow breath. "It didn't sound like a warning. It sounded like bait."

"Exactly," Sadie said. "She practically dangled it in front of us like a shiny key."

Clara didn't respond straight away.

Sadie turned to her. "You felt it, too, right? The way she said it? Like it wasn't just a story—it was a message."

Jasper nodded. "And coming from Valen? That's not nothing. She doesn't waste words. If she mentioned that study, she wanted someone to hear it."

Clara slowed to a halt. Her gaze drifted across the sun-dappled leaves. "I don't know if it was meant for all of us," she said quietly. "But it felt like it was meant for me."

Sadie raised a brow. "You mean because of the locket?"

Veilborne

Clara nodded once. "Maybe. Or maybe I'm imagining it. But something about the way she looked at me... it didn't feel like a coincidence."

Jasper tilted his head. "You think she knows what it is?"

"I think she wants to know what I'll do with it," Clara replied. "And if that study's connected to Emberlain, then it might be the only place left that hasn't been scrubbed clean or sealed away."

They walked on in silence, the path curling through the undergrowth like an old scar in the land.

Then, the trail opened into a small glen.

Outside a domed greenhouse, half-swallowed by ivy and crowned with stained-glass sunbursts, crouched a familiar figure.

Fennrick Bramble was muttering to a translucent toadstool while poking it with a twig.

"Gently, you spiteful jellycap... we've talked about this..."

Sadie blinked. "Is that...?"

"Yep," Jasper sighed. "That's Fennrick."

"Of course it is."

"Ah!" Fennrick exclaimed, not looking up. "Starfire strays! Was wondering when one of you might come poking after legends."

Clara frowned. "What?"

Fennrick delicately deposited the toadstool into a jar, then stood and dusted off his moss-splotched sleeves. His eyes twinkled behind a tangle of wild hair and a bark-flecked beard.

"You've got that look," he said, pointing at Clara. "Like you're about to dig up something that prefers to stay buried."

Sadie crossed her arms. "You mean the study?"

Fennrick's grin widened. "Ah. So she brought it up, did she? Knew she would eventually."

"So it's real?" Clara asked.

Fennrick tilted his head. "Depends on your definition of real. There was something. Built into the bones of the Keep. Emberlain's private sanctum. The official word says it was sealed off—or never existed at all. But secrets like that… they don't go away. They wait."

Sadie stepped forward. "Did anyone ever find it?"

"No one who kept their eyebrows intact," Fennrick said lightly. "But you lot? You might just be the right kind of wrong to try."

He crouched again and plucked a bright green sprig of fern from beneath the moss, then held it out to Clara.

"If you're going to chase ghosts," he said, "take something living with you."

Clara stared at the fern. "What does that mean?"

Fennrick winked. "You'll know when it matters."

And with that, he turned and wandered off into the tall grass, humming to himself, his satchel squeaking softly—as though something inside it shuffled.

****

The Keep's library was more cathedral than an archive.

Vaulted ceilings soared above them, ribbed with arched beams of living wood entwined with silver veins that shimmered softly with residual magic. Towering shelves stretched into the shadows above, some vanishing into the gloom where floating crystal lanterns drifted like tethered stars. A crisscross of silver and brass chains spanned the vast ceiling, suspending enchanted ladders that glided silently between shelves—guided, Jasper whispered, by reader intention.

Whispers clung to the silence like breath to a mirror. Somewhere, a page turned on its own. Dust floated through slanted beams of light, stirred by invisible eddies. Books shifted gently as if asleep, spines twitching mid-dream.

Veilborne

Clara had never seen anything like it. She hadn't known it was possible for a place to remember.

Jasper, on the other hand, was practically vibrating with excitement.

"This way," he said, barely above a whisper, and led them deeper into the eastern wing. The air grew cooler and older. The polished floors gave way to uneven flagstones, their centres worn smooth by time and footsteps long faded. Thin traces of warding glyphs shimmered on the stones—half-active, half-lost.

"Jasper…" Sadie muttered, slowing as they passed beneath a faded arch etched with runes. "Are we supposed to be in this section of the library?"

"Nope," Jasper said brightly. "But as long as we don't touch anything cursed, cast light directly at the chainwork, or speak the phrase 'unlock full sequence,' we're fine."

Sadie stared. "Why does that sound like something you've actually tested?"

"I have theoretically tested it," Jasper replied, already ducking into a narrow stairwell hidden behind an angled shelf of oversized atlases. "This way."

Clara followed in silence, one hand curled loosely around her satchel strap. The stone grew damper as they descended, and the air turned dense—muffled as if the sound itself hesitated to linger. They passed alcoves with brass plaques: Cartography of the Second Epoch, Collapsed Wards and Structural Failures, Classified — Restricted Access.

They didn't slow their pace.

Finally, Jasper led them through a rust-hinged gate into a narrow chamber with a vaulted ceiling, its shape reminiscent of a ribcage. Scroll tubes lined the walls like bone flutes. A long display case glimmered faintly beneath an enchantment, its contents protected behind glass fogged with dust.

"This is it," Jasper whispered. "Restoration and Reconstruction Archives—third epoch and earlier. Most of this hasn't been copied or catalogued. Some of it's not even listed in the current records."

Sadie frowned. "Is that supposed to mean something important?"

"Yes," Jasper murmured, already moving toward the oldest shelving unit. "It means if the truth's buried somewhere… this is where we start."

They split up.

Time blurred around them.

Clara lost track of how long they'd been digging. Her fingers were stained with soot and ink. Her eyes itched from the dry air. Scrolls snapped like dried leaves when unrolled. A thick hush blanketed the space, broken only by the occasional scrape of parchment or Jasper's whispered muttering as he translated tangled Aurical shorthand.

Twice, they froze at the sound of movement overhead.

Once, a robed figure passed directly across the mezzanine above them. Jasper extinguished his orb so fast it singed his thumb. They crouched in a shadowed alcove, hearts hammering, until the figure vanished.

"We're going to be expelled," Sadie hissed at one point, clutching a book wrapped in flaking bark. "Or hexed. Or expelled by hexing."

Jasper didn't look up. "I'm already emotionally invested in this particular crime."

"You need help," she muttered.

But Clara barely heard them. She was absorbed in a cracked leather ledger marked with constellations—until Jasper suddenly made a noise.

"Found something," he said.

They crowded around him quickly.

He sat on the floor beside a lopsided shelf labelled Post-Fracture Floorplans: Northern Towers. In his lap was a massive, ring-bound

Veilborne

ledger stamped with an ancient Calendor crest—a tower wreathed by thirteen stars. He opened it cautiously.

Inside, diagrams and soot-ink sketches spilled across the pages. Jasper flipped through slowly until a folded floor plan crackled loose from the spine and opened with a reluctant sigh of dust.

"There," he breathed, pointing at a barely legible corridor. "Tower 7-C. Collapsed during the siege. But look—this passage doesn't appear in the current maps. It's faint—drawn in red ink—but it runs along the wall that connects to the east turret."

Sadie leaned in. "Secret chamber?"

"Or lost," Jasper said. "But if that's the study Lirah hinted at—this might be the only record of it."

Clara's eyes locked onto a circular symbol near the base of the page.

It matched the pattern etched onto the back of her locket.

Her heart missed a beat.

She didn't speak—just reached forward and touched the parchment lightly, tracing the faded ink.

"It's connected," she whispered. "This isn't coincidence. It's not just history. This is… personal."

Jasper nodded. "This whole volume looks like it was misfiled. No index tag. Half the glyphs are degraded. No one's touched this in years."

Sadie tapped the page. "So this is it. The place no one talks about. The place they were willing to bury and forget."

Clara's fingers closed around the map's edge. "And we found it."

No one spoke for a long beat.

Then Sadie broke the quiet. "Well… what's the worst that could happen?"

Jasper sighed as he closed the book and tucked it into his cloak. "We really have to work on your timing."

But he didn't put it back.

And none of them turned around.

****

That Night – Starfire Dormitory

Rain tapped gently against the canopy windows, casting streaks of silver light across the curved beams of the Starfire dormitory. The enchanted runes above their beds shimmered faintly, responding to the soft storm outside—not in alarm, but in recognition. It was a kind of hush Eryndor seemed to honour. A time to listen. To pause.

Clara lay in her bed, still fully clothed, one hand resting lightly over the locket beneath her tunic. She could feel the beat of her heart, steady beneath her palm, but something beneath it whispered—a quiet tension, like the stillness before a door swings open.

Across the room, Jasper was half-sitting on his cot, mumbling to himself through a half-asleep haze.

"No way that corridor still exists... foundation's unstable... unless they reinforced it post-siege with a layered barrier ward..."

Sadie's pillow sailed through the dark and smacked him squarely in the face.

"Shut up," she whispered hoarsely. "Some of us are trying to pretend we're not planning to die horribly tomorrow."

"I'm not planning to die," Jasper mumbled into the blanket, adjusting his glasses without opening his eyes. "I'm planning to be... deeply inconvenienced."

Clara smiled faintly, but the ache in her chest didn't ease. She turned her face toward the high window, where rain ran in thin, glowing streaks. The stars beyond were blurred by clouds, but she could still see a few constellations shifting, ever so slowly, in the heavens above.

A storm in the sky.

And something else brewing beneath.

Veilborne

She reached again for the locket, fingers curling around it.

It was cool.

Still.

Then—

A tremor. Not in the stone. Not in her hand.

In the locket.

A single shiver, like it had drawn a breath.

Clara froze.

Her heart skipped once, then surged back to life. She sat up slowly, careful not to wake the others, and held the locket out in front of her, letting the blanket fall away.

It pulsed. Just once.

A shimmer of light flickered over its surface—thin as a breath. Not the warm thrum she had felt before, but something sharper. Focused. Like recognition.

Then—silence.

No more glow. No hum. Just the faint sound of rain and the soft rhythm of Jasper's snoring.

She stared at it, eyes wide in the dark.

"Are you... trying to tell me something?" she whispered, voice barely audible.

The locket didn't answer.

She clutched it gently in both hands, pressing it to her forehead.

"You know something," she murmured. "Don't you?"

No reply. No flash of memory. Only the weight of it. Heavy not in metal—but in meaning.

She sank back into her bed, curling around the warmth of it, her thoughts spinning too fast to catch.

Beneath her, the wood of the dormitory creaked softly with the storm. A lullaby of roots and rain. But Clara didn't sleep easily. Not that night.

Because something was waking.

Something long buried.

And tomorrow, the door would open.

****

The next morning came slow and grey, as though the storm had left a hangover in the skies above Calendor.

Clara sat at the edge of her bed in the Starfire dormitory, already dressed, her boots laced tight. The others were stirring gradually—Sadie buried beneath a heap of quilts, one sock sticking out like a forgotten flag of surrender; Jasper blinked sleep from his eyes as he adjusted his crooked glasses and reached blindly for his notebook.

They hadn't spoken about the library.

Not yet.

The silence stretched until Sadie finally groaned and threw off her blanket. "Alright," she said, voice thick with sleep, "is this the part where we pretend last night was just a very dusty dream?"

Clara stood and crossed to the window, where faint morning light filtered through the canopy. "We found something real," she said quietly. "That corridor exists. The plans were too detailed to be a coincidence."

"Which means the sealed tower's real too," Jasper added, sitting upright. "And whatever's down there… it's never been retrieved."

"Or maybe it was," Sadie muttered, rubbing her face. "And the people who went looking didn't exactly walk out smiling."

There was a long pause.

Then Jasper said, more hesitantly, "We don't have to go today."

Clara turned. "But we want to."

Veilborne

Sadie raised an eyebrow. "Want? Or need?"

Clara didn't answer at first. She reached into her satchel and pulled out the fern sprig Fennrick had given her. It was already beginning to curl at the edges, but it still held its pale-green glow.

"I didn't come here looking for relics or secret stairwells," she said. "I just wanted answers. About the locket. About my parents. I've spent my whole life not knowing who I am or where I come from—and now there's a chance, even the smallest one, that this study is connected to them. To all of it. If we don't go now... someone else might find it first and I can't risk losing that chance."

Jasper leaned back against the headboard, silent for a moment. "We're really doing this," he said finally.

Sadie flopped onto her back and sighed toward the ceiling. "Well... I do enjoy a good near-death detour."

Clara smiled faintly.

Jasper rose from bed with a groan. "I'll get the map."

They dressed quickly, checked their bags twice, and agreed to skip lunch entirely. Less chance of someone asking where they were headed.

By the time the bells struck midday, the plan was set—simple in theory, treacherous in reality.

Find Tower 7-C.

Get inside.

And find whatever Emberlain had left buried in the dark.

They met beneath the arch of the east courtyard, half-shadowed by the overgrowth of flowering ivy and the weight of everything unsaid. Jasper handed Clara the rune-glass orb. It shimmered faintly as she took it.

"Ready?" she asked.

Sadie flexed her fingers. "Never."

Jasper nodded once. "Let's go."

****

The afternoon sun broke through scattered clouds, casting streaks of gold across the ageing battlements of Calendor Keep. Warm light spilled into quiet halls that hadn't seen student footsteps in decades. These corridors—forgotten, ivy-choked, and haunted by echoes—stretched into a part of the Keep that even the Auricals rarely mentioned.

Clara, Jasper, and Sadie moved through one such hallway, their footfalls muffled by dust and moss-softened stone. Shadows clung to the edges of the passage. The air smelled faintly of mildew and something older—like the breath of time held in stone.

"This part of the Keep gives me the creeps," Sadie muttered, glancing up at the warped rafters above. "Tell me this isn't the setup for a missing-students ghost story."

"It's probably just the humidity," Jasper said, though his voice lacked conviction. He adjusted the rune-glass orb in his hand, its amber light flickering uneasily. "Old sections like this tend to collect atmospheric residue. Magical backwash. Wards that failed years ago but never fully cleared."

Clara said nothing. She walked slightly ahead, her hand closed around the fern sprig tucked into her sleeve, the locket warm beneath her collarbone. It hadn't pulsed again, not since the night before. But she could still feel something—like a pull. A direction. As if her body were tuning to a note only she could sense.

They turned a final corner and came to a halt.

The corridor ended in a dead wall of grey stone. Broad. Uneventful. Framed on either side by two ancient sconces whose brackets had rusted nearly in half. A faint shaft of light filtered down through a narrow window far above, illuminating the space in pale gold.

"This should be it," Jasper said, checking the old schematic he'd brought along. The map crackled softly as he unfolded it, the corners stained with ink and time. "Tower 7-C. Or what's left of it. The structural notes end here."

Sadie scanned the floor, crouching to inspect something near the base of the wall. "Drag marks," she said, running her fingers along a shallow groove in the stone. "Something used to move here. A door? Hidden entrance?"

Jasper joined her, frowning. "You're right. And there—see the chisel gouges in the mortar? Someone sealed this. Sloppily, too. Like it was done in a rush."

Clara took a slow breath. Her heart was drumming now—not with fear, but anticipation. She stepped forward, leaving the others behind, and rested her palm against the cold stone.

It was smooth. Unbroken.

But she could feel it again—that hum beneath her ribs. The warmth in her chest. The sense that something was watching… listening.

"I still don't get it," Jasper said behind her. "Why hasn't anyone found this before? We're first-year students using publicly available records and half a map. You'd think—"

"Maybe they did find it," Clara said softly, still staring at the wall. "Maybe others got this far… and couldn't go through."

Jasper's brows drew together. "Then why can we?"

Sadie answered before Clara could. "Because this time, we've got a Holloway."

A silence followed.

Clara's hand drifted up and closed around the locket. It was warm now. Steady. Almost… welcoming.

Without thinking, she pulled it from around her neck.

The air shifted.

She stepped to the wall again and reached for a faint seam in the stone—one that hadn't been visible before. As her fingertips brushed the surface, a soft click echoed through the corridor.

A small section of the wall slid inward with a hiss of dust and stale air, revealing a shallow, circular indentation. The rim was lined with silver and etched with a glyph Clara didn't recognise—but the shape was unmistakable.

A perfect fit.

Clara held her breath. She raised the locket, hesitated only a heartbeat, then pressed it into the recess.

It locked into place with a muted chime—like a key turning in a long-forgotten door.

And the wall began to shimmer.

Not crack or crumble—shimmer. The surface blurred, like heat rising off stone, until the solidity of it faded into illusion.

Before them now stood a narrow passageway, descending in a gentle spiral into the earth. The air beyond was colder, touched by a scent of rust and memory. There was no light inside—just a depth that seemed to draw them inward.

Sadie stared. "...Well. That wasn't creepy at all."

Jasper was wide-eyed. "That mechanism... it required your locket. No wonder no one else ever made it past the wall. They didn't have the keypiece."

Clara gently pulled the locket free, and the hidden opening remained. She tucked it back beneath her tunic, heart racing.

Sadie gave her a sideways nudge. "Guess there's no turning back now."

Clara stepped forward.

And the three of them disappeared into the dark.

Veilborne

The corridor was narrow and choked with cobwebs, each one glistening faintly as if threaded with silver wire. The stone underfoot was cracked and uneven, worn by time and untouched for what felt like centuries past.

Jasper reached into his satchel and pulled out a small metallic sphere etched with concentric rings. With a muttered phrase and a sharp flick of his wrist, the orb floated free from his palm and flared to life—casting a soft, golden glow around them.

The faint light revealed more of the passage: walls etched with ancient glyphs, many faded, some still humming softly with lingering magic.

"Can't believe this thing still works," Jasper murmured, keeping his voice low. "Old apprentice lamp from the Gilded stockpile. Basic light, minor warmth, faint warding. I think it has attitude problems, though."

Sadie raised an eyebrow as she brushed away a dangling thread of cobweb. "How can a lamp have issues?"

Jasper gave her a pointed look. "It flickers when I'm nervous."

As if on cue, the orb's glow stuttered—pulsing once, twice—before steadying again.

Sadie snorted. "Well, that's comforting."

"Hey, it's better than nothing," he muttered, holding it aloft as they descended the narrow, spiralling stair that curved deeper into the earth. Each step echoed like a distant drumbeat, swallowed by the pressing silence.

Clara said nothing. She moved quietly, one hand brushing along the wall for balance. The closer they got, the heavier the air felt—not just in weight, but in intent. A strange stillness clung to the walls, broken only by the quiet insistence of their footsteps.

The passageway narrowed almost immediately, its stone walls damp and cold to the touch. The air grew heavier with each step, thick with the scent of earth, metal, and something older—an alchemical sharpness laced with the musk of forgotten decay.

The orb stuttered with faint, anxious light.

Sadie gave it a look, then Jasper. "Hey, you two... deep breaths."

Jasper didn't look away from the glyphs. "Tell him that. I'm doing my best."

Clara said nothing. The deeper they went, the more she felt it—the pull of something buried in the bones of this place. Her locket was silent now, but her pulse drummed with a rhythm that didn't feel entirely her own.

They reached a spiral staircase carved directly into the rock. It curved steeply downward, vanishing into darkness.

Clara hesitated at the top step.

"Ready?" Sadie asked, her voice hushed but steady.

"Not even slightly," Jasper answered, adjusting the orb in his grip. It gave a low, uncertain flicker—almost as if it, too, was holding its breath.

Clara nodded. "Let's go."

The stairs creaked faintly underfoot, not with age, but with strain—like something in the stone resisted their passage. Cobwebs laced the corners of the walls, their threads unusually thick and faintly luminous, as though they too had once been touched by spells.

The descent seemed to go on longer than it should. The walls curved tighter, and the air became thinner, colder. And then, just as Jasper muttered something about spatial compression wards, the stairway stopped.

The corridor levelled out into a short landing... and beyond it, an arched doorway stood open.

Clara stepped through.

Her breath caught.

The chamber beyond was vast—a circular vault built deep within the Keep's foundations. The ceiling stretched high above, supported by

Veilborne

ribs of metal and stone interlaced with dormant crystal lenses. Once, they might have channelled light. Now, they only stared blankly downward.

Desks and tables ringed the outer wall, each cluttered with the wreckage of forgotten work: cracked beakers, gears fused to parchment, scrolls browned with time and curled at the edges. Some relics floated in containment fields that flickered uncertainly, while others lay shattered beneath collapsed mechanisms.

In the centre of the room was a dais—low, circular, rimmed with ancient copper. On it sat a wide metal desk, eerily clean amid the dust. Above it loomed a massive mirror, darkened with age, so soot-stained it reflected nothing at all.

Sadie's voice came out in a whisper. "It's like someone locked this place up and hoped no one would ever come searching."

Clara walked slowly toward the dais, her boots brushing across a layer of fine grit that coated the floor. Around her, strange machines whispered with long-dead purpose—clicks, hums, the occasional flicker of forgotten wards.

Jasper trailed a hand over a spiralling coil of etched brass. "Some of this looks like Gilded tech. But it's older. Twisted. Like he was splicing theories."

Sadie picked up a disc-shaped object with tiny etchings on the rim. The moment her fingers closed around it, it emitted a soft, musical tone.

She yelped and dropped it.

The tone continued for a second longer—then stopped.

"Nope," she muttered. "Didn't like that!"

Clara was no longer listening. She had reached the central desk.

Unlike the others, it was pristine. No dust. No decay. Only a single object lay in the centre—a book. Its cover was deep green, bound in leather so dark it looked black in the low light. No title. No markings.

Clara approached it with slow steps, heart pounding in her chest.

"It's not decayed," Jasper said from behind her. "That shouldn't be possible."

"Protective ward?" Sadie offered, crouching beside him.

"Maybe," he said slowly, then added, "Or someone's been here recently—"

Sadie shot him a look. The kind that didn't need words.

"Don't be stupid," she said flatly. "We're the first ones down here in ages."

Jasper raised his hands in mock surrender. "Just covering all the worst-case scenarios."

"Save that for after we open the creepy book," she muttered.

Clara reached out.

Her fingertips brushed the cover.

The book felt warm.

Alive.

She opened it slowly.

The pages were impossibly neat—handwritten in ink that hadn't faded a drop. Diagrams filled the margins: runes, spirals, star-maps, mathematical formulas woven with arcane notes. She flipped to a page marked by a small fold in the corner. Her eyes moved across the text.

The Veil is thinning. The anchors between worlds aren't holding. Current readings still hovering around 0.73 — not stable, but close enough to try again. Most of the realms I've found are empty. Nothing. Dust, rock, airless voids. One had tiny life forms, barely worth noting. Another had creatures, small and fast. But one…

One looked promising.

Veilborne

Mark those coordinates. If I can tune the device properly, I might be able to reach it again. The tethering isn't perfect. Still jumps. Still flickers. But the door is there.

If it breaks completely, I'll have to collapse it and start over. Or risk opening it wide.

And if it doesn't close the way it should...

I might not get back.

Her hands trembled.

"This is his," she whispered. "This is Emberlain's. The real thing."

Jasper was beside her in an instant, peering over her shoulder.

"I recognise that handwriting," he said breathlessly. "There are reproductions in the Lorehall, but this... this is the source. It has to be."

Clara turned the next page—and froze.

A diagram showed a locket.

Not hers—but similar.

Labeled: "Personal Anchor — Subject H."

Before she could say anything, a low click echoed through the room.

The ground beneath them gave a faint jolt.

Jasper's head snapped up. "Clara... what did you just do?"

"I didn't do anything—" She looked down. The book. "I just picked it up—"

From all around them came the hiss of long-dormant mechanisms awakening. A sharp shkkt as metal slats along the walls peeled back like eyelids opening after centuries of sleep.

Inside each alcove stood a tall figure. Humanoid. Motionless.

Mechanical.

They began to glow.

Sadie stepped back. "Oh, no."

Jasper's voice rose in panic. "Those are sentries—archaic defence constructs. Military-grade. Not Gilded. Aurical-built."

The sentries turned.

Their eyes—red slits of molten light—blinked to life.

One by one, they stepped forward.

The nearest sentry leapt from its alcove.

Its feet struck the ground with a boom that cracked the stone tiles beneath. From its forearm, a long, narrow blade snapped forward with a chilling snikt, glowing faintly with arcane charge. The red light in its visor narrowed like a focusing lens.

The orb's light trembled as if in panic.

"Yup. Nervous."

Jasper rummaged through his satchel with frantic precision, fingers closing around a familiar shape. Without a word, he thrust the relic toward Sadie.

Sadie raised the relic Jasper had given her—an odd, twisted wand-like rod with a stone core—and jabbed it toward the charging sentry.

"Let's rattle those gears a bit!"

A pulse of crackling blue light shot forward in a jagged arc, striking the sentry square in the chest. It staggered, steam hissing from its joints.

But it didn't fall.

It raised its arm, spinning the blade in a wide arc—and charged again.

Clara gripped the book tight and looked at Jasper. "Run?"

The orb blinked, harder, faster.

"RUN!!" Jasper shouted.

Veilborne

"GO!" Sadie shouted, grabbing Jasper's cloak and dragging him after Clara, who was already halfway up the stairwell.

Another sentry moved to intercept—leaping onto the wall and scrambling sideways like a spider. Its hands split open to reveal clawed digits sparking with volatile magic.

Clara turned on the stairs just in time to see it pounce.

She threw up her arm instinctively, the journal still in her grasp—but before the construct could reach her, the locket ignited.

A soundless flash of blue-white light erupted from her chest. Electricity arced through the air, striking the sentry mid-lunge and blasting it backward with a concussive bang. Its body slammed into the far wall, arms and legs convulsing violently.

Clara gasped and stumbled, catching herself against the stair rail.

The others paused in stunned silence.

"Did you—" Sadie started.

"I didn't do anything!" Clara shouted. "It just—reacted!"

Jasper looked between the journal, the locket, and the glowing security glyphs below.

Another pulse echoed through the chamber—this time from the walls themselves.

Orange light began seeping through the seams of the stone. A soft, whirring crack travelled along the supports above. One of the glowing ceiling lenses shattered inward, letting in a rush of arcane fire.

"It's all unravelling!" Jasper choked out. "The wards, the machines—everything's turning on itself! We have to get out before the whole place collapses!"

The remaining sentries surged up the stairwell.

Sadie threw a handful of reflective shards behind them—mirrorburst fragments she'd lifted from the dormitory relic bin weeks ago. They detonated in midair with a concussive pop, briefly blinding the sentries in a shimmer of light and magnetic static.

"Don't stop!" she screamed.

Clara led the way, lungs burning, legs aching. The walls shook. Dust cascaded from the archways above. From below, the shriek of metal grinding against stone pursued them upward.

Jasper clutched the flickering orb in one hand, muttering fragments of half-formed warding spells under his breath.

"Come on, come on—don't die on me now, glowy ball."

They reached the corridor just as the hidden passage began to reappear, stone folding inward again with the same clicking rhythm it had used to open.

The last sentry lunged after them—closer than the others, arms outstretched, blade arm glowing with a pulse of red.

Clara turned back, heart pounding. It was nearly through the barrier.

But the locket flared again.

This time, the light didn't burst—it drew in. A sudden gravitational pull, like air sucked from a room, yanked the sentry to a halt mid-leap. Its limbs jerked as though resisting an unseen force.

And then it imploded—folding in on itself with a shriek of metal and light, collapsing into a fist-sized coil of blackened circuitry that clattered harmlessly to the floor just beyond the seal.

The shimmering veil shimmered again... and sealed itself shut.

Then silence.

The three of them collapsed into a heap on the corridor floor, gasping, shaking, bruised but breathing.

But the danger wasn't over.

A deep rumble gathered behind them, low and rising, like a storm rolling through stone. The shimmering wall—the one Clara's locket

Veilborne

had opened—flickered wildly. Its surface rippled with unstable light, as if something enormous was clawing its way up from beneath the Keep.

Then came the fire.

It wasn't a flicker. It wasn't a flame.

It was a wave.

Arcane fire, thick and seething, surged upward from the spiral stair. It twisted with gold and white heat, laced with crackling arcs of violet lightning. It poured through the hidden corridor, hungry and alive—obliterating the air, devouring shadow, scorching its way toward them.

Sadie dragged Jasper closer, flattening herself against the wall. Clara shielded her head, curling in on herself as the roar swallowed everything. They had no time. Nowhere left to run.

The wave struck.

It hit the barrier like a hammer of the gods, a thunderclap of heat and force. The magic flared—a dome of trembling light that pulsed and held against the inferno pressing against it. The flames recoiled, folding in on themselves, slamming into the invisible wall again and again. The air howled. Heat rippled outward in waves.

But the barrier held.

Each blast echoed down the hall like cannon fire, but slowly—inch by inch—the magic began to fail. The light dimmed. The edges of the shimmer frayed. One final pulse trembled through the stone, and with a sound like a breath being let go after centuries, the barrier shattered.

The fire was gone.

The study was open.

The hidden wall no longer shimmered. No longer cloaked. It stood as stone now—solid, scorched, and bare. The entrance to Emberlain's lost sanctum was no longer hidden from the world.

Clara lifted her head, dazed, blinking through the haze.

Jasper slumped back, still catching his breath. "Just for the record, I did say this was a terrible idea. I whispered it. Firmly."

Sadie let out a choked, half-delirious laugh. "Yeah, and we ignored you. Look how well that turned out."

She flopped onto her back, arms spread across the cold stone like she might dissolve into it. Her hair was singed at the ends. One boot was missing a strap. She looked both triumphant and completely done with the day.

Clara didn't say anything at first. She just sat there, knees drawn to her chest, clutching the journal under her cloak with both arms. Her hands were still trembling.

But after a long silence, Clara looked up—eyes wide, face streaked with soot—and said quietly, "We found it."

The words barely left her lips before the sound of approaching footsteps echoed down the corridor—heavy, swift, deliberate.

Jasper tensed. Sadie turned sharply toward the noise, already half on her feet.

A moment later, six figures swept around the corner of the hallway—robes flaring, boots striking stone, the silver thread of their Aurical insignia catching what little light remained. They moved with quiet command, their presence undeniable.

They stopped when they saw the three of them—dust-streaked, wide-eyed, huddled near the wall where the shimmering barrier had once stood.

Except there was no wall anymore.

The illusion was gone.

Behind them, the entrance to the study now stood fully exposed—no longer hidden from the world, the charred stone edges still pulsing faintly with heat and disrupted magic.

For a moment, no one spoke.

Veilborne

And then the tallest of the Auricals stepped forward, eyes narrowing as he took in the scorched floor, the raw scent of burned air, and the three students crumpled in its aftermath.

"What in Eryndor's name have you done?" he murmured.

Behind the line of Auricals—arms folded, jaw clenched, expression carved from stone—stood Eldric Ducart.

Clara froze at the sight of him. His gaze met hers. He didn't speak. Didn't need to. The weight in his stare said enough.

Beside him, leaning slightly on his walking stick, hair wild and boots still damp with mud from whatever forest corner he'd crawled out of, stood Fennrick Bramble.

He looked like he might've just rolled in from a nap in the moss and was chewing on something—possibly a liquorice root, possibly the handle of a much-abused pipe.

"Step back," one of the robed women ordered sharply, stepping forward. Her tone snapped like breaking ice. Her robes bore black stitching and a crimson sash—clearly marking her as a senior enforcer.

Clara, Sadie, and Jasper obeyed without a word, retreating several paces as the Auricals moved past them and into the opened chamber.

But they weren't left behind for long.

"Come," said the woman with the crimson sash, her voice clipped. Two Auricals moved behind the trio, gesturing them forward with curt nods. Another led the way down the stairwell. The unspoken message was clear: You're still involved.

They descended slowly, hemmed in on both sides by silent, watchful figures. The spiral steps groaned underfoot, their edges slick with dust and soot. Clara's heart thudded with each step, the journal still pressed beneath her tunic, its weight somehow heavier now.

The moment they passed through the threshold, the heat hit them.

The chamber had changed.

The low glow of containment runes had guttered out, replaced by a dull, sickly shimmer that pulsed through cracks in the floor. Smoke curled from collapsed tables. Relics had been shattered—twisted metal, scorched parchment, warped crystal. The central desk was charred along one edge. The mirror behind it was cracked, its surface veined with black and red like shattered obsidian.

A coppery haze lingered in the air. The scent of overburned magic was thick—acrid and electric. Like burnt wires and forgotten rituals.

Clara swallowed hard.

Sadie made a faint noise in her throat and muttered, "Stars…"

Even Jasper, normally so curious, stood stunned. His eyes swept the wreckage, and he slowly shook his head. "It's all ruined," he whispered. "All of it."

An Aurical knelt beside the remains of a containment field, now flickering uselessly. Another prodded a scorched gear assembly with the tip of their staff, brow furrowed.

And then the crimson-sashed woman turned to face them fully.

"You will bear witness to this," she said, voice sharp as flint. "The knowledge that was lost. Do you understand the magnitude of what you've done?"

Clara didn't answer. Her throat was too tight. She could still feel the echo of the locket's pulse, the memory of flame pressing against the threshold.

She felt Eldric's presence beside her before she heard his voice.

"You could've been killed," he said quietly, his tone a slow burn of reprimand, worry, and something harder to name. "And you nearly brought the whole Keep down with you. But gods help me… I'm glad you're still standing."

Fennrick, still chewing his root, gave him a glance out of the corner of his eye but said nothing.

Sadie shifted her weight, opening her mouth to speak—

Veilborne

Jasper, without even turning his head, nudged her sharply in the ankle.

Sadie closed her mouth again, muttering something that sounded suspiciously like "ow."

The sharp-featured Aurical with the crimson sash turned toward them fully now, gaze cold.

"Students," she said, her voice carrying easily through the corridor. "You are hereby confined to your dormitory until further notice. You will not speak of what occurred here. You will not enter restricted wings. And you will not leave the grounds without permission from a senior Aurical."

Her eyes swept across them, lingering for half a breath longer on Clara.

"This will reflect on your team. Severely. Mark them."

She turned toward Eldric without another word.

He gave a single nod.

Clara lowered her gaze—but she didn't let go of the journal beneath her cloak. Her fingers stayed wrapped tight around the binding.

She didn't know yet if what they'd salvaged was worth the cost. But the truth—whatever shape it took—was now hers to carry.

****

Back in the Dormitory

They barely spoke on the walk back.

No scolding. No whispered arguments. Just the quiet sound of boots on stone, breath still catching now and then in their throats, and the weight of what had been lost pressing against their backs.

By the time they reached the door to the Starfire dormitory, even Sadie's usual swagger had worn down into something slower, more sober.

Once inside, Clara sat on the edge of her bed and turned the dried fern sprig over in her fingers. It had survived the flames—singed at the tips, but still whole.

Fennrick's words rang back in her mind: If you're going to follow ghosts, take something living with you.

She didn't know if it had saved her. But in the middle of chaos, she had run, not frozen. She had chosen.

A soft knock interrupted the silence.

Clara looked up as the door creaked open. Fennrick stepped in, alone, holding a scroll of parchment in one hand and chewing thoughtfully on his ever-present liquorice root.

"Well," he said mildly, his eyes scanning the room. "Good. You still resemble people."

Sadie groaned from her bed and pulled a pillow over her head.

Clara stood slowly. She held up the singed sprig. "What was the point of this?"

Fennrick paused, his smile softer than usual. He stepped closer, squinting at the little branch in her hand.

"Clarity sprig," he said. "Old forest trick. Grows near ley-spring roots. Grounds the nerves. Keeps panic from swallowing your mind in high-magic places."

He tilted his head slightly. "Not foolproof, mind you. But enough to keep your feet moving when instinct says hide."

Clara thought about the fire. The sentries. The journal. The moment the locket had lit up like a storm inside her chest.

"You're saying this helped me stay calm?"

Fennrick gave a small shrug. "Helped you choose. That's more important."

He glanced toward the window, then chewed the root again.

"There's old magic," he murmured, "and then there's Emberlain's kind. Some doors aren't meant to be opened just because you have the key."

Veilborne

Clara nodded. "Noted."

****

Later That Night

The dormitory was quiet. Shadows stretched long across the wooden beams as the lantern by the window guttered softly in its frame.

The trio sat cross-legged on the floor near the fire pit, wrapped in a silence that was heavier than before.

"So…" Sadie said at last, prodding the flickering embers with a stick. "That's going to haunt us forever."

"They're marking our team," Jasper muttered. "You heard her. 'Reflect poorly.'"

Clara looked over. "Reflect how?"

He adjusted his glasses, then pushed them back up again with a sigh.

"End-of-year evaluations. It's not just classwork. They assess field performance, conduct, magical growth, capacity for teamwork—and yeah… mistakes."

"Sounds like a lot," Clara said quietly.

"It is," he replied. "Think of it as reputation. Everything we do shapes what training we're allowed to pursue. What doors stay shut."

Sadie flopped back against the rug, arms behind her head. "Well, that's fine. I plan on being equally reckless in every branch."

Clara smiled faintly. They laughed—just a little—but it was tired laughter. A threadbare patch in a worn-out quilt.

She looked down at the pack resting beside her bed. The journal was inside, carefully wrapped.

She hadn't told them yet.

But she would.

Just not tonight.

Mark Peters

Chapter 10
Embers and Echoes

Morning After the Collapse

The dining hall at Calendor Keep had never been loud—not truly. It buzzed with a kind of gentle, scholarly energy most days: the scrape of cutlery on stoneware, the murmur of students trading notes, the occasional peal of laughter rising like birdsong beneath the high-vaulted ceiling of living wood and rune-carved beams.

But this morning, that warmth was gone.

Clara felt the shift the moment they stepped through the threshold.

The air inside was thinner somehow, stretched taut over the tables like a skin that might tear at any moment. Words were still spoken, spoons still stirred bowls of spice-dusted grain, but everything was… aware. Every glance held just a second too long. Every voice quieted just a note too early.

She walked between Jasper and Sadie, the three of them unconsciously aligned—shoulders squared, eyes forward, matching pace without a word. It wasn't for effect. It was armour.

Still, the stares came.

Dozens of them. Too many to count.

They passed one table, then another. Conversations dipped. Clara saw a boy in indigo sleeves lean toward his mate and whisper something behind a cupped hand. A girl from their theory class lifted an eyebrow, then quickly looked away.

It hit Clara in the chest before she could name it.

This silence—this brittle, purposeful quiet—she'd known it before. The weight of it. The shape of it. It was the same hush that had followed her down the halls of Morrowmere after something had gone wrong. When other kids pressed against doorframes and let her pass like a storm they hoped wouldn't touch them.

Veilborne

She half-expected to look up and see Miss Wren standing at the back of the hall, arms folded, expression unreadable.

But there was no Wren. No cracked linoleum. Just stone and stares and the same cold knowing.

The silence wasn't total—but it was surgical. Deliberate. Like the Keep itself had decided to rearrange its attention.

They sat near the end of their usual bench. No one else from their assigned team joined them. No one even sat within arm's reach.

Their plates had already been laid out—elegant stoneware nestled against crystal-glass goblets that shimmered faintly with chill enchantments to keep water crisp and cool. A folded napkin shaped like a moonflower perched beside a polished fork. On the plate, coils of stewed emberroot glistened with syrupy glaze, releasing slow tendrils of spice-sweet steam that carried hints of nutmeg, gingerbark, and fire-thistle.

Delicate wedges of sunfruit—cut into perfect spirals—sat atop a drizzle of sugared frostmilk, their golden flesh glowing like captured sunrise. Beside them, a trio of folded breads—each a different shade of grain—rested warm in a nest of linen. One was filled with spiced tuber mash, another with softleaf cheese and green chive, and the last still breathed with the scent of honeyed airflour and salt crystal.

But none of them moved to touch a single bite.

The food might as well have been glass.

Jasper was the first to speak.

Jasper didn't look up. He absently poked at a curled spiral of candied duskroot with his fork, watching it slowly uncurl and then re-curl as if sulking.

"Well," he said quietly, "we've gone from curious to contagious."

Sadie reached for her fork, prodded a hunk of rye crust, and shrugged. "Could be worse."

Jasper gave her a look. "Could it?"

Sadie didn't blink. "Could be worse. Varek Draven could've decided we're his new best mates."

A quiet snort escaped Clara, but it died quickly. Her hands stayed in her lap. She could feel the heat creeping up her neck again, not from embarrassment—though there was plenty of that—but from anger. From the weight of being seen. Judged. And not being able to explain.

It wasn't shame. Not exactly.

It was something heavier.

A scraping sound pulled her attention up—and her stomach dropped.

Striding between the tables with the effortless confidence of someone born to command attention came Varek Draven, his silver-threaded robes catching the morning light like a challenge. His two ever-present shadows flanked him, moving in perfect sync—though their presence was more for show than necessity.

Varek didn't need guards.

He had a tongue sharp enough to do the cutting himself.

Jasper nudged Sadie with his elbow, not bothering to hide the grimace on his face. "You spoke too soon," he muttered, tilting his head subtly toward the approaching figure.

"Wonderful. I've always dreamed of joining the Varek Draven Appreciation Society."

"Well," he said, stopping just short of their table. "If it isn't the Veilborne and her demolition crew."

Clara looked up, calm on the surface, silent within.

Varek offered a half-smile, not kind. "I must say, I'm impressed. I didn't think you'd manage to disgrace your team so quickly. That takes a special sort of… enthusiasm."

"Go away, Varek," Sadie said, not even glancing up from her bread.

Veilborne

"I simply had to see the aftermath for myself," Varek murmured. "It's not every day someone rewrites the handbook on how to humiliate a House."

That one landed.

Jasper stood. His chair scraped loudly against the floor—an audible protest.

Clara didn't move.

But someone else did.

A shape passed behind Varek, quiet as falling dusk.

Eldric Ducart.

He didn't speak. He didn't need to. He simply came to a halt behind Varek, placed one hand—large, callused, and steady—on the boy's shoulder, and applied the sort of pressure that said enough.

Varek flinched, only slightly.

Eldric leaned down, voice low enough that only the nearby students heard. "You don't belong here. Off you go."

There was no threat in the words. Just gravity. A weight that didn't need raising.

Varek turned—expression tight, teeth clenched—and walked away. His shadows followed, just a fraction slower than usual.

Eldric watched them leave, then shifted his gaze to the trio.

"I take it," he said, voice dry as old paper, "that the lesson in subtlety hasn't landed."

Sadie turned halfway in her seat. "He started it."

"I wasn't talking about him."

That shut them up.

Eldric stepped around the bench and sat across from them, his presence quiet but grounding. He didn't speak straight away, just offered a nod—less like a teacher and more like a guardian checking on those who'd weathered a storm. There was no judgement in his eyes. Only the calm of someone who'd seen worse and still chose to believe in second chances.

For a moment, he just studied their faces.

Then, without preamble: "If you're set on chasing things that shouldn't concern you... then it's time you learned how to survive what you insist upon chasing."

Clara blinked. "What do you mean?"

"Your training schedule's changed," he said. "Combat basics start tomorrow. After breakfast. Be there."

Jasper raised a tentative hand. "Are you teaching it?"

Eldric smiled, barely. "I'll be leading your training. Not just for the three of you—for your whole team. If one of you stirs up hornets, the rest had better learn to deal with the stings."

He stood smoothly.

"Questions?"

Jasper raised his hand again. "Do we get helmets?"

Eldric gave him a long, flat look. "That depends on how attached you are to your skull."

Then he was gone.

And just like that, the attention in the room shifted again.

Clara exhaled.

This was far from over.

They left the dining hall in silence.

****

No one followed them as they left the dining hall. No one called out, or asked where they were going. The sea of quiet stares parted wordlessly, letting them pass like ghosts through a place that no longer claimed them.

Veilborne

And the whispers—those ever-present whispers—stayed behind this time, trapped in the long, echoing bones of the Keep.

Clara was grateful for that. Even whispers could bruise, if enough of them landed in the same place.

The trio wandered the paths without speaking, until the winding walkways gave way to stone steps and the steps gave way to dirt, and finally, they stood at the edge of one of the oldest trails behind Calendor Keep. It led away from the main towers and toward the cliffs beyond—toward a place few remembered and fewer bothered to visit.

It wasn't marked on any map.

Sadie had named it.

Emberbridge Overlook.

A narrow bridge of weathered stone stretched across a shallow gorge here, flanked by ruins of ancient arches half-consumed by moss. Trees arched above in crooked halos, their branches knotted with vines that shimmered faintly in the light, as if dew had memory.

They sat beneath one of the gnarled trees, where the moss was soft and the stone warm from the sun.

Below, silver streams braided through the valley floor—thin, glimmering ribbons that caught the light like threads being pulled tight. Wind moved slowly here, curling through grass in long sighs and bringing with it the scent of rain-damp roots and something older still.

They didn't speak at first.

Jasper sat cross-legged, plucking pebbles from the ledge and flicking them into the gorge with too much precision for someone claiming not to care.

Sadie chewed a honeyfruit stem down to the bitter core, spat it into the wind, and scowled as if the sky had insulted her.

Clara hugged her knees to her chest, her chin resting just above the fabric of her robes. The locket sat against her collarbone, still warm. Not pulsing. Not warning. But aware. It felt like it was listening.

Mark Peters

Not to the wind. Not to the valley.

To *her*.

"Do you reckon they'll actually kick us out?" Jasper asked eventually, not looking up.

Sadie answered with a snort. "Doubt it. We're too valuable. Bold, reckless, and just stupid enough to open things we shouldn't. They'll want to keep us close. That's how institutions work—punish the curiosity while quietly filing it away for later use."

"That's comforting," Jasper muttered.

"I didn't say it was comforting. I said it was how it works."

Jasper dropped another pebble. It bounced twice, then vanished into the gorge.

Clara hadn't spoken. Not since they sat down. But her silence wasn't the same one she'd worn in the dining hall. This was something more internal. More uncertain.

"They're mad because we destroyed something irreplaceable," Jasper said after a pause. "We're lucky they didn't feed us to the gliders."

Clara looked up. "Gliders?"

Sadie perked up immediately. "You haven't heard the bedtime stories?"

"They're not stories," Jasper muttered darkly.

"Depends on how good your imagination is," Sadie said, waving a hand. "Picture a six-legged bat the size of a stablebeast—you know, those massive shaggy things they use to haul timber near the Glimmerden ridge? Wings like veined silk, jaws that unhinge twice, and talons sharper than mirrorsteel. Moodier than Varek and with breath to match."

Clara blinked. "Wait… you have bats here too?"

Sadie grinned. "Course we do. My cousin tried to tame one once. He's… quieter now."

Veilborne

Clara blinked. "That's... deeply unsettling."

"Gliders live in the southern cliffs," Jasper said. "They used to be aggressive, but the Auricals managed to train a few. Now they're used to scout the outer territories—sometimes even deliver messages."

Clara blinked. "People ride them?"

Sadie nodded. "Apparently. Some people ride giant sky-lizards with wings like nightmares. Others prefer to keep their bones unshattered."

"Or stupidity."

"Same coin," she said, lying back and watching the clouds pass like forgotten thoughts.

Silence stretched again.

Then Clara spoke, her voice barely more than a breath.

"There was something in that study. I don't just mean the relics or the machines—it felt like... like we were standing in the middle of something bigger. Like we brushed up against a story that hasn't finished being told."

Sadie didn't answer right away.

Eventually, she rolled onto her side and stared at the sky. "Yeah. I've done reckless before. But this? This felt different. Bigger. Like the kind of mistake that changes things."

Clara turned toward her. "Do you regret going?"

Sadie shrugged. "Not yet. Ask me again when the Council decides what to do with us."

Jasper finally looked up, expression unreadable.

"Whether we were supposed to or not," he said, "we've changed something. And I don't think it can be undone."

The words sat heavy between them.

Clara lowered her gaze again. She reached up and touched the locket through her robes.

It had shielded her in the study. Acted without command. Like it cared about what happened to her.

She still didn't know what it was.

But she was beginning to understand what it wasn't.

It wasn't ordinary.

And it wasn't finished.

****

Rain whispered against the dormitory windows that night, soft as secrets.

The usual nighttime sounds—creaking rafters, distant owl calls, the rustle of sleep-heavy blankets—folded into the hush of the room.

Sadie was already asleep, sprawled diagonally across her bed like she'd fought off the day and won. Jasper had slumped over his notes again, ink smudged across his sleeve, one hand still resting on the edge of his flickering orb.

But Clara lay awake for a while longer.

Eyes wide open. Hand resting lightly over the locket at her chest.

It was warm again. Not pulsing. Not urgent. But steady—like something listening. Watching.

She didn't try to fight sleep when it came.

And when her eyes finally closed, it was without fear.

Because sleep, for her, no longer meant rest.

It meant waiting.

Across the room, the dormitory settled. The storm rolled softly against the walls.

And on Clara's chest—just beneath the fold of her blanket—the locket stirred.

A single arc of blue lightning flickered silently across its surface.

Veilborne

Barely a breath.

Gone before it could wake her.

But it had reached for her.

And whatever memory it carried… was beginning to rise.

****

Clara was standing in a forest clearing she didn't recognise—yet somehow felt as if she'd been there before.

The trees around her rose in twisted spirals, their bark etched with spiralling grooves that glowed faintly in the moonlight. The air was heavy with mist, damp with magic. Leaves shimmered silver. Roots tangled like knotted cords beneath her boots.

She blinked—but the body wasn't hers.

Her hands moved without her will—calloused, steady, clad in fingerless gloves. Her limbs were lean, strong. Familiar with movement. There was a satchel slung across her back, the leather worn and patched at the corners. Its weight was comforting. Heavy with purpose.

As she moved, she caught a glimpse of her chest—of the chain that hung there. The locket swayed gently with her stride, its surface scuffed but unmistakably hers.

She didn't stop. Her boots struck stone. Somewhere distant, the wind howled low through broken arches, and a lantern flickered to life beneath her fingertips without her needing to touch it. She kept walking. Forward, always forward—through a space that felt both ancient and waiting.

She heard footsteps crunching through the underbrush.

Two figures stepped into view near the edge of the clearing.

The first was the man.

The courier.

Clara recognised him instantly—though he looked younger here. His short-cropped hair was darker, the white streaks at his temples not yet earned. He moved with cautious authority, like someone used to navigating danger. His cloak was damp with mist, his eyes sharp.

The second figure stood behind him, face obscured by the angle—but tall, and still.

The courier approached her—no, the person she was within—and stopped just a pace away.

"Is this everything?" he asked.

She felt herself nod. Then she—they—reached into the satchel and produced a sealed parchment. The courier took it without hesitation, tucking it into a hidden fold of his cloak.

"They'll come looking for it soon," he said.

"That's why it can't be found," came the reply—Clara's voice, but not. Soft, resolute. Female.

The courier shifted his stance, lowering his voice. "Does anyone else know?"

A pause.

"No," the figure replied. "Not yet."

Wind stirred the mist.

The moment hung like a blade, suspended between past and present.

Then the courier gave a single nod and turned, vanishing back into the trees as silently as he'd come.

The clearing dimmed. The air grew heavy.

The forest dissolved.

****

Clara gasped awake.

The dormitory was still dark. Rain tapped softly at the high windows, a hush of sound like pages turning in the dark. Sadie's slow, steady

Veilborne

breathing drifted from the bed beside hers. Jasper mumbled something incoherent, kicked off his blanket, then fell quiet again.

Clara sat up slowly, one hand already clutching the locket at her chest.

It was cool now. Still. As though it had done what it came to do—and gone quiet again.

But something lingered beneath her skin. A hum. A pressure. Like smoke that clung long after the fire had gone out.

She swung her legs over the side of the bed, bare feet brushing against the chilled stone floor. Her breathing was shallow, but steady. Her thoughts spun too fast to catch—except one.

It hadn't been a dream.

Not like the others.

The images still pulsed behind her eyes: the satchel, the gloves, the lantern flaring to life without touch. The steady stride through stone corridors. The locket, swinging gently against her chest—not this chest, not this body, but one she'd moved through like a second skin.

It had felt real.

Too real.

The man—the courier—he'd been there. Not in the dream, but in the classroom days ago. She'd seen him. Felt the locket react the moment he'd entered. She hadn't known why.

Now she did.

It hadn't been her recognising him.

It had been the locket.

And that parchment... that warning... whatever message he'd carried in that moment—it had been significant.

She pressed the cool metal to her forehead and closed her eyes.

Was it a memory?

Had she witnessed someone else's past—someone the locket had once belonged to?

Or was it something else?

A future?

She opened her eyes slowly, her heart suddenly heavier.

It didn't make sense. The courier had appeared younger—far younger than he had in the classroom. Too young. If that was her future… how could he be younger?

Unless…

She didn't finish the thought.

Instead, she lay back down slowly, wrapping the blanket tight around her, the locket still pressed to her chest. She stared at the ceiling for a long time, watching as faint runes above her bed blinked gently with the stormlight.

No answers came.

Only questions.

And the quiet certainty that something—someone—had reached through the veil of sleep to find her.

And that next time… it might come closer.

****

The breakfast hall of Calendor Keep glowed with golden warmth, a soft contrast to the brooding skies outside. Arched windows, veiled with condensation, caught the early light and diffused it across long stone tables, their surfaces smoothed by centuries of meals and hushed conversation. High above, lantern-globes floated between the curling beams of the vaulted ceiling, trailing wisps of cinnamon-scented steam as they pulsed with gentle magic to chase away the gloom.

Plates clinked. Cups hummed faintly with temperature-preserving spells. Enchanted trays drifted from the kitchen alcoves like drowsy birds, delivering fresh fruit slices and rolls that steamed with spice-

Veilborne

filled fillings. From the hearths at the far end of the hall, the rich scent of baked grains, seared mushrooms, and ember-roasted roots filled the air—comfort food valiantly trying to smother the morning's unease.

Clara sat at the end of one of the longer tables near the House Starfire banner, hunched over a plate of untouched fruit-filled grain rolls dusted in crystal sugar and warm cloves. Her tea sat beside them, barely rippling, as she turned the spoon in slow, aimless circles. Her elbow was propped against the table, cheek resting in her palm, gaze distant. The chatter in the room passed over her like smoke—present but unattainable.

Across from her, Sadie had already eaten half of a honey-glazed root pastry and now, with great concentration, was balancing the other half atop the rim of her teacup like a structural challenge issued by the gods of breakfast. One of the flaky layers sagged perilously.

"Hold," she whispered, eyes narrowed. "The moment of truth approaches."

Jasper, on the other hand, was multitasking at lightning speed—one hand buttering a chunk of dark rye, the other holding open a creased parchment map that kept curling back on itself.

He paused mid-smear and glanced up.

"You're awfully quiet."

Clara blinked. "Huh?"

Sadie leaned forward, eyebrow arched. "That roll's dead, Clara. You gonna eat it, or just keep hoping it comes back to life?"

Clara hesitated, glanced around to make sure no one was close enough to overhear, then leaned in.

"I saw something. Last night."

Sadie stopped mid-bite. "Like… a vision-saw, or a dream-saw?"

Jasper dropped his butter knife. "You don't mean just a dream, do you?"

Clara nodded. "It was... different. Like I was inside someone else. Watching through their eyes. But not just watching—I was them. I could feel what they felt."

Sadie slowly lowered her pastry. "Okay, that's full-on creepy."

"I was in a forest," Clara continued. "Old. Deep. The trees looked like they were made of braided silverwood—"

She paused. "At least, I think that's what it was. I don't even know where that name came from. I've never heard it before. But somehow... I just knew."

Jasper's brow furrowed. "What happened?"

"There were two people," Clara said. "One of them was a man. Tall, cloaked, a scar through one eyebrow. He handed a scroll to the other person—who I think was... me. Or, the person I was inside."

Sadie's eyes widened. "Wait. That guy—wasn't he the one who came into our relics class last week? The one who gave a message to Professor Valen?"

Clara nodded. "That's what I thought too. Except... he looked younger in the vision. Like it was a memory from years ago."

Jasper was already scribbling something on the map's margin. "If that was real—and not just your brain being creative during REM sleep—then that means your locket didn't just recognise him. It remembered him."

"Residual energy imprint," Sadie muttered. "Like relic echoes."

Jasper looked up. "Exactly. Some relics can retain impressions—memories tied to powerful events or emotional states. Especially if they were crafted with binding materials like bloodglass or weeping stone."

Clara raised an eyebrow. "Those are real things?"

"Unfortunately," Jasper said. "And usually illegal."

Veilborne

Sadie pointed her pastry at Clara. "But the locket isn't just echoing. It's showing you things. Like it's... guiding you."

Clara looked down at her plate. "It didn't feel like a message. More like... a warning. Or a clue."

There was a moment of thoughtful silence.

Then Sadie smirked. "So what you're saying is, your mysterious inherited necklace just beamed a magical spy memory into your head while you were sleeping and now we're supposed to act normal?"

"I mean, we could try," Jasper offered.

Sadie nudged Clara's plate. "Eat something before your locket sends you a dream about starvation. Seriously."

Clara smiled faintly and broke off a corner of a grain roll. The taste of honeyed pear and warm spice filled her mouth, but her thoughts were still elsewhere.

Somewhere, in a forest she'd never seen. With a man she'd never met. Holding a secret she didn't yet understand.

****

The courtyard reeked of moss and wet wood. Rain had passed through before dawn, leaving the stones damp beneath Clara's boots and the air cool enough to make her fingertips tingle. A line of gnarled trees arched overhead like sentinels, their twisted trunks interwoven with lantern vines that pulsed faintly in the morning haze.

It was not the sort of place she'd imagined being trained for combat.

No iron rings or sandpits. No bellowed orders echoing off walls of steel. Just a broad, pale wooden platform at the centre of the courtyard—circular, etched with chalk glyphs that glowed softly underfoot. Around it, natural terraces formed seating ledges shaded by vine-draped canopies. It felt more like an outdoor amphitheatre meant for rituals than for bruises.

And yet… students stood there. Nearly twenty of them in quiet groups, some yawning, others stretching or fidgeting with their sleeves. All of them waiting.

Clara spotted her team easily—five others from Starfire House, gathered near a flowering archway. None of them made eye contact. One boy nodded faintly, but another turned away as if embarrassed to share a uniform.

Sadie rolled her eyes. "Oh look, it's our fan club."

"They're just scared of being next to us," Jasper muttered, arms folded. "Might catch some of our recklessness."

Clara didn't respond. Her eyes had already found him.

Varek Draven.

He stood a little apart from the others, spine straight, hands clasped behind his back. His training robes were spotless—of course—and his boots barely touched the damp earth, as if the ground wasn't fit for him. His two usual lackeys flanked him: one sharpening a mock-blade unnecessarily, the other muttering about something Clara couldn't make out.

Varek didn't smile this time.

He simply watched her.

And then, as if the weather itself responded to the tension, the wind shifted.

Leaves rustled.

And Eldric Ducart appeared.

Not with ceremony. Not with sound.

One moment the courtyard was empty—and the next, he was there. Cloak catching the wind, hands behind his back, eyes cutting through fog and youth alike with quiet precision.

The murmurs died immediately.

Veilborne

"You will all fail today," he said.

A few students shifted uncomfortably. One actually laughed—until Eldric glared at him.

"That is not a threat," he continued. "It is a promise. You are meant to fail. Because if you cannot learn from failure, you will not survive what waits beyond these walls."

Clara straightened slightly.

Eldric stepped onto the ring's edge and gestured toward a tall wooden rack that had stood unnoticed until now. With a smooth motion of his hand, it opened—retracting like puzzlewood—to reveal an armory's worth of practice tools.

Blunted blades, ashwood staves, leather-bound training shields. Curved batons, sand-weighted rings, and strange paired rods that sparked faintly as if alive.

"You will each choose one," Eldric said. "You have ten seconds."

Someone near Clara whispered, "Ten what?"

"Begin," Eldric said.

And the courtyard erupted into chaos.

Students surged forward—not running, but jostling, elbowing for the best spots like scavengers at a relic auction. Clara moved with the flow, flanked by Sadie on one side and Jasper on the other.

"Low centre of gravity," Jasper muttered, already reaching for a long, slightly tapered staff. "Good reach. Even balance. Minimal training curve—ah-ha!" He seized it with both hands and spun it like a baton. "Excellent."

Sadie snatched up a short, curved blade and gave it a test swing. "Sleek. Stylish. Would look deadly in a rooftop duel."

Clara hesitated.

Her fingers skimmed the row of weapons. A polished wand? Too formal. A pair of leather-bound chakrams? She couldn't even juggle.

She settled finally on a simple baton—smooth, straight, a little longer than her forearm. Not flashy. Not dangerous. But balanced. Familiar, somehow.

She gripped it and turned.

Eldric was already watching her.

"Back to the ring," he called. "Now. Pair off."

The students shuffled into new groups. Some confidently bumped fists or nudged each other with grins. Others looked around awkwardly, clearly trying to avoid anyone who might bruise them more than a lesson required.

Clara's heart jumped when she realised she was face to face with a lanky boy she didn't recognise—tall, sharp elbows, and wide eyes like he'd been dragged into battle by accident.

He raised a short staff hesitantly. "Uh... hi?"

Clara lifted her baton in a mirroring stance. "Hi."

Eldric's voice cut across the ring again.

"Combat begins with intention. The moment you draw your weapon, you make a choice—not just to fight, but to declare why. Your stance speaks. Your strike speaks louder."

He nodded once.

"Begin."

Clara's opponent struck first.

It was a hesitant swing—more instinct than training—and she blocked it with a sharp clack of wood against wood. The vibration ran down her wrist, jolting her. She winced but kept her grip tight.

They circled. His stance was unsteady, knees locked too straight. Clara shifted without thinking—feet planting, weight balanced—as if her body remembered something her mind didn't. He came at her again, staff aimed high. She ducked low, brought her baton up—and knocked his strike aside.

Veilborne

"Oh," he said, sounding surprised.

Clara didn't reply. Her pulse was quick, but her focus stayed razor-sharp. When his next swing came low and wide, she was already moving—dodging back with a sharp pivot as his staff whooshed past her hip.

Around the ring, other matches echoed:

Sadie laughing mid-swing as she danced around her opponent with loose-limbed grace, blade flashing in playful arcs.

Jasper awkwardly wielding his staff like a broom, spouting theories mid-fight. "Leverage is key! If I angle from—Ow! Hey, I'm explaining!"

A girl with braided copper hair knocked her opponent flat with a spinning shield manoeuvre and shouted, "Oops!" a bit too gleefully.

Clara barely registered it.

Her opponent lunged again, faster this time.

She dropped into a crouch, her baton sweeping low. She caught him off balance, striking the back of his knee, and he tumbled with a surprised yelp. The glyphs surrounding their spar flared softly.

Match over.

Clara straightened, chest heaving.

She'd won.

She blinked, startled by her own balance, the way her body had moved before her thoughts had caught up.

The boy on the ground grinned up at her. "Good match," he said, rubbing his shin. "Didn't think you'd be that fast."

Clara offered him a hand. He took it, and she helped him up.

A voice rang out—calm and cold.

"Again. Switch partners."

Eldric's tone brooked no argument.

The students shifted, swapping places, offering brief nods or awkward smiles. Clara turned, unsure where to go next—until a shadow stepped into the ring opposite her.

Varek Draven.

He offered no greeting. No smile. Just that sharp, unreadable look, like he was already calculating the precise moment she'd fall.

Sadie caught Clara's eye from the sidelines and mouthed, Kick his teeth in.

Clara lifted her baton.

Varek raised his training blade—blunt-edged and perfectly balanced.

"Try not to embarrass yourself," he said quietly, so only she could hear.

She set her feet, heart hammering.

Eldric's voice echoed through the courtyard.

"Begin."

Varek moved like water poured into a sword's mould. Smooth, fast, merciless.

Clara barely blocked his first strike, the baton jarred in her grip. She stepped left, ducked, parried—barely keeping pace. But she was still upright.

She feinted and struck his side with the baton.

A spark flared in the glyphs.

Point: Clara.

Gasps rippled through the ring.

Varek's jaw twitched.

He didn't speak.

He came at her again.

Harder.

Veilborne

Now his strikes were unrelenting—controlled, but brutal. Clara fell back, blocking, dodging, losing ground. Her shoulder screamed where he clipped her with a glancing blow. Her ribs ached from a jab that caught her off guard.

She managed one more swing—but he intercepted it mid-arc, twisted, and sent her baton flying. In the same breath, he swept her legs out from under her.

Clara hit the ground, hard.

The glyphs flared.

Match over.

For a moment, everything stilled.

Varek loomed over her, breathing evenly, blade lowered. "Almost," he murmured. "But not quite."

Without a word, he turned, leaving her there without offering a hand.

Clara lay on the cold stone for a second, winded, gasping.

Then Eldric stepped into view, arms crossed, expression unreadable.

"You held your footing longer than most," he said. "But you shifted your weight too soon."

He extended a hand.

Clara took it, letting him pull her to her feet.

As he did, he added, "Pain teaches. But only if you listen to its lessons."

Clara nodded once, absorbing the weight of his words.

****

The corridor outside the training courtyard was eerily quiet, lined with ancient stone arches that opened onto gardens cloaked in soft mist. The lanterns on the walls cast a steady golden glow, their light blurring into halos across the worn flagstones.

Clara limped slightly as she walked, her shoulder stiff, ribs aching with each step. Sadie supported her on one side, while Jasper hovered anxiously on the other, arms half-outstretched as though expecting her to collapse any moment.

"I'm fine," Clara said for the third time, though her breath caught a little at the end of the sentence.

"You're not fine," Jasper muttered under his breath. "He's had years of training. You lasted longer than most would've."

"He fights like someone who's never been hit," Sadie remarked, voice low but amused. "Not properly, anyway. Might do him some good."

"I bet he practices in front of a mirror," Jasper muttered. "Probably compliments himself between strikes."

They reached the door to their dormitory wing, and Sadie nudged it open with her shoulder. Inside, the room was dim and warm, the lanterns flickering softly, the beds neat—except for the pile of cushions Sadie had claimed as her 'study fort.'

Clara eased herself down onto her mattress with a quiet groan.

Sadie crouched to unlace her boots. "You did great, by the way. For someone who's never fought before, you actually held your own."

"She scored a point on Varek," Jasper added, visibly impressed. "That alone should earn her a statue. Or at least a fruit tart."

Clara smiled weakly, pressing a palm to her ribs. "I didn't think I'd last at all."

Sadie stood, hands on her hips. "You did more than last. You showed up. And don't forget the part where you knocked that first guy on his arse."

"He was polite about it," Clara said with a faint grin. "That helped."

Jasper crossed to the side table, rummaged through a drawer, and pulled out a wrapped compress. "Here—cold rune. Put this on your side."

Veilborne

Clara accepted it gratefully and pressed it to her ribs. "Thanks."

A silence settled over them as the warmth of the room softened their edges.

Then Clara spoke quietly. "There's something else."

Sadie and Jasper both looked up at her.

Clara hesitated, fingers brushing the locket at her collarbone. She reached down, pulled a worn cloth-wrapped bundle from beneath her bed, and unwrapped it carefully.

The journal.

She set it down on the bed between them.

"You kept it?" Sadie asked, voice low, not accusing but tinged with curiosity.

Clara nodded. "I couldn't leave it. Not after everything. It felt like it was meant to be found. Meant to be read."

Jasper leaned forward, his eyes wide behind his glasses. "You haven't opened it?"

"Not yet," Clara said. "I wanted to tell you both first."

Sadie studied the worn cover, then glanced at Clara. "Well, looks like we're in this together. Again."

Clara offered a small, tired smile. "Yeah."

Jasper adjusted his glasses and rubbed his hands together. "Right. Let's find out what nearly got us turned to ash."

Clara opened the journal.

The journal smelled of ash and the weight of time.

Its cover was well-worn but still intact—charcoal leather etched with faint sigils that shimmered under the lantern light. The clasp, a simple loop of copper set with a dull blue crystal, clicked softly as Clara undid it. A small breath escaped her lips, as if the sound alone might wake the book from whatever slumber it had been in.

She opened the cover.

The first few pages were blank.

No ink. No indentations. Just clean, rough paper—faintly yellowed and soft at the edges. Jasper leaned in closer, brow furrowed.

Clara flipped ahead, skimming through more empty pages—until one finally shimmered beneath the lantern's glow.

Text bloomed faintly across the surface, not written in ink but appearing as if dusted with starlight. The words curled in an elegant script—neat, exact, and unmistakably deliberate.

Clara read aloud:

"Resonance detected. Entry keyed to bloodline cipher. Observation priority: Veil tension remains unstable. Secondary note: drift increasing. Subject link unconfirmed."

She looked up at them. "Does that mean anything to you?"

Jasper's mouth opened. Then closed. Then opened again. "Uh… maybe? It sounds like a diagnostic entry—like someone tracking the Veil's condition, or testing access protocols."

Sadie leaned over her shoulder. "Wait. That first line. 'Bloodline cipher'? You think it's reacting to you?"

Clara hesitated, then touched the locket beneath her collar. "Maybe. It didn't glow or anything—but when I picked up the journal back in the study… that's when the security triggered."

Sadie frowned. "So it didn't just let you in. It tried to stop you too."

Jasper nodded slowly. "Which might mean the study wasn't meant to stay sealed. Just… selective. Only someone with the right link could trigger the next phase."

"Someone with a link," Clara whispered, looking at the journal in her hands, "To him. To Emberlain."

Clara turned the page. More glowing text appeared—some clear, some fractured, flickering like light on shattered glass.

Veilborne

Jasper leaned in closer, his brow furrowed. "That's an encryption weave. It's trying to show us something, but... the pattern's unfinished. Like it's waiting for something to fully unlock it."

Sadie pointed to a patch where the letters fluctuated in and out of focus. "A trigger, you mean? Something personal?"

Jasper nodded. "Yeah. Blood, bonded artefact, perhaps an aura signature—whatever Emberlain trusted to last long enough to complete the link."

Clara's hand instinctively moved to the locket beneath her tunic.

Sadie caught the motion. "You think it's that?"

Clara didn't reply immediately. She pressed her palm against the locket, feeling its consistent warmth.

"I think it's part of it," she said at last. "But perhaps not all of it."

Jasper tapped the page again, deep in thought. "We might need something to reinforce the link. A catalyst. Maybe a relic tied to the same weave."

Sadie leaned back in her chair, stretching. "Great. We need a magic key for the magic key."

She grinned sideways. "I say we raid Fennrick's cottage. If anyone's accidentally hoarding ancient artefacts in a biscuit tin, it's him."

Jasper stifled a laugh. "Or braided into that disaster he calls a beard."

Clara flipped another page.

This time, the diagram was clearer—etched in strands of light. Circular formations. Crystal matrices. Lines of runes spreading outward like veins across a translucent outline of the Veil itself. The sketch pulsed faintly, as if alive.

Her chest tightened.

Whatever Emberlain had been trying to construct—it wasn't just a door.

It was something far larger.

She ran her fingers along the lines.

It pulsed beneath her touch. Just once.

Like the journal was breathing.

Sadie leaned in closer. "Is it just me, or is this whole thing starting to feel like the opening act of a much bigger blunder?"

Clara didn't respond.

She closed the journal carefully, wrapping it back in the cloth.

Then she looked at her friends—wide-eyed, fatigued, loyal.

"I think this is just the beginning."

Sunlight filtered into the dormitory like honey through gauze—soft, golden, and serene.

No horns. No footfalls echoing in the hallway. No urgent knocks at the door.

Just birdsong. And stillness.

Clara stirred slowly beneath her blanket, blinking up at the wooden canopy of the Starfire dormitory ceiling. The rune-etched beams above glimmered faintly in the morning light, their protective patterns calm and undisturbed.

Across the room, Sadie was sprawled on her bed like a starfish, one leg hanging off the edge, hair a wild halo of tangled gold. Jasper had fallen asleep half-sitting, half-slumped over a pile of parchment and diagrams at his bedside. One of the scrolls had slipped to the floor, crumpling beneath the heel of his boot.

Clara sat up slowly, muscles sore from the previous day's training. Her ribs ached, a dull echo of Varek's final blow, but it was the weight at her collarbone that truly woke her.

The locket was warm.

Not urgent. Not pulsing.

But aware.

Veilborne

She touched it gently, then glanced down at the folded cloth bundle beneath her bedroll. The journal lay tucked inside—no longer untouched, but still holding more secrets than answers. Waiting.

****

"Morning," Sadie mumbled, stretching like a cat before flopping onto her side. "Please tell me that was all a dream and we're actually somewhere dull, like stuck in lecture with Professor Snoreval."

Clara smiled faintly. "Afraid not."

Jasper rubbed his face. "I had a dream where the sentries were librarians. They didn't attack—they just kept shushing me until I cried."

Sadie sat up and rubbed her face. "Recovery day, then?"

"Looks like it," Clara said, gesturing toward the window. The campus outside lay still, the morning mist still hanging over the trees like mist-woven shawls. Distantly, she could see students moving through the courtyards at a relaxed pace, some in small groups, others reading beneath the archways.

No drills. No combat training. No reprimands—yet.

Jasper blinked hard and sat up. "We should go back over the journal today. Cross-reference any readable entries with the archive indexes."

Sadie rolled her eyes. "Or, and hear me out, we could nap in the garden and pretend we didn't nearly vapourise ourselves in a forbidden hidden study two days ago."

"I'm not saying we skip the nap," Jasper muttered, already scanning a nearby list he'd compiled the night before. "I'm saying we do both."

Clara stood and stretched, walking over to the tall windows and pulling them open just enough to let the breeze in. The morning air was cool, carrying the faint scent of dew-damp stone and blooming vale-root—a flower that only grew in the cracks of Calendor's high walls.

She closed her eyes.

In the stillness, she could almost hear the flutter of turning pages.

Almost.

Sadie appeared at her side. "You alright?"

Clara nodded slowly. "Yeah. Just thinking."

Sadie didn't press. She just bumped her shoulder gently against Clara's and said, "We'll figure it out. Whatever this journal is, whatever's in that locket of yours—we'll figure it out together."

Clara smiled. "Thanks."

Behind them, Jasper stood up too quickly and knocked over a mug. "We should ask Fennrick what relic might help decode veil-based scripts. And we need to check if the northern record hall still has those old star charts from the expedition archives—maybe they'll match what's in the journal."

"We'll do it after breakfast," Sadie said firmly, tugging him toward the door by the sleeve. "You're not saving the world on an empty stomach."

Jasper grumbled but didn't resist.

Clara followed them, the journal secure in her satchel, the locket a warm pulse beneath her collar.

****

Outside, Calendor Keep basked beneath the grey-gold sky, its ivy-clad towers rising like spires in an ancient hymn. Wind swept across the upper terraces, carrying the scent of rune-moss and the distant chime of skyloft bells—an old Aurical signal used to mark shifts in weather and wandering thoughts.

And somewhere beneath it all, magic hummed—not loud, but alive.

They found Fennrick Bramble exactly where Sadie predicted he'd be: off the eastern ridge trail, knees-deep in brambles, arguing with what appeared to be a badger.

Veilborne

Not just any badger—a silver-furred, antlered creature with bright violet eyes and a surprisingly expressive scowl.

"I told you," Fennrick said, hands on his hips, "you can't hoard all the glowberries. The grove's shared territory. And no, I don't care if the fox owes you favours."

The badger snorted and flicked its tail, then waddled off with unmistakable indignation.

"Diplomacy," Fennrick muttered. "Completely wasted on woodland royalty."

He turned to the trio just as they stepped into the clearing.

"Ah, the singed survivors," he said, brushing off a twig. "Glad to see you made it. Figured the training yard would've turned you to ash by now."

"Nearly did," Sadie replied. "But we punched it in the metaphorical teeth."

Jasper adjusted the strap on his satchel. "We need your help. Again."

"Doesn't everyone?" Fennrick said, brushing bark dust from his sleeves. "Come on then. Walk with me, the forest's always chatty this time of year."

He led them down a winding track that twisted beneath arching trees and sun-dappled vines. The canopy above filtered the light into shifting patterns—green and gold and copper, like stained glass woven by wind. Birds sang in distant loops, and the air smelled of damp earth, citrus bark, and whatever wildflower was currently dominating the seasonal battle for supremacy.

Clara felt her tension slip away with every step. The locket was warm again—noticeable, but soft. A quiet hum, as though it recognised the land.

Fennrick glanced at her sideways. "You're walking lighter than yesterday. Did something settle in you overnight?"

Clara offered a small shrug. "Sort of. Maybe."

He nodded as if that explained everything. "Well, whatever it is—hold on to it. Peace doesn't visit often. Best not to question it when it does."

She was quiet a moment longer, then spoke. "I think I saw something last night. In a dream, maybe. But it didn't feel like mine."

He nodded, plucking a leaf from his sleeve. "Relics have moods, some more than others. Especially ones that remember things."

Clara hesitated, then said softly, "I think it showed me something. Last night. A vision—or a memory. But it wasn't mine."

Fennrick slowed his pace, brows knitting. "Not yours?"

She shook her head. "It felt like… I was someone else. Just for a moment. I looked down, and it was still my hands—but older. Different. There was a satchel. Boots I've never worn. And the locket—it was there too."

Fennrick hummed low in his throat. "That happens with old relics. Especially ones bound to the living. Memory echoes. You're not just carrying it—it's carrying you, too."

They reached a break in the path where a cluster of stone steps led down into a shallow glade surrounded by whisper trees. Their leaves never stopped moving, even without wind.

The moment Clara stepped into the clearing, the locket flared with warmth.

It wasn't pain. It wasn't fear.

It was recognition.

She stopped at the edge of the grass.

Fennrick watched her closely. "This place remembers things. Has for centuries. Auricals used to train here before the Keep was fully built. We call it the Grove of Telling. It's where old truths rise to the surface."

Clara moved slowly into the heart of the glade. The air shimmered faintly, like heat rising from stone.

And then she saw them.

Veilborne

Not with her eyes—but as if a memory had risen through the dark.

Ghosts of people standing where she stood. Young men and women in long robes, hands clasped over relics, faces lit by silent understanding. Their outlines flickered like candlelight. One of them turned—toward her—and smiled before fading.

Clara gasped softly.

Jasper and Sadie said nothing. They saw the change in her posture. Felt it in the stillness that followed.

"Let it come," Fennrick said gently. "Whatever it wants to show you."

The warmth of the locket deepened—pulsing once, like a heartbeat against her skin.

And then—

A voice. Not loud. Not strange. Familiar.

"If I fall... don't let them forget."

It wasn't a command.

It was a promise. A last breath tucked into metal and magic, meant to endure.

Clara's eyes filled with tears. She didn't know why. The words weren't hers. But the weight of them settled deep, like a hand placed gently on her soul.

When the warmth faded, it didn't disappear entirely. It just quietened—content, for now.

Clara turned to face the others.

Sadie stepped forward and reached for her hand. "What was that?"

"I don't know," Clara whispered. "But I think... someone's counting on me."

Fennrick nodded slowly. "Then you'd best be ready. Because memories like that don't survive by accident. They survive because something's coming."

He turned toward the trail, pausing just long enough to glance over his shoulder.

He turned toward the trail, pausing just long enough to glance over his shoulder. "What comes next... isn't forgiving."

****

The trio sat huddled in the library's upper alcove—a narrow nook nestled between shelves of old spellcraft journals and alchemical recipe folios, warmed by a single floating globe-lantern that drifted overhead like a lazy firefly. A carved stone table lay between them, its surface scratched with initials and chalk-glyph doodles from long-forgotten students.

Clara placed the journal on the table with reverence, its rune-bound cover dull now but still pulsing faintly if you stared long enough. They had only just begun unlocking its secrets this morning—she hadn't dared open it again since.

Jasper leaned in, a quill tucked behind one ear and smudges of charcoal on his fingers. "Alright," he said, "let's review what we know."

"We know it belonged to Emberlain," Sadie said, tipping her chair back. "We know it's hiding half the story—and we're missing the decoder ring."

Jasper muttered, "Fantastic. Guess we'll just check the lost-and-found for ancient decoder rings."

Sadie gave a mock-salute.

Clara gently unlatched the cover. The pages inside responded instantly—glowing at the seams, letters blooming into visibility before fading like mist. Some entries were written in visible ink, while others swam in and out of perception.

"It's like it's waiting for something," Clara murmured. "Something we don't have yet."

Sadie tapped a finger on the table, frowning. "Then we'd better figure out what it's waiting for—before someone else does."

Veilborne

Jasper leaned in. "See this?" He pointed to a margin scribble beside a spiral rune. "This wasn't written at the same time. Different pressure. Different ink quality. Could be weeks—maybe months—apart."

"So, he came back," Clara said. "He wrote in it over time."

Jasper brightened. "Exactly. He didn't just leave a record—he left a puzzle. One that only makes sense once you find the missing piece."

Sadie raised an eyebrow. "Like what, exactly? A blood moon? Standing on one foot while reciting Veil theory?"

"No," Jasper said, eyes gleaming now. "Another relic. Something tied to this one. Without it, we're only seeing part of the picture."

Clara stared at the pages, a knot tightening in her stomach. "So, we're still missing something."

Jasper nodded. "Exactly. Emberlain was a master of personalized encryption. He wouldn't leave this lying around unless it was meant to be unreadable without the right—" He snapped his fingers. "Relic resonance. A magical object imbued with his signature."

Sadie leaned forward. "Okay, so... what kind of relic would do that?"

Jasper grinned. "There's a theory—unverified, obviously—that Emberlain created a device called the Monocle of Reflection. Not literal reflection—magical. A lens that could read the unseen. Decode illusions, wardings, even memory echoes stored in magical constructs."

Clara blinked. "Wait—seriously? A monocle?"

"Don't laugh," Jasper said. "It was reportedly used during the Silent Rebellion. Let Aurical scouts read hidden trails. Rumor says it could even show the imprint of old spells cast in a location."

"Sounds convenient," Sadie said. "Where is it now?"

"Lost," Jasper shrugged. "Or stolen. Or buried. Accounts vary. Some say it was smuggled off-campus during the last major purge of Gilded tech. Others claim it was hidden inside Calendor itself. Maybe wherever Emberlain went, he took it with him."

Clara tapped the journal's edge. "If that relic really exists—and if it's what he used to read his journal—then we need to find it."

Jasper nodded. "Assuming it's still in one piece and not rotting in some cellar."

Sadie cracked her knuckles. "Because obviously, nothing says adventure like chasing a monocle. I'll grab the snacks."

Jasper pulled a folded parchment from his satchel. "I've got a few leads. There's an artifact ledger from the Rebellion that might still be archived in the vault wing. No promises, but it could mention Emberlain's items."

"And if it doesn't?" Clara asked.

He gave a crooked smile. "Then we follow the oldest trick in the book."

Sadie raised an eyebrow. "Bribery?"

"Rumors," Jasper said. "And a lot of pestering librarians."

****

The vault wing of the Calendor Library was nothing like the airy, rune-lit chambers Clara had grown used to. It was lower—older—buried deep beneath the main archives and sealed behind a heavy door veined with arcane locking sigils. A quiet place. A forgotten place. The kind of place books went when even history stopped asking questions.

"This place gives off the kind of vibe that makes you walk faster without knowing why," Sadie muttered, peering around the corridor's curve. The only light came from Jasper's rune orb, flickering gently as it hovered beside them, casting long shadows that danced across the stone walls.

"I double-checked the cataloguing ledgers," Jasper said, holding up a parchment scribbled with notes. "The artifact registry from the Rebellion was transcribed into codex form, then stored in—" He scanned a nearby placard etched in rusted iron. "—Vault C. That's this one."

Veilborne

They reached the vault door. It wasn't locked—at least, not physically. But a shimmering sheet of protective glyphs wavered just an inch above the handle, like the air itself was reconsidering their presence.

"Please tell me you know how to get past that," Sadie said.

Jasper adjusted his glasses. "Well... not exactly. But it's a standard recognition ward. Usually responds to Aurical signatures. I was hoping..." He turned to Clara. "You should try."

"Why me?"

"Because your locket's already opened a sealed door. If this relic is tied to the old Auricals somehow, it might recognize something in you."

Clara gave him a look. "That's comforting."

Jasper shrugged. "Magically speaking."

Clara stepped forward, nerves prickling. She reached out and hovered her fingers near the glyph-veined field. The locket, warm beneath her shirt, pulsed once.

The barrier shimmered—then vanished with a soft sigh, like the vault itself had just exhaled.

Sadie blinked. "Okay, not gonna lie. That was creepy."

They stepped inside.

The vault smelled of old parchment and the sharp tang of air before a thunderstorm. Rows of narrow shelves stretched into the gloom, each stuffed with scroll cylinders, leather-bound ledgers, and relic storage crates sealed with brass buckles. Above them, the ceiling disappeared into shadow.

"This place is massive," Clara whispered.

Jasper held up his orb, rotating slowly as he scanned. "The codex should be labeled *Artifact Ledger: Post-Gilded Submissions, Year 1–12 AR*."

Sadie picked her way down one aisle. "AR stands for *After Rebellion*, right?"

"Right," Jasper called back. "They reset a lot of recordkeeping systems after the final treaties. Time, magic calibration, rank structures—everything."

Clara wandered to a shelf and ran her fingers along a row of books wrapped in enchanted linen. Her eyes landed on a thick spine etched with a faded title: *Aurical Anomalies: Classified Entries—Restricted*. She didn't touch it.

Jasper made a triumphant sound. "Found it!"

He dragged a heavy codex from a low shelf and thumped it onto a nearby table. The cover creaked open, pages brittle with age but preserved by binding wards. Names and item descriptions filled the ledger in neat columns, each line referencing a tag number and status.

"Let's see," Jasper murmured, flipping. "Monocle... monocle..."

Clara leaned over his shoulder.

"'Object 217B—Personal Viewing Lens, Gilded make. Allegedly in possession of Nikolas Emberlain. Recovered fragments suggest the original item is capable of refractive memory analysis. Listed properties: passive illusion dispels, temporal afterglow tracking, resonance amplification...'"

"Sounds promising," Sadie said.

"Condition," Jasper continued, "unknown. Final entry: item requisitioned by Aurical R. Holloway for containment assessment. Relic never returned to the central inventory. Presumed missing."

Clara's breath caught. "Holloway."

Jasper glanced at her. "Same as your name."

Sadie shifted uncomfortably. "Doesn't mean it's close by. If it went missing back then... it could be anywhere now."

Jasper nodded grimly. "Across the Veil, even. Lost for centuries."

Veilborne

Clara stared down at the entry. Her heart thudded with the weight of it. Another thread. Another secret. And now, another piece of the past scattered beyond her reach.

"What's this here?" Sadie pointed near the margin, where a faint stamp overlapped the final line. It was shaped like a sunburst, but twisted. Its rays bent in strange directions, and a fine crack ran through the symbol like a fracture in glass.

Jasper's face darkened. "That's not good."

Clara looked at him. "What is it?"

"That's a ward seal used for corrupted relics," he said. "It means the item was either too unstable or too dangerous to store conventionally. Relics marked like this usually end up in containment vaults… or buried."

"So, someone thought the monocle was cursed?" Sadie asked.

"Or it started behaving like it was," Jasper said grimly.

Clara's fingers drifted to her locket.

"Then we find it," she said. "If it's here—if it's anywhere—I want to know."

Jasper nodded. "We'll start cross-referencing known containment sites and see what lines up with the Holloway circle's old haunts."

Sadie grinned. "Monocle hunt officially begins."

Jasper closed the codex with a puff of dust. "Let's just hope whatever's attached to it isn't still… watching."

****

Later That Night – Starfire Dormitory

The common room was dim, lit only by the soft amber glow of a single hovering lantern near the bookshelves. Rain tapped lightly against the windowpanes, threading quiet through the stone like a whisper. Jasper sat at the reading nook table, cross-legged, flipping through notes he'd scribbled on the artifact ledger. Sadie lay sprawled across the rug, tossing a cushion in the air and catching it with alternating hands.

Clara sat curled in one of the deep armchairs, the journal still resting on her knees. She hadn't opened it again since the vault. The image of the monocle's corrupted seal wouldn't leave her mind.

Sadie reached over and snagged a small wrapped treat from the stash they'd smuggled in earlier—something chewy and cinnamon-scented from the breakfast hall, now slightly flattened but still edible. She bit off half and offered the rest to Clara.

"Want?"

Clara shook her head.

"You sure?" Sadie waved it. "Emergency rations for emotional meltdowns."

"No, thanks."

Sadie shrugged and finished it in one bite.

Jasper leaned over the back of his chair. "I've started a cross-reference list. Known containment vaults from the Rebellion, relic misplacement reports, old Aurical records... but it's a lot. This might take weeks."

"Weeks?" Sadie groaned. "Can't your brain just... shortcut us to the cursed monocle already?"

Jasper raised an eyebrow. "Unfortunately, no. Magic leaves breadcrumbs, not roadmaps."

Sadie flopped dramatically onto her stomach. "So, we're on a possibly cursed scavenger hunt for an unstable memory lens that may or may not be rotting in a vault full of rejected war trinkets."

"Correct," Jasper said brightly. "Also, possibly haunted."

Sadie buried her face in the pillow. "Excellent. I feel reassured."

Clara hadn't moved. Her fingers tightened slightly around the edge of the journal.

Veilborne

"I don't think it's fruitless," she said quietly.

Sadie lifted her head.

Clara's voice trembled—but didn't waver. "I know you're both trying to keep it light. I appreciate that. But this isn't just some curiosity to me. It's not about relics or echoes or school points."

She stood, the journal clutched tight against her chest. "After thirteen years of nothing-no—no faces, no stories, not even a rumor—this is the first thread I've had. Ever."

Her breath caught, and for a heartbeat, she saw Miss Wren's face in her mind's eye—stern, silent, a door that had never opened.

"I need to know," she said, the words scraping free. "Not for House points. Not for the Council. For me. I need to know who they were. Who am I?"

Her voice cracked, but she didn't look away. "And if I have to dig through every cursed vault, chase every broken piece of the past, then fine. I will."

Silence held the room.

Jasper slowly set his notes down.

Sadie sat up, her expression softening into something fierce. "Then we're with you. No jokes."

Clara let out a breath she hadn't realized she was holding. Her arms dropped to her sides, the journal still pressed close.

Jasper nodded. "You're not doing this alone."

A few heartbeats passed—then Clara smiled faintly. "I know."

Chapter 11
Gilded Horizons

The bells rang early that morning—sharp, silvery tones that sliced clean through the usual hum of dawn.

At first, Clara thought she'd dreamed it. But when the sound came again, echoing down the high-vaulted corridors like a ripple through still water, she bolted upright in her bed. Across the dormitory, students stirred with sleepy confusion, groaning as blankets were thrown back and slippers were hunted for in half-darkness.

Jasper sat up with a yawn. "That's not the breakfast bell."

"It's the Gathering chime," Sadie muttered, already halfway through tugging on a pair of boots. "Haven't heard that one since orientation."

The air buzzed with the collective energy of something unusual. Excitement? Dread? Clara couldn't quite tell.

Within minutes, the trio joined the stream of students flowing through Calendor Keep's inner halls, lit by flickering glyph-lanterns that adjusted to the dawn's approach. The murmurs grew louder as they descended toward the Grand Hall—a sprawling chamber with stonework so old it whispered stories of forgotten centuries. A great mosaic of the Veil, inlaid with silver and moonstone, shimmered beneath their feet as they entered.

All four Aurical Houses were represented now, gathering in loosely formed clusters—Starfire, Dawnspire, Ironwake, and Mistmere. The colors of their robes painted the room like scattered ink: deep indigos, burnished golds, crimson-grays, and ocean greens.

Clara spotted Varek Draven near the front of the Dawnspire contingent. As always, his dark hair was tied neatly at the nape of his neck, and his silver-trimmed robes looked like they'd never known a crease. He stood with his arms folded, flanked by two other students, Clara recognized but didn't know by name.

And he was looking directly at her.

Veilborne

Not a glare. Not a smirk. Just a long, unreadable stare—like he was trying to figure out where her edges were so he could press against them later.

Clara didn't flinch. She lifted her chin a little higher and looked away.

A hush fell as the tall doors behind the dais opened.

From them emerged the Head Aurical, Master Vaelryn, cloaked in robes the color of hammered steel, trimmed with pale gold. Her hair was streaked with iron and silver, and her presence alone seemed to command silence. Behind her stood several senior mentors, including Archivist Heren and Eldric Ducart, their expressions unreadable.

Vaelryn raised one hand, and when she spoke, her voice echoed with a clarity that no normal throat could summon.

"Students of Calendor," she began, "for many of you, this year has already tested courage, curiosity, and consequence. The fabric of our world grows thinner, yes—but so too must our knowledge deepen, our bonds strengthen."

She let that settle.

"It is in this spirit that the Council has approved a rare opportunity. Today, you will journey beyond these walls to a place unlike Calendor Keep. A place where steam dances with spellcraft. A living city built of brass and thunder. Today, we visit Glimmerden."

A rush of whispers broke through the crowd—some thrilled, others shocked.

Glimmerden. Clara thought she'd heard the name before—once, in passing from Sadie, and maybe scribbled in the margin of a book about Gilded trading posts. A hub of invention and commerce, tucked into the mountains far beyond Calendor's cliffs.

But she didn't know it. Not yet.

"Glimmerden?" Jasper echoed, blinking. "Wait—the place with the clockwork messenger rats? And the market towers that shift floors?"

Sadie grinned. "The very same. Also, home to the best sweetroot toffee this side of the Veil. If you don't mind a little soot with your sugar."

Clara tilted her head. "And we're just... being taken there? For a visit?"

"Think of it as an educational excursion," Jasper said, adjusting his spectacles. "A field trip. With a mild risk of explosion."

"Moderate risk," Sadie corrected, deadpan. "Gilded engineering standards are more like suggestions."

"Your mentors will accompany you," Vaelryn continued. "You will travel by mag-lev train from the undercroft platform. Mind your belongings. Mind yourselves. Departure is in thirty minutes."

With a flick of her hand, a series of arcanely scribed sigils flared into view above the dais—hovering departure times, mentor groups, and safety notices drifting in pale light like translucent scrolls.

Dismissed by the bell again—this time with a single deep chime—the students erupted into motion.

****

Descent to the Train Station

"Did he say mag-lev train?" Jasper asked as they filed down the outer staircases that curled like stone ribbons along the cliffside.

"He did," Sadie replied, barely concealing her grin. "Old Gilded tech—well, newer-old. Electromagnetic propulsion. They hover above the rails using repulsor fields. You'll love it."

"I already do," Jasper said, practically bouncing.

They passed through ancient stone arches into the mountain's base, where a once-sealed cavern had been repurposed into the Undercroft Station—and it was unlike anything Clara had ever seen.

The walls glowed with soft amber glass veined in filigreed copper. Brass piping snaked through the rock like arteries, hissing with low bursts of steam. Suspended from the ceiling hung an enormous

Veilborne

glowing orb of rotating runes and interlocking rings—a wayfinder compass, humming faintly with magical energy. The whole place smelled of warm metal, machine oil, and something faintly sweet, like burning honeycomb.

Students gathered on broad stone platforms overlooking a wide stretch of smooth black metal, broken only by narrow seams where luminous glyphs and copper spires pulsed with a gentle electric light. There were no old rails here, no iron tracks—only a network of hovering pads, thrumming softly with restrained power.

The track itself buzzed with quiet anticipation.

"Here she comes," Sadie whispered.

Far down the tunnel, a sound like a rolling storm began to build, rising in pitch. The glow shifted from amber to white-blue, and a gust of wind surged toward them.

Then the Glimmertrain arrived.

It didn't run on wheels. It hovered just above the rail, suspended by invisible force. The body was sleek and gleaming: brass-edged panels, long glass windows, and an undercarriage that shimmered with arcs of contained lightning. Intricate etchings crawled along its sides—part rune, part circuitry, pulsing with life. Steam curled from roof vents, vanishing into mist.

A symphony of metal and magic.

With a hiss, the doors slid open as the train came to a perfect, floating stop—never once touching the platform.

Clara stared, wide-eyed. "This is... amazing."

Sadie nodded. "Told you. Welcome to the Gilded Age."

Inside, a corridor lined with polished brass and smooth paneled walls that seemed to glow from within. Arcs of soft blue light pulsed along the edges of the floor, guiding students to their cabins. Overhead, gears clicked and rotated behind transparent panels—mechanisms built more to impress than function, a flourish of Gilded pride.

Clara, Sadie, and Jasper stepped aboard, swept into the flow of students down the central aisle. The interior smelled of warm cedar and wild mint—like a forest glade hidden inside a clockmaker's dream. Every footstep landed with a softened echo. Velvet-cushioned seats curved around brass-framed windows that stretched nearly from floor to ceiling, offering panoramic views of the tunnel beyond.

They slid into a semicircular booth near the center of the third cabin. Around them, voices rose in a blend of laughter and hushed awe.

Then, with a low chime and a lurch so gentle it felt like a breath, the Glimmertrain began to move.

There was no jolt, no clatter—just a rising hum beneath their feet and a sensation of smooth, gliding speed. The windows blurred with streaks of light as the train sped through the mountain.

Jasper pressed his palm to the glass, frowning in wonder. "No rattle… no vibration. It's like we're just hanging in the air."

Sadie smirked. "Careful. Press any harder and you'll either flatten your face or end up flying through it."

A small group of students passed their booth and did a double-take.

"Hey," said a boy with sandy hair and round glasses slightly askew. "You're Clara Holloway, right? From the collapsed study hall?"

Clara blinked. "Uh… yes?"

"I'm Renley. That was mad, what you did. The whole barrier thing—surviving it, I mean. Everyone says you somehow got through it." He turned to Jasper. "And you—I heard you decked one of the sentries with a book or something!"

Jasper blinked. "I—well, sort of. I mean, I panicked."

Another girl stepped in beside Renley. She wore dark green robes trimmed with fine bronze threading, a thick braid of silver-dyed hair draped over one shoulder. "I'm Lira," she said, not unkindly. "I'm in Mistmere. You three aren't nearly as disastrous-looking as I expected."

"We try to contain it to weekdays," Sadie offered.

Veilborne

That earned a few laughs. Soon they were joined by Renley, Lira, and a third boy—Caz, short for Casrield, apparently—who sat backward on the booth bench with a crooked grin and no concept of personal space. He kept tossing small enchanted stones between his fingers, each one flickering a different color as it moved.

"So what's Glimmerden like?" Clara asked as the train entered a vast crystal-lit cavern. "Has anyone been before?"

"Oh, absolutely," Caz said. "My sister lives there. Works in a potion-tech garage—fixes hybrid bikes and alchemical boilers. Glimmerden's noisy, it's weird, and you can buy pocket clocks that sprout legs and sprint away when the alarm goes off. You have to chase them down to turn them off."

Jasper lit up. "I need one. For Sadie."

Sadie snorted. "Please. You're the one who needs it—to remind you when it's time to put the books down and go to bed." She shrugged, a smirk tugging at her mouth. "Not that I wouldn't mind one myself. Maybe then I'd get some sleep."

Clara smiled—a real one, small but steady.

Moments like this—easy, laughing, alive—would never have happened back at Morrowmere. There, life had meant gray corridors, cold stares, and a kind of silence that gnawed at the edges of her heart.

Here, even with the dangers, even with the uncertainties, she had friends. She had a place.

And for the first time she could remember, she was exactly where she wanted to be.

As the train moved from a mountain tunnel to a glass-sided sky bridge, the view burst open—rolling clouds and sprawling valleys below, threaded with coppery rivers and tiny villages nestled in forests. In the far distance, pale mountains rose like sleeping giants, and a line of smoke marked some unseen forge.

But it wasn't long before the mood shifted.

Clara noticed the temperature drop—not in the air, but in the energy.

She glanced up just in time to see Varek Draven approaching their booth, his usual two companions close behind.

He didn't smile. He flicked his gaze to each of them in turn—first to the broad-shouldered one, then the slighter, sharper figure at his side.

"Crayle. Sorn," he said, voice smooth as silver but twice as cold. "Look who it is."

Then he turned his full attention to Clara, his expression carved from disdain.

"I see they let you board after all," Varek said. "Though I imagine the safety wards were doubled."

Clara straightened, her voice cool but steady.

"What's the matter, Varek?" she said, lifting an eyebrow. "Spotlight not bright enough for you anymore? Must be hard, having to share the stage."

Jasper snorted. Sadie outright laughed—and so did a few other students nearby, heads turning at the jab.

A flush crept up Varek's neck, quickly masked by a thin, icy smile. His two shadows—Crayle and Sorn—shifted behind him, uneasy.

"I simply thought it worth reminding you," Varek said, voice like a blade drawn too slowly, "that this is a diplomatic outing. A public-facing one. No spontaneous collapses. No tampering with ancient wards. And please—try not to embarrass the Keep."

Sadie leaned forward, still grinning. "We'll do our best to disappoint you."

Crayle shifted awkwardly, glancing at Sorn, who stared fixedly at the floor.

Varek's gaze lingered on Clara a moment longer—not glaring, not mocking. Just... weighing.

Veilborne

His jaw tightened almost imperceptibly. Then, without a word, he turned.

As he walked away, Clara caught the slight flick of his eyes toward Crayle and Sorn—a silent, sharp reprimand without a single word spoken.

They followed him at a pace just a fraction too fast, as if trying to outrun the weight of their failure.

"Is it wrong that I hope a gear falls off and hits him in the head?" Renley whispered.

"Nope," said Lira brightly.

The whole booth laughed—light and easy, the tension breaking like a cloud releasing the sun.

The train continued its journey through rising terrain. Outside, the air turned bluer, sharper. Snow-dusted peaks came into view, jagged and gleaming under the rising sun.

Cold mist coiled behind the hover pads, swirling in long ghostly trails, where the heated rail plates met the morning air's chill.

For a time, even Clara forgot the weight of questions and locket dreams.

****

The mist thickened as the train climbed higher, coiling around the windows like restless smoke.

Through the shifting haze, shapes began to form—first vague, then sharpening with every second.

Spindly towers pierced the sky, their sides plated in copper and etched with winding glyphwork that caught the morning light. Steam vents hissed from rooftops, releasing plumes that curled into the cold air like breath from sleeping giants.

Crane arms swung lazily over distant warehouses, their frames stitched from black iron and burnished brass.

Above it all, bridges of glass and gear-linked trusses arched between buildings, glittering like spider silk spun by a mad architect.

And in the distance, Clara caught the faint flicker of clockwork birds weaving between the spires—small, metallic things with brass-feathered wings and gemstone eyes that gleamed in the sun.

Glimmerden.

A living city of invention and impossibility, where magic and machinery stitched the world together in ways the rest of Eryndor barely dared to imagine.

For a moment, Clara simply stared, mouth slightly open, forgetting even to breathe.

Sadie pressed her forehead to the glass, grinning.

Jasper just whispered, "This is... incredible."

The train began to slow, its hum deepening into a resonant pulse as it prepared to dock.

Around them, the other students gathered their satchels and cloaks, voices rising in excitement and awe.

The city of gears awaited.

The train entered its final descent, curving through an arch of ribbed steel and alchemically glazed stone. Lanterns hung like pollen-dusted pods along the tunnel walls, each one flickering with glyphlight that shifted colors in response to the train's passing.

As the Glimmertrain glided to a perfect stop, the platform came into view—a massive circle of polished bronze, etched with concentric symbols and veins of circuitry that pulsed faintly underfoot as the students began to disembark.

Clara stepped down and immediately noticed the change.

The air was warmer, rich with the scent of oil, scorched metal, and something sharper—like cinnamon mixed with singed citrus peel. Steam hissed nearby in short, high bursts, and voices called out across the station in a dozen dialects—some clipped and brisk, others lilting like music.

The buzz of invention thrummed through every corner of the soundscape—alive and electric.

Even the ground hummed faintly beneath her boots—not stone, but layered copper and pale brass plates, engraved with spirals and thin channels of runic light. Pipes disappeared into the walls. Chimneys ticked and exhaled. Signs rotated themselves overhead, swapping languages in real time as they spun.

Above them, in the distance, rooftops glittered with solar mirrors and spincrank devices, while narrow streets ran like veins between workshops, cafés, and towers strung with suspended glass walkways.

"It's... alive," Clara murmured, her eyes wide.

Sadie grinned. "Told you Glimmerden was different."

Students filtered into groups under the supervision of their mentors. An enormous, rust-red automaton in a top hat and brass-trimmed vest held a placard labeled:

'CALENDOR DELEGATION – FOLLOW FOR ORIENTATION' in neatly etched lettering. Its inner gears clicked and turned behind a glass-paneled chestplate as it began waddling down the ramp.

The trio joined the flow of bodies, passing under an arch where charms fizzled like soap bubbles in the air, scanning students for concealed enchantments.

Eldric stood to one side, arms folded, gaze cool and calculating, while Archivist Heren appeared deep in conversation with a wiry woman selling pressed flower scrolls that changed scent as you read them.

They stepped out into the street.

And then the city opened.

Glimmerden's main thoroughfare was a riot of motion and light—towering signs spelled out names in flickering glyphs above vendor stalls built into the undersides of gear-halls. Pipes arched overhead, carrying steaming liquids in glass tubes that lit the street with a warm, alchemical glow. Mechanical birds fluttered between perch-lanterns, tweeting out the day's headlines in rhyming couplets.

And then—

A faint clicking.

Clara looked down.

A small brass creature with glowing blue eyes scuttled across the cobblestones in a perfect figure-eight. It had the body of a rat, but its joints clicked with mechanical precision, and its tail was a segmented antenna ending in a tiny lantern that blinked once before it darted off down a drainpipe.

Jasper froze mid-step, eyes wide.

"Is that—"

Sadie grinned, already following his gaze. "Clockwork rat. Told you they were real."

Another one zipped up the side of a lamppost, its tiny gears whirring faintly before it vanished into a chute.

"That's even better than I imagined," Jasper breathed. "We're getting one. I don't care what it costs—I need one."

Sadie elbowed him lightly. "What for? Planning to raid the kitchen after hours?"

Jasper gave her a glazed, distracted look—like he hadn't even heard—and turned back toward the last disappearing clockwork rat, completely enraptured.

Clara laughed. "Do you think they're... for sale?"

"You can buy one," Sadie said, glancing after the rat. "But there's usually a wait. They're made to order—keyed to your magic signature. Sometimes it takes weeks. They'll send it out once it's ready."

Jasper's eyes shone. "Perfect. Absolutely perfect."

Veilborne

The students had been given a generous amount of free time to explore before the formal tour began— "an orientation through immersion," one mentor called it, though Eldric had simply grunted and waved them off with a warning to "stay visible and stay alert."

Which most of the delegation promptly ignored.

Clara, Sadie, and Jasper stuck together at first, weaving into the current of foot traffic that flowed through Glimmerden like a river of robes, boots, and gliding brass footwear that hovered just above the ground. Signs pointed in every direction: Runeweavers' Walk, Emberglass Plaza, Coil & Charm Books, The Whistlepot Café, Clock & Kindling.

Everything clicked and spun and whispered with purpose. Steam curled from hidden grates. Scent charms burst in the air like citrus fireworks. Above them, laundry flapped from spindly brass clotheslines stretched between towers like high wires, casting patchwork shadows below.

A street performer in a long, grease-stained coat twitched copper wires strung from his gloves to a dozen clockwork marionettes.

The tiny figures danced across a spinning platform—soldiers, wolves, dancers—all moving with eerie grace to the rhythmic clack of hidden gears.

With a few flicks of his fingers, the puppets wove brief, silent battles and crumbling cities into the air—phantoms of motion and memory, dissolving into steam before the next story began.

Jasper nearly walked into a streetlamp, eyes locked upward.

Then he spotted it.

"There," Jasper gasped, grabbing Clara's sleeve and pointing. "Look!"

A narrow stall was tucked between two brass-shelled cafés, its canopy stitched from worn velvet and braided copper chain. Hanging from slender struts were cages—not crude iron, but delicate frames of wire and glass, each one humming faintly with layered enchantments.

Inside: clockwork rats.

Some balanced on spinning spools. Others darted across tiny treadmills, their brass paws clicking in perfect rhythm. A few sat perfectly still, gemstone eyes tracking the crowd with unnerving precision.

Jasper barreled forward, barely stopping himself from pressing his face to the glass.

"I need one," he blurted. "Absolutely. Immediately. At any cost."

The vendor—a stout woman in soot-streaked leathers and oversized bronze goggles—raised an eyebrow, unimpressed.

"You looking to buy, or just to daydream?" she asked, voice dry as powdered ash.

"Buy," Jasper said fervently. "Please. How do I get one?"

The woman chuckled—a low, crackling sound—and beckoned him aside with two crooked fingers.

"Come here, boy. We'll talk business."

Jasper practically stumbled after her, nodding so fast his glasses nearly slipped off his nose.

Clara and Sadie hung back a few steps, exchanging smirks.

"Look at him," Sadie murmured. "Like a kid in a candy shop."

Clara grinned. "I don't think I've ever seen him this happy."

They watched as Jasper leaned in close, whispering questions while the vendor rattled off terms with the ease of someone long used to negotiating with the desperate and wide-eyed.

As Jasper stood mesmerized, Clara let her gaze wander. The city stretched in all directions, like a living labyrinth. She could see spire-markets climbing in spiral staircases, floating shops drifting just above the street, and glass elevators filled with glowing fog ascending on cables that looked too thin to hold them. Her locket gave the faintest flutter against her collarbone—as if stirred by the city's static.

She turned to say something to Sadie—

Veilborne

And saw her frozen.

A few paces away, at a corner stall shaded by brass-leaved awnings, stood a tall man in a long moss-green coat. He wasn't watching the mechanical pets. He wasn't scanning the street.

He was staring at Sadie.

Clara followed his gaze.

He looked older than most in the crowd—not a student, but not quite middle-aged either. His skin was umber-toned, his jaw sharp beneath a neatly trimmed beard streaked with copper gray. One gloved hand rested atop a cane of spliced wood and steel, etched with ivy motifs.

When he noticed Clara watching, he turned and slipped into the crowd.

Sadie blinked. "Let's keep moving."

"You knew him," Clara said softly.

"No," Sadie replied. Then added—too quickly, "He just looked like someone."

Jasper reappeared, breathless and beaming, clutching a folded receipt.

"Guess who's officially on the list?" he said—then frowned, catching the tension. "Wait—what happened?"

"Just some guy," Clara said, watching Sadie's posture. Tense. Guarded.

But Sadie was already walking, braid swinging behind her as she headed toward another row of shops—this one humming with music boxes and gear-chimes, their delicate melodies spinning into the misty air.

The moment passed. But not unnoticed.

The street narrowed as they moved beyond the market stalls. Light from Glimmerden's upper walkways filtered down in shifting tones—gold, rose, violet—like the city itself couldn't settle on one color at a time.

Clara slowed as they approached a shop with no sign.

Mark Peters

It was wedged between two towering brassworks, nearly invisible but for its round archway rimmed with polished obsidian, stitched through with delicate copper filigree. The metal pulsed faintly, alive with slow, rhythmic beats.

She felt a tug—so subtle it might have been imagined—and stepped inside.

The others followed without hesitation.

The air was thick, muffled—as if sound itself moved slower here. The floor was tiled with overlapping clock faces, their hands frozen at different hours. The walls were lined with glass orbs suspended by thin copper threads.

Each orb shimmered faintly, as if breathing.

As Clara passed the nearest one, it flickered—and a scene bloomed inside the glass: a rooftop at sunset, a blurred hand reaching toward her, a half-formed laugh snatched by the wind.

She stumbled back, breath catching.

Jasper moved closer to another orb. It flickered to life, showing a younger version of himself poring over a battered book in a dusty library, his nose smudged with ink he hadn't even noticed.

Sadie stood frozen before one, her hand hovering inches from the surface.

Inside, a younger Sadie laughed as a gear-driven dragonfly buzzed around her in a sun-drenched garden.

In the distance, a cloaked figure watched.

Above the counter, a brassplate sign reconfigured itself with soft mechanical clicks:

ECHOES OF ELSEWHEN — LOST MOMENTS FOR SALE

Another plate snapped into view underneath:

WARNING:

Veilborne

ONCE REMEMBERED, AN ORB MOVES ON.

NOT RESPONSIBLE FOR PERSONAL CONSEQUENCES.

Clara stepped closer to the counter, her gaze skimming a neat list of prices—and nearly choked.

No wonder the shop was empty.

The cost of one orb could buy half a workshop in Glimmerden. These were luxury artifacts—crafted to pull forgotten memories from anyone nearby, storing them until recognition unlocked them again.

Once reclaimed, the memory would dissolve into a swirling void at the orb's core, vanishing like smoke—released to drift until it found another bearer.

Sadie's hand dropped away from the orb, her face pale.

"Let's go," she said quickly.

Jasper backed off too, rubbing the back of his neck. "Yeah. Before my whole childhood gets put on display."

Clara lingered a moment longer, eyes catching a glint deep inside one of the orbs.

A flicker of something—a woman's hand reaching toward a silver chain.

She felt a lurch deep in her chest—but turned away before the memory could take hold.

She wasn't ready. Not yet.

They stepped back out into the street, the hum of Glimmerden roaring back around them like a flood.

For a moment, none of them spoke.

The weight of what they'd almost remembered clung to them like mist.

Then—

A bell rang overhead, three clear notes echoing through the air.

The sound was followed by a ripple of blue light—an enchantment projected in the sky, displaying the Calendor sigil surrounded by arrows pointing toward the central plaza.

Mentors were already gathering, forming small clusters of students around various automaton markers. The trio made their way toward a group led by Eldric, who stood in front of a gently ticking clock-pillar etched with glowing lines.

He looked them over once. "Still behaving. Good."

"Barely," Jasper muttered.

Around them, other students buzzed with excitement—some waving newly acquired gadgets, others comparing sketches or samples. One had a birdcage with a floating marble that sang sea shanties. Another wore a set of mechanical wings strapped awkwardly to their back.

Eldric raised a hand for silence.

"You've had your first taste of Glimmerden," he said, voice calm but steady. "For some of you, it's a glimpse of home. For others, a world you've never walked. Either way, remember this: invention without purpose builds nothing that lasts. Let this city remind you that magic—even refined through gears and steam—remains a force of will."

His eyes swept the group. They landed briefly on Clara, then on Sadie—who hadn't spoken since they'd left the shop.

"Invention changes everything," he finished. "Even us."

Archivist Heren approached from behind, adjusting the cuff of his rune-etched sleeve.

"You'll have another hour to explore," he said crisply. "After that, return here for departure. Don't be late. Or lost."

With a tap on a sigilplate embedded in his wristguard, a shimmering countdown appeared in the air: numbers ticking steadily from **01:01:00** downward.

Clara glanced up instinctively, along with half a dozen other students.

Veilborne

It wasn't like the slow, shifting sky-signs back at Calendor—this was sharper, faster, more mechanical. The numbers clicked down with a soft stutter, like the heartbeat of a machine.

She exchanged a look with Jasper, who gave a low whistle.

Sadie nudged Clara with her elbow.

"Let's go. Clock's ticking," she said, nodding toward the hovering numbers.

"Literally."

The trio stepped away from the group, quiet again for a moment.

"What now?" Clara asked softly.

"Now," Sadie said, her voice regaining its usual tone, "we find the perfect place for tea and something ridiculous."

And with that, the city welcomed them once more.

They parted from the mentor circle with an hour left to explore, the crowd dispersing like threads unwinding from a spool. Glimmerden was shifting again—glass bridges retracting, new stalls rotating into place, alleyways reshaping like the city had somewhere else to be.

"Still want that tea?" Clara asked.

"Definitely," Jasper said, eyes still tracking every glimmer of brass and motion.

Sadie gave a vague nod, but she wasn't listening. She stood a few steps back, posture rigid, eyes narrowed.

Clara followed her gaze—and felt her stomach dip.

There he was again.

The man in the moss-green coat. Just at the edge of the crowd near a column of chime-lamps. Same copper-streaked beard. Same etched cane. His eyes met Sadie's.

Then he turned—stepping behind a vendor's rolling shutter.

Gone.

Sadie didn't hesitate. "I'll be right back."

"Sadie—wait—" Clara started, but her friend was already slipping into the tide of foot traffic.

Jasper frowned. "We're not letting her go alone, right?"

"No," Clara said. "But give her a moment."

They lingered near a rotating signpost, the market's current swirling around them—until something changed.

It wasn't the wind.

It wasn't the temperature.

It was the air itself—heavier, charged, like a pressure drop before a storm. The hairs on Clara's arms stood on end.

Light shimmered across the plaza—brief, like a ripple through glass.

And for a heartbeat, the ground seemed to slip sideways—like a gear grinding out of place.

Jasper stepped closer, fingers brushing Clara's sleeve.

"Did you feel that?" he muttered.

Clara nodded once, barely breathing.

Then it split open.

A jagged rift tore into the air above the square, the world warping as violet, green, and electric blue light spilled out in ragged threads.

Sparks of white flickered like dying stars, bleeding into daylight—then vanishing.

From the heart of the rupture, black tendrils began to unfurl—thin at first, like smoke, then thickening into clawed shapes that writhed against the edges of the tear.

The temperature dropped.

And from that breach in the world—they came.

A sharp scream cut through the square.

Veilborne

Students stumbled back from the plaza's center, knocking over crates, scattering goods.

Someone shouted for a mentor. Another just ran.

Clara froze for half a second, heart hammering—

Then Sadie was there, grabbing her arm and yanking her sideways, away from the spreading shadows.

Three pale, jagged creatures leapt from the tear like rats from a fire.

Their limbs were long and clawed, their movements twitchy and unnatural. Heads tilted too far with every step. Their eyes were deep black—slick and glinting like glass.

Clara's heart dropped.

She knew them.

The same kind of creatures that had torn through the orphanage—room by room, hunting with cold precision. One had flipped her bed across the floor like it weighed nothing, driving her into the corridor in a blind sprint.

That night, her locket had burned against her skin—flaring to life, as if it had sensed the threat before she could.

These weren't accidents.

They were hunting.

They had killed Miss Wren—the closest thing Clara had ever had to a mother, even if she hadn't known it then.

And now they were here.

Screams tore through the square. Shopkeepers fled their stalls, bolts of fabric and crates of gears crashing to the cobblestones. A floating café tray clattered down, tea and biscuits scattering across the ground.

Clara grabbed Jasper and yanked him behind a gear-crate just as one of the creatures skittered past, claws carving deep furrows into the copper-plated street.

Then came the sentinels.

Three Glimmerden city automatons dropped from above—one landing in a crouch with a thunderous clang, the others bursting from hidden alcoves in the walls.

Each stood at least eight feet tall—humanoid, but eerily alien, their frames a fusion of polished copper, arcane crystal, and rune-etched armor. Core runes flared brilliant white. Their eye-slits blazed red.

One sentinel surged forward, metal fists swinging in a brutal arc—smashing the nearest creature with enough force to crack the cobblestones.

Another raised a gauntlet and unleashed a web of searing sigil-light, snaring a second beast mid-pounce.

For a moment, Clara dared to think they had it under control.

Then it turned.

The creatures moved with impossible speed, their bodies warping and flexing like living shadows stitched together with bone and hunger.

The first sentinel grappled with one—but a second creature barreled into its side, and together they dragged it down in a snarl of flashing claws and rending metal.

Sparks exploded into the air. The automaton's core flickered wildly—then went dark.

Its body collapsed with a grinding shriek of gears, steam venting from its ruined joints.

Clara gasped.

Jasper yanked her back as the two victorious creatures turned, oily-black tendrils flickering from their bodies like smoke, ready to strike again.

But the second sentinel charged—moving faster than any machine its size should.

Veilborne

A piston-arm slammed the first creature into the wall with a crack that echoed across the plaza.

The third sentinel surged in from the side, sigil-cables whipping outward to bind the last attacker. With a roar of metal, it dragged the thing down, slamming it into the ground until it burst apart in a sickening cloud of blue mist and unraveling magic.

For a moment, Clara thought it was over.

Then the third creature moved.

Not toward the sentinels.

Toward her.

It skittered low across the ground, claws clicking against the metal, mouth stretching wide in a soundless, yawning howl. Its eyes burned a sickly green, locked on her like a hawk zeroing in.

Clara backed away instinctively, fumbling for anything to defend herself. Her heel caught on the edge of a toppled cart, sending her stumbling sideways.

The creature stalked after her, its form contorting and flickering at the edges, struggling to maintain solidity.

It was fast.

Too fast.

Jasper shouted something—words lost beneath the roar of blood in Clara's ears. Sadie called out as well, her voice distant, swallowed by the pounding of Clara's heartbeat.

The creature lunged.

Clara ducked instinctively, the creature's claws slicing through the air mere inches above her head. She stumbled across the debris-strewn ground, her boots sliding on shattered pottery and spilled tea.

The Sentinel surged forward, a metallic blur intercepting the Revenant—but this time, the creature twisted unnaturally mid-leap, evading the automaton's strike. With unnatural strength, the beast slammed into the Sentinel, hurling it violently against a reinforced pillar. Stone cracked and metal shrieked as the automaton collapsed to the ground, sparks flaring from its damaged joints.

Clara scrambled backward, the air around her growing bitterly cold as the Pale Revenant turned toward her once again, its hollow gaze fixed on her locket.

Then, from the shadows—a flash of steel.

Eldric surged forward, coat billowing, his dagger glinting sharply as he closed the gap in seconds. He struck swiftly, the blade slicing deeply into the creature's shifting torso. But the Revenant twisted viciously, letting out a piercing shriek. Its long, sinewy limb whipped around with blinding speed, claws raking across Eldric's side and tearing open his coat, a spatter of blood darkening the stone beneath them.

Eldric stumbled back, grimacing from the impact. For a heartbeat, he seemed to falter, breath hissing through gritted teeth.

The Revenant lunged again, sensing weakness.

But Eldric met it head-on, teeth bared in determination. He thrust forward again, his blade driving straight and true into the creature's core with renewed strength.

This time, the Pale Revenant convulsed violently, limbs flailing—then shattered into fragments of dissipating magic and icy mist.

Above, the Veil tear spasmed once more, edges writhing wildly, before finally folding inward with a gut-deep, wrenching snap. Silence slammed down across the square, broken only by the hiss of cooling metal and the faint clatter of debris.

Eldric stood amid the thinning mist, dagger gripped tightly, shoulders heaving slightly with exertion. Blood seeped steadily from the wound at his side, but his gaze remained fixed protectively on Clara, fierce and unwavering.

Students and shopkeepers stared, wide-eyed and stunned. Somewhere, a dropped gear clinked against the stones, the sound sharp and distant.

Veilborne

Clara couldn't look away.

She had seen magic before. She had seen fear.

But she had never seen resolve like this.

Then came the footsteps.

Several Auricals swept into the plaza, robes trailing faint light, hands raised in practiced readiness.

One led the way—a tall woman with silver-threaded hair and a face carved into permanent disapproval. She paused mid-stride when she spotted Clara, Jasper, and Sadie reuniting at the edge of the square—breathless, bruised, but still standing.

She exhaled through her nose—a sound more dangerous than any shout.

"Why," she asked the air, "is it always you three?"

Clara opened her mouth to protest—

But Eldric was already moving.

He stepped between the students and the Auricals. His coat hung in tatters at the sleeve, the fabric still smoldering where a claw had grazed it. His jaw was set like stone, and for one sharp, defiant beat, he locked eyes with the silver-haired Aurical.

No words were needed: *They're mine.*

"They weren't involved," Eldric said, voice calm but carrying. "The tear didn't originate from them. They were caught in the radius—same as everyone else."

The Aurical studied him for a long, tense moment. Measuring. Weighing.

Then she gave a sharp nod.

"Make sure it stays that way," she said curtly—and turned, barking orders as the first restoration wards ignited across the damaged plaza.

The Auricals moved to inspect the scene. The sentinels slowly deactivated, their limbs folding into neutral stances, red eyes dimming.

The crowd began to settle again, though many still stared at the trio.

Sadie looked shaken.

Clara caught Eldric's eye as he passed. He gave her the smallest nod—approval, maybe relief—before vanishing into the tide of cloaks and magic.

They slipped away, ducking into a shadowed alley lit by half-tinted skylights and a vendor hawking mistglass.

"I've seen them before," Clara whispered. "Those things. They're the same ones that attacked the orphanage. I know it."

"They came through the Veil," Sadie murmured. "They weren't just passing through. They were looking for something."

"Or someone," Jasper added, eyes fixed on the space where the tear had been.

Clara touched the locket at her collarbone. It felt warm.

Too warm.

But not like before.

Back at the orphanage, the locket had burned against her skin the moment the creatures drew close—sparking, pulsing, almost dragging her awake.

Here, in the chaos of the square, it had stayed quieter.

Was it the crowd? The noise? The sheer weight of magic in a place like Glimmerden?

Or maybe the creatures hadn't been looking for her this time.

The thought chilled her more than the air.

"They didn't attack us at Calendor Keep," she said. "They've never come near."

Veilborne

"Because they can't," Jasper said, frowning. "Calendor's layered in protections. Wards in the walls, glyphs in the walkways. Even the windows are laced with enchantments."

"But Glimmerden doesn't have that," Clara realized.

"Which might be," Jasper said slowly, "why Eldric keeps such a close eye on us all the time."

No one spoke after that.

The return platform felt colder now, though the same amber-glow lanterns burned overhead and steam hissed from the brass vents as if nothing had changed.

But everything had.

The Glimmertrain waited—sleek and silent, but not untouched. Even here, the air felt different. Heavier.

The trio boarded without a word, finding the same booth they'd used earlier. This time, no one else joined them.

The windows reflected their faces—drawn, quiet, still jittering with the aftermath.

Clara sat with her arms folded tightly over her middle. Sadie hadn't looked up once since they left the plaza. And Jasper, who normally couldn't sit still for five seconds, stared out the window in total silence.

Only the soft, steady hum of the train filled the space as it began its slow rise through the mountain tunnels.

"I keep thinking about the locket," Clara said finally. "It reacted that night at the orphanage. Right before the creatures came. And now... they're back."

"Drawn to it," Jasper murmured. "That's what you're saying."

"They were looking for something," Sadie added, her voice barely above a whisper. "They came through that tear like they were... chasing a scent."

"I thought this trip was supposed to be safe," Clara said. "Normal."

"Yeah," Jasper muttered, slumping. "We really nailed that."

That earned the faintest smile from Sadie. But it faded quickly.

Clara looked down at the locket. It was quiet again. Cool. Innocent.

But she could still remember the heat. The pulse. The warning.

The train slipped into shadow, entering the last tunnel before Calendor Keep.

"I think someone's watching us," Clara said softly.

Sadie looked up. "You mean the Auricals?"

"It feels like we're being followed," Clara said quietly. "Like there's something just out of sight. Waiting."

No one disagreed.

The rest of the ride passed in silence, the city of gears fading behind them like a memory they weren't sure had ever been real.

Chapter 12
Silent Divides

The rain had returned overnight.

Not a storm—just a soft, whispering drizzle that tapped against the windows of Calendor Keep like it was trying to be let in.

Clara sat on the edge of her bed, wrapped in her blanket, boots half-laced and forgotten.

The world outside was gray and blurred, like even the mountains were trying to disappear behind the rain.

She hadn't slept. Not really.

Not after Glimmerden.

Not after the creatures.

They were the same.

The slick black eyes. The wrong-angled limbs.

The way they moved—twitching, hungry—like puppets yanked by too many strings.

The same ones that had come for her at the orphanage.

That night.

When her bed had been thrown across the room like a toy.

When she'd run barefoot down cold hallways, heart battering against her ribs.

When she'd smelled smoke and blood.

And Miss Wren—

Miss Wren had died.

The thought sliced sharper than she expected.

She had never said it aloud.

Not to Sadie. Not to Jasper.

Maybe not even to herself.

Miss Wren, cold and stern and worn thin by years of keeping too many children alive with too little.

Miss Wren, who made sure Clara had clean socks.

Who remembered her birthday.

Who left the hallway light on when the wind howled at night.

Not warmth.

Not softness.

But something steady. Something real.

And now—

Clara twisted the blanket tighter around herself until her knuckles ached.

The ache was easier than the hollow.

She blinked hard, pushing the sting away.

The rain kept tapping at the glass.

Soft. Relentless.

Unforgiving.

She reached up and wrapped her fingers around the locket resting against her collarbone. It was cool now. Inert. Just a trinket to anyone else.

But to her, it was weight and memory and mystery—and sometimes, when she was very still, she thought it felt… aware.

She closed her eyes.

"I miss her," she whispered.

A gentle warmth pulsed beneath her hand. Not hot, like it had burned before—just warm. Comforting. Like sitting too close to a sunlit window. Like a memory leaning against her shoulder.

Veilborne

It was the closest thing to a hug she'd had in a long time.

Her breath caught.

The ache in her chest eased—not gone, but quieted. Like someone had whispered *I'm still here* without needing words.

She opened her eyes slowly.

The rain had eased, and a shaft of pale morning light spilled across the stone floor. For the first time since their return, Clara didn't feel like she was carrying it all alone.

She stood, tucking the locket securely beneath her shirt, and finished lacing her boots.

Somewhere down the hall, she could hear Sadie's laughter echo faintly. A heartbeat later, Jasper's voice followed—something about toads and cinnamon, as usual.

Clara smiled faintly.

Time to face the day.

Sadie and Jasper were already waiting near the west stairwell—dressed, unusually subdued.

"Did you get a summons too?" Sadie asked as Clara approached.

Clara nodded. "Eldric's handwriting. Hard to miss."

"Same." Jasper held up a parchment still faintly steaming from the messenger pipe. "Mine was still warm. Either he sent it this morning, or Eldric writes in dragon ink."

They walked together through the curving hallways, boots tapping softly on smooth stone, the walls glowing faintly with morning runes.

Calendor Keep always felt calm in the early hours—like the building itself was still dreaming.

But today, the silence carried weight.

As if the Keep had woken—and was listening.

When they reached the north turret conference chamber, the oak door was already open.

Eldric Ducart stood near the arched windows, arms folded, expression unreadable. Archivist Heren paced beside the long table; parchment rolls and polished memory stones arranged in careful lines.

"Come in," Heren said without preamble. "Close the door."

They obeyed. Jasper shut it gently behind them, and the three stood in a line before the mentors like students waiting to be tested.

"First," Eldric said, "you did well."

That caught them all off guard.

"In Glimmerden," he clarified. "You remained calm. You observed. You didn't engage unless forced. I've seen senior Auricals crumble under less."

Jasper blinked. "Is this… praise? Are we dying?"

Heren shot him a sharp look. "Don't interrupt."

"Right. Sorry. Please proceed with the dying."

Heren ignored him. His voice remained steady, deliberate.

"There's something you need to know," he said. "Something we've kept from the student body at large. Until now."

Clara felt her shoulders tense.

Heren stepped forward.

"We believe someone within Calendor Keep is working against us. A traitor."

The words landed like a dropped stone.

Clara glanced at Sadie, whose face had gone very still.

Jasper's mouth was half open.

Veilborne

"We can't say who," Eldric added. "We don't know yet. But we suspect that certain... occurrences—strange readings, passive Veil activity, ward disruptions—have not been accidents."

"Glimmerden?" Clara asked. "Was that—?"

"Possibly connected," Heren said. "It was too precisely timed to be ignored. The creatures emerged when security was at its thinnest—during a student excursion. Either we were remarkably unlucky... or someone wanted them to find you."

Clara's hand went instinctively to the locket beneath her shirt.

"We took you to Glimmerden for two reasons," Eldric said. "One, because it was promised. And two—because we hoped the traitor might make a move if they thought you were vulnerable."

"Did they?" Sadie asked quietly.

Eldric's eyes flicked to her.

"We don't know," he said. "But someone breached the Veil. Not from the outside—from here."

A silence fell over the room.

Then Heren added, "We're monitoring all internal enchantment logs. Nothing you three did caused it. But you were at the center of it—again. And that tells us you're still a target."

Jasper scratched his head. "So, what happens now? We start reporting on our professors? Join an Aurical spy ring? Get monocles and cool aliases?"

Heren sighed. "You go to class. You keep learning. But you stay alert. If you notice anything strange—especially from those you trust—tell us."

Clara nodded slowly.

"Do you think the man I saw..." Sadie began, then trailed off.

Eldric's brow furrowed. "What man?"

Sadie hesitated. "In Glimmerden. Before the Veil tear. I... saw someone. Twice now. Long coat. Copper in his beard. He stared at me like he knew me."

"You think he triggered the breach?"

"No," Sadie said quickly. "It wasn't him. I just... thought you should know."

Eldric's expression didn't shift, but Clara caught the glance he exchanged with Heren. It wasn't surprise. It was concern.

"Thank you," he said finally. "We'll look into it."

"This does not leave this room," Heren added. "The wrong whisper could compromise everything."

He dismissed them with a nod. "You're due in your next class—Protections and Wardwork, with Instructor Dorran Nym. Don't be late."

Jasper muttered, "Can't even skip the fun stuff during a magical conspiracy," but Clara didn't laugh. Not this time.

As they left the chamber, Clara touched the locket again.

It was warm.

Not like before—this warmth had a pulse. A rhythm.

Not comforting.

Warning.

The council chamber door clicked shut behind them, and the noise of the corridor seemed to fall away. The three of them walked in silence for several paces, the low amber light of the Keep stretching ahead of them like a path—or a warning.

"Okay," Jasper said finally. "So... there's a traitor."

"Keep your voice down," Clara hissed.

He raised his hands. "Right. Whispering. Secret. Treasonous infiltrator inside the walls. Casual stuff."

Veilborne

Sadie walked with her arms crossed, eyes fixed ahead. "Do you think it could actually be... someone we know?"

"I don't know who else it would be," Clara murmured. "Someone knew exactly when we'd be vulnerable—and made sure those things found us."

They stopped near one of the window alcoves overlooking the inner courtyard. The sun had just begun to warm the spires.

Jasper rubbed the back of his neck. "I can't be the only one thinking this, but... Varek?"

Sadie arched a brow. "Draven?"

"He's smug. Elitist. Knows way more than he should. And his mother's Obsidian Court." He paused. "Like, actual Obsidian Court."

"She's on the ruling seat, isn't she?" Sadie asked.

Jasper nodded. "Lady Selvara Draven. Cold as her son and twice as venomous."

Sadie looked unconvinced. "He's unpleasant. That doesn't make him guilty."

"No," Clara agreed. "But it means we should be careful."

She glanced down the hall. "And we absolutely don't mention the meeting. To anyone."

They all nodded.

Clara added, "If someone inside the Keep really is working for MalVaran... we don't know who's listening."

They stepped away from the window and continued toward the warding classrooms. As they turned a corner, voices echoed from behind—

"Clara!"

She turned just as Renley jogged up, waving, trailed by Lira and Caz, each with new gear strapped to their bags and the faint post-excursion glow of people who'd almost died but now had stories to tell.

"There you are," Renley said, grinning. "We've been looking for you since yesterday."

"Didn't get a chance to debrief after all the... well... you-know-what," Caz added, glancing around like the cobblestones themselves might be listening.

Clara gave a small smile. "We're fine. Bit of a whirlwind, but fine."

Lira stepped closer, voice low. "Is it true? You were right there when the Veil tore? You actually saw the creatures?"

Sadie folded her arms. "Saw them. Dodged them. Nearly got flattened by one."

Jasper gave a theatrical shudder. "Up close and personal. One tried to turn me into floor polish."

Renley winced. "That bad?"

"Bad enough," Jasper said. "I don't recommend it. Ten out of ten—terrible life choices."

"But you're all right?" Caz asked, tone more serious now.

Clara nodded. "We got lucky. And the sentinels showed up in time."

"And Eldric," Sadie added quietly.

For a moment, the group went quiet. The memory settled over them like a brief shadow.

Then Caz grinned and nudged Renley. "Told you they'd have a better story than anyone else."

"Show-offs," Renley said with mock accusation, though the smile didn't hide the relief in his eyes.

They all fell into step together, and for a moment, the heaviness from the meeting lifted. There was something grounding in the casual chatter of allies—not strategists or mentors. Not Aurical suspects. Just students. Just friends.

That peace lasted exactly thirty seconds.

Veilborne

"Draven at nine o'clock," Caz muttered.

Varek Draven appeared at the far end of the corridor, gliding like he owned it. His expression was, as usual, unreadable and vaguely disdainful.

As he passed, he looked directly at Clara. Then at Sadie.

"Making friends, are we?" Varek said, glancing at the others. "Hope they know what they're walking into."

Clara didn't wait for him to pass.

As Varek took a step forward, Clara lifted her hand and began mimicking an exaggerated talking mouth—thumb and fingers opening and closing like a gossiping puppet—while rolling her eyes in slow, dramatic circles.

Sadie caught it first and nearly choked on a laugh.

Lira elbowed Renley, who turned just in time to see it too.

Varek's head snapped around—sharp and sudden.

For a beat, he stared directly at Clara.

She simply lowered her hand and gave a slow, almost innocent blink, as if daring him to say something.

The corner of Varek's mouth twitched—not a smile, not exactly. More like a grimace trying to become one.

He shook his head, a small, stiff motion that the entire group could see. An expression that said clearly: *She doesn't fear me anymore.*

Then he turned and stalked off, his cloak flaring slightly behind him.

Lira let out a low whistle.

Jasper leaned closer, grinning. "You're either very brave or very stupid. Probably both."

Clara just smiled, heart pounding but victorious.

The Protections classroom was unlike the others.

It wasn't even in the main towers.

Tucked behind a hinged stone arch near the eastern ramparts, the warding hall felt more like a dueling arena than a classroom—its walls marked by scorch scars, impact dents, and carved glyphs still pulsing faintly in the stone. Crystal sconces flickered above racks of staves, mirrored panels, chalk-dusted relics, and velvet-lined drawers that buzzed faintly with latent magic.

The trio stepped inside just as the last bell chimed.

Students filed in and spread out across the stone floor, forming loose rows while enchanted training dummies flickered into place at the edges. The air smelled faintly of slate dust and lemonroot polish.

"Who's this class with again?" Jasper whispered.

As if in answer, a side door burst open in a gust of peppery incense.

A tall, angular man strode into the hall, wrapped in a long brown coat, moving with the brisk efficiency of someone used to moving from one task to the next without pause.

"Good morning, hopefuls," he said, clapping twice. The torches flared brighter. "I'm Instructor Dorran Nym. Welcome to Protections and Wardwork."

He had a voice like cracking parchment—sharp, dry, fast—and eyes that sparkled like everything amused him just a little more than it should. A constellation of charm pins clattered faintly on one shoulder of his coat, beside what looked like a fire-damaged Aurical patch.

"You'll learn to defend yourselves," he went on. "Not just from bandits, curses, or falling bookshelves—but from Veilborne corruptions, relic misfires, and yes—rampaging horrors that try to eat your face. It happens. Ask the third-years."

A few students chuckled nervously.

Dorran smiled. "Now. First rule of wardwork?"

He pointed dramatically at the floor.

Veilborne

"Protection isn't about walls. It's about awareness."

He snapped his fingers—

Three illusionary arrows launched from hidden glyphs in the wall, aimed straight at the front row.

Gasps erupted. A few students ducked.

But the arrows froze midair, then burst into harmless mist.

"Good. You flinched," Dorran said brightly. "Means you're still alive."

The class moved quickly into demonstrations.

He showed them the basic *Weaving Sigil*—a swirling, looping glyph designed to deflect low-force magical projectiles. Then the *Brim-Ward*, a shield against short-range curses. Each student received a faintly glowing rune-disc for practice.

Clara traced the Weaving Sigil in the air, her fingers glowing faint blue.

Sadie's first attempt flickered—then sputtered out.

"Try again," Clara whispered.

Sadie nodded and tried—only for her rune-disc to spark too brightly, crackle, and snap in two. The pieces hissed and vanished in a puff of smoke.

Dorran appeared beside them in an instant, crouching next to the fading glyph with a sharp, analytical look, as if piecing together a puzzle only he could see.

"Interesting," he murmured. "Not a failure. An overload."

He straightened, eyes locking on Sadie.

"You've experienced wild magic before," he said. Not accusing—just curious. "Unpredictable. Dangerous in the wrong hands. But with the right training…"

He trailed off, unreadable.

Sadie hesitated. "I don't know," she said, her voice thin.

Dorran nodded slightly, like he'd expected the answer.

"Try again," he said, handing her another rune-disc. "Gently this time."

And then he was gone, moving on before anyone could ask more.

Jasper leaned in. "Was that normal? That didn't feel normal."

Sadie didn't answer.

The rest of the lesson blurred in a haze of sigils and slow-blinking rune circles.

By the end, only a third of the class had managed to raise a full Brim-Ward. Clara was one of them.

So was Sadie—on her third attempt. Her shield held steady, though her hands trembled afterward.

As they filed out of the hall, Instructor Nym called after them:

"Next time—bring questions," he said, voice rougher. "Magic doesn't favor the obedient. It favors the ones who look twice, who doubt, who ask *why* when everyone else nods and moves on. Curiosity's not a flaw. It's survival."

The midday sun poured through high, circular windows, casting gold light across the corridor. Dust motes drifted in the air like slow-falling glyphs. Around them, students chatted in quiet tones—some proud of their glowing sigils, others nursing magical burns or bruised egos.

The trio said little.

Clara walked between Sadie and Jasper, her hands still tingling faintly from the spell work. The Brim-Ward had held—she'd even earned a quiet nod from Nym.

But she couldn't stop thinking about Sadie's disc. The way the light had flared—too fast, too hot.

Ahead, the Keep's corridors twisted upward toward the Lorehalls and the spire libraries, bathed in green and gold.

Veilborne

Clara touched the locket through her shirt, fingers resting lightly.

Something's changing, she thought.

In the Keep.

In Sadie.

In her.

And if someone really was working for MalVaran from inside these walls...

How long did they have before it all came undone?

Chapter 13
Between Reflections

It had been several weeks since Glimmerden—since the creatures had broken through the plaza, since Sadie had seen the man in the green coat vanish behind a plume of hissing steam, like Glimmerden itself had swallowed him. Since Clara's locket had pulsed against her skin like a heartbeat not her own.

Life at Calendor Keep had drifted back into rhythm. Mostly.

The air had taken on a crisper bite in the mornings. Students bundled in layered cloaks walked the garden paths, steam rising from their breath and their mugs. Lessons returned to their usual rotations—defense, relic theory, Veil stability, and magical ethics—though the instructors seemed more alert. Less patient.

The name *MalVaran* was never spoken aloud. Nor was *traitor*.

But Clara could feel it, hovering in the air like smoke, clinging to every closed door, every whispered conversation.

Still, no one had come looking for the journal she kept hidden beneath her bed. No one had asked about the locket. And sometimes, that silence felt louder than anything else.

****

It arrived on a quiet midweek morning—Jasper's parcel, small and, brown, tied with gold thread and stamped with the insignia of a Gilded artisan collective: *Crimp & Clatter's Compendium of Curious Companions.*

Jasper held it carefully, eyes fixed on it like he was memorizing every detail. The excitement was there—bright, eager—but held in check, just for a few more seconds.

He tore it open on the dormitory floor, grinning like it was his birthday and nobody had forgotten.

"It's here. I've been checking the mail like a madman for two weeks."

Veilborne

Clara and Sadie sat nearby, cross-legged, sipping apple-blossom tea while he carefully unwrapped the contents. A small brass cage unfolded like an origami box, and inside, nestled gently...

"Percival," Jasper breathed, lifting the little creature with reverent hands.

The clockwork rat was smaller than Clara had expected—sleek and bronze, with articulated paws, a delicately coiled tail, and soft-glowing eyes the color of candlelight. Its ears were leaf-shaped gears, its whiskers fine silver wire. It blinked once, chittered, and turned its head toward Jasper, as if waiting for instructions.

"Oh, he's perfect," Jasper whispered.

The rat clambered up his sleeve, sat on his shoulder, and gave a faint mechanical chirrup that made Sadie smile.

Clara leaned closer. "I didn't think it would be this detailed."

"It's Gilded," Jasper said proudly. "They don't do things halfway."

For five minutes, the rat performed flawlessly. It scurried in figure eights on the floor. It fetched a pencil Clara had rolled away. It even bowed—jerkily—when Jasper asked for "formal behavior."

Then, with no warning, it stopped mid-turn.

Its eyes dimmed.

Its tail sagged.

It tipped slightly forward on its paws like it had simply... given up.

Jasper blinked. "No, no, no. Percival?"

He tapped the rat gently. Nothing.

"Come on, little guy. Wake up."

He opened the small hatch along its back and fiddled with the inner gear dial. Still, nothing. The rat remained slumped like a child's toy abandoned mid-play.

Sadie raised an eyebrow. "Is it... supposed to do that?"

"I—I don't think so," Jasper said, crestfallen. "Maybe he's just tired?"

"Jasper," Clara said gently, "it's not alive."

"I know that," he muttered, "but he's just... temperamental."

He cradled Percival in both hands, like a wounded bird.

"I'll fix him. He just needs a little care."

Sadie smiled softly. "He's lucky to have you."

****

That evening, Clara sat by the window, watching the fading light outside as Jasper tinkered quietly in the corner. Percival lay on a folded cloth, tiny tools scattered around him like surgical instruments. Sadie was flipping through her spellbook, muttering incantations with furrowed brows.

But Clara's mind kept drifting.

Not forward—but back. To the mirror chamber. To the strange flickers in the glass. To the warmth she'd felt, though it hadn't come from the torches. It was a feeling that hadn't left her—like the memory of being seen by something that shouldn't have known her at all.

She stood abruptly.

"I'm going for a walk," she said, reaching for her coat.

"Want company?" Sadie asked, looking up.

Clara shook her head. "I think I just need to clear my head."

"Clear your head," Jasper murmured. "But if you need us, we're here."

Clara smiled faintly and slipped into the corridor.

The halls were quiet at this hour—too late for structured classes, too early for curfew. Just the hum of old enchantments in the walls and the occasional flicker of torchlight catching on polished stone.

Clara moved through the lower levels of Calendor Keep with practiced steps. She didn't need a map anymore; her feet remembered the way on their own.

Veilborne

Down the spiral stairwell near the lore annex.

Past the half-faded tapestry of the First Weaving.

Right at the hall where the sconces burned blue instead of gold.

And there—tucked behind a narrow door of oak and iron—waited the chamber of mirrors.

It hadn't changed.

Clara stepped inside slowly, closing the door behind her with a soft click. Its walls were lined with towering, mismatched mirrors—some pristine, some cracked at the edges, others fogged, as if they hadn't seen light in decades.

And all of them quiet.

Waiting.

She moved deeper into the room. Her boots barely made a sound against the floor. Her reflection followed, multiplied and fractured across dozens of warped panes.

She found herself drawn to the same mirror as before—the tall, narrow one edged in silver ivy. Its glass was still, too still—like water that hadn't been touched in years.

Clara stared at her reflection.

At first, she saw only herself: hair a little messy, coat slightly wrinkled, eyes tired but clear.

Then... something shifted.

Not in the mirror.

In her.

The locket warmed.

Not a warning, not a flare—just a quiet presence. As though it sensed something she hadn't yet noticed.

And then the mirror began to cloud.

A pale mist crept across the surface, veiling her reflection. Clara took a step back—but didn't run.

She didn't call for help.

She was ready for this.

The mist parted slowly... and a figure appeared.

Not a ghost. Not quite an image.

A woman—standing tall, half-turned as if caught mid-step, her face lit by some inner glow. Her features were indistinct, like trying to remember someone's face from a dream. But her presence...

Clara felt warmth rise in her chest. Not heat. Something else.

A feeling of familiarity so strong, it made her breath hitch.

Her heart tightened. She didn't know this woman. Had never seen her before.

And yet—

Something deep inside her whispered: Safe.

The woman turned slightly, as if she might look Clara's way.

But then the glass shimmered—and she was gone.

The mist retracted like breath on a windowpane. The mirror cleared. Only Clara's reflection remained, blinking back at her with wide, uncertain eyes.

Clara took a shaky step backward.

The locket pulsed once, warm and slow.

Then still.

Clara didn't know how long she stood there after the vision faded.

Long enough for her heartbeat to steady. Long enough for the warmth of the locket to fade back into stillness, as though it had never been.

She turned from the mirror and crossed the chamber, her steps soft against the stone, her hand lingering at the chain around her neck.

Veilborne

But when she opened the door—

She nearly collided with Professor Lirah Valen.

The relics instructor stood in the doorway, holding a slim bundle of parchment, her expression carrying the faintest trace of surprise. Her robe sleeves were dusted with chalk, and her brow was furrowed with the weariness of long hours spent in thought.

Clara froze. "Professor—I—"

Lirah tilted her head, her gaze flicking past Clara into the room behind her.

"The mirror chamber," she said softly, her voice measured. "Not a place most students wander into after hours."

Clara's throat tightened. "I wasn't doing anything wrong. I just... needed to think."

Lirah studied her for a long moment—perhaps too long—and then nodded, a small, reserved gesture.

"Be that as it may, you should return to your dormitory. We have class in the morning."

"Yes, Professor."

Clara stepped aside, brushing past her with a fleeting glance over her shoulder. Lirah remained still, her eyes never leaving the mirror. She didn't turn to watch Clara go.

Only after Clara's footsteps had faded into the hall did the professor step fully into the doorway.

She stood there, unmoving, for several seconds.

Then a few more.

Her eyes drifted from mirror to mirror, as though tracing something invisible in the air—some echo Clara hadn't noticed, some whisper of a secret not yet fully revealed.

And then, so softly it might have been a thought spoken aloud:

Mark Peters

"What did you see, Clara Holloway?"

She didn't step inside.

She didn't need to.

She simply stood there, gaze fixed on the silver glass, lost in her own reflection—and whatever secrets it might still be holding.

Chapter 14
Hidden in Plain Sight

Morning light filtered through the dormitory windows in thin, silver beams, catching on dust motes and faint traces of magic—soft glimmers in the air, like heat haze or the sheen of oil on water, barely visible unless you were looking for them.

Calendor Keep felt quieter today—damp from the morning mist, with a chill in the walls that hadn't quite lifted.

Jasper was already awake when Clara stirred.

He sat cross-legged on the floor, with Percival sprawled out in front of him like a patient on a tiny surgical table. Gears and etched rune plates lay scattered on a cloth beside him, along with a magnifying lens and an unlabeled jar of enchanted oil.

"He twitched twice during the night," Jasper said, not looking up. "I think he's responding to tone inflection now. I whispered 'wake up, brave soldier,' and he flinched. So… progress?"

Clara rubbed her eyes, still half-lost in the fog of sleep. "Or trauma."

"Could be both," Sadie said from across the room. She sat by the wardrobe, her hair half-braided, boots on only one foot. "He's clearly broken and confused. He fits in."

Clara smiled faintly. The warmth from the night before still clung to her—the memory of the mirror, the woman's face, the way the locket had stirred like a sleeping heartbeat. She hadn't told the others yet. Not because she didn't want to—but because she still didn't have words for what she'd felt.

"Come on," Sadie said, standing. "We've got Valen first thing. If we're late, she'll make us diagram thirty relics from memory and glare at us like we tampered with her wards."

****

The relics lecture hall was already half full by the time they arrived—rows of long wooden tables facing an elevated stone dais, cluttered with relics locked in glass, chalk glyphs from last week's lesson still etched into the board.

Professor Lirah Valen stood at the front, organizing a stack of vellum notes with precise, almost mechanical movements. She didn't look up as they entered.

Clara slid into a seat near the center, the faint buzz of the locket beneath her collar just barely noticeable.

"Today," Lirah said, her voice cool and clipped, "we'll continue our discussion on relic interaction theory—specifically, how relics with sensory enhancements affect magical perception."

She tapped the board with a long stylus tipped in rune-carved silver. Behind her, a shimmering projection appeared—rotating diagrams of lenses, runes, and focus arrays.

"In earlier centuries, objects known as *perception relics* were used by wardmakers and arcane historians to observe residue—magical fingerprints left behind by spells, portals, or rift disturbances."

She paused, glancing briefly at the class.

"Some of the more refined models—such as the Emberlain Monocle—allowed users to detect unstable Veil currents, identify hidden enchantments, even bring clarity to arcane scripts obscured by time or intent."

Clara's head lifted slightly.

Lirah moved on without pause, as if it had been any other example.

"Most of these relics were lost or locked away due to misuse, but the theories remain essential to our understanding of aura manipulation and spell-layering…"

Clara barely heard the rest.

The *Emberlain Monocle.*

Veilborne

She didn't look at Sadie or Jasper. Not yet. But the pattern was clear now, like threads drawing tighter. The hidden journal with answers no one else had. The mirror that had revealed more than reflection. And Lirah's pointed lecture—measured, deliberate, and far too precise to be coincidence. Too carefully delivered to be offhanded.

Lirah continued the lesson, unfazed. No accusatory glances. No narrowed eyes. Just the same sharp control and smooth cadence she always had.

And yet...

Clara's fingers closed over the locket beneath her shirt.

She knows.

Clara barely moved, but she could feel Sadie shift beside her.

Professor Valen continued, gesturing toward a projected schematic of a crystalline lens etched with fine runes.

"Ocular relics were often crafted for very specific purposes—some to read a single inscription, others to reveal hidden layers in maps or detect enchantments long faded from view. Many were bound to a particular magical essence—sometimes even a bloodline. In the wrong hands, they simply don't work. In some cases, they mislead."

Sadie raised her hand.

"Yes, Miss Faelyn?" Valen asked, her tone neutral.

"Could relics like these be used to read... hidden text? Say, runes that had been erased or cloaked?"

Valen nodded once. "Under the right circumstances, yes. If the relic was designed to reveal hidden text—and it's used by the right individual—it can work. But most were crafted with specific magical bindings. In the wrong hands, the text remains unreadable. Or worse—it appears altered."

Sadie leaned forward slightly. "What about encrypted texts? Could they—"

Valen cut her off with a faint, dry smile. "If you're asking whether a relic will do your homework for you—no. They reveal. They don't interpret."

A few chuckles scattered through the class.

Valen's gaze lingered on Sadie for a moment too long before she turned back to the projection.

"Let's move on."

Clara didn't breathe for a beat. She could feel the air shift around them—as if they'd drawn attention they weren't meant to.

Beside her, Sadie's face was unreadable. But Clara could sense it in her posture: tense, focused, already connecting dots the rest of them hadn't seen yet.

Not fear.

Certainty.

The quiet kind that settles in your bones and doesn't let go.

****

The day had brightened since morning, crisp with the scent of drying leaves and distant chimney smoke. The trio wandered the outer walk, a winding path along the Keep's northern terraces, bordered by low walls and bronze-leafed trees. Beyond them, the valley rolled into misted forest and glimmering hills.

Clara kicked a pebble down the path, her hands buried in her coat pockets. "She wanted us to hear that."

Sadie didn't even argue. "She picked that relic, that name, that moment—no way that was just a lecture."

"She said it like it was just another name. But it wasn't. Not to us," Jasper added. "Like she wanted to see if it landed."

"She knows I have the journal," Clara said quietly.

"She suspects," Sadie corrected. "There's a difference."

Veilborne

They paused at a bench near a low, ivy-draped wall. Jasper sat down with a sigh and pulled out a tiny screwdriver to fidget with Percival's spine. The little rat still wouldn't stir, no matter how gently he coaxed its gears.

Clara lowered herself beside him, staring out over the golden-dappled hills.

"I think she wants me to find it."

Sadie blinked. "The monocle?"

Clara nodded. "I don't know why. But the way she said it... it felt intentional."

Jasper muttered, "Subtle clues from suspicious professors. Classic start to a terrible idea."

"Should I be worried about all this muttering?" came a familiar voice behind them.

They turned to see Fennrick Bramble standing under the overhanging branches, cloak half-unbuttoned, collar sticking up, a sprig of something leafy tucked behind his ear as if he'd forgotten it was there.

"How long have you been listening?" Clara asked warily.

Fennrick shrugged. "Long enough to hear the words 'monocle,' 'Emberlain,' and a very dramatic 'she knows I have the journal,' which, I assume, was meant to be whispered in a far more private setting."

Clara glanced at Sadie, then at Jasper. Carefully, she said, "We found something. In the study beneath the Keep."

Fennrick's expression didn't shift, but his gaze sharpened. "Found what, exactly?"

"A journal," Clara said. "Emberlain's. We still have it."

He exhaled through his nose—a slow sound, more thoughtful than surprised. "So that's where it ended up."

Sadie narrowed her eyes. "You knew about it?"

"Knew of it," Fennrick corrected, easing down onto the stone wall across from them. "The Auricals swept the ruins after the collapse. They thought everything had been destroyed. Odd they haven't searched your rooms."

He shrugged. "Suppose they still trust you. Or someone—or something—is keeping them distracted."

"We didn't know who to trust," Clara said.

"That's wise," he said. "Still is."

They sat in silence for a moment, the wind rustling through the trees overhead.

"Do you think Lirah was trying to tell Clara to look for the monocle?" Jasper asked. "Without actually saying it?"

Fennrick scratched his chin. "Hard to say. But if I were trying to discreetly point someone toward a dangerous relic without letting anyone else notice—that's how I'd do it."

"You don't think it was just a coincidence?" Sadie asked.

Fennrick raised an eyebrow. "Coincidence is finding a coin in your pocket you didn't know you had. Not an Emberlain artifact getting name-dropped in class right after a hidden study goes up in smoke."

Clara hesitated. Her gaze dropped to the moss-lined stones beneath their feet. "We found a journal." she said quietly. "We've kept it hidden."

Fennrick's gaze sharpened. He nodded but didn't ask to see it. Didn't press.

"The monocle," Clara said. "Do you know where it is?"

Fennrick exhaled, rubbing a hand along his jaw. "No. Not exactly. It vanished around the same time Emberlain did. One day it was under Council protection—the next, gone. Some say it was moved to a secure vault. Others think it went with him. For all we know, it's in another realm—maybe even yours, Clara."

Veilborne

He looked at her, something unreadable in his expression. "I'm not saying you should look for it. But if anyone's likely to stumble across it—it's the three of you. Especially with that thing you wear."

He paused, then added more softly, "Or maybe you should just leave it right where it is. Hidden. Safe. Sometimes not knowing is the better path."

Clara shook her head. "I'm not looking for power. Or to unlock something dangerous. I'm looking for answers."

She glanced down, fingers brushing the locket beneath her collar. "The journal—it talks about Veil breaches. About energy patterns. Stabilization attempts. It might have theories, even instructions, on how to fix the damage. Or at least stop it from getting worse."

Her voice steadied. "If there's even a chance it holds a way to stop what's coming, then I can't ignore that. I won't."

Fennrick studied her for a moment, then gave a slow nod.

"Your heart's in the right place," he said quietly. "Just make sure your feet don't follow it straight into something you can't walk back from."

Clara's hand moved to the locket at her collarbone. "You recognize it?"

"Not exactly," Fennrick said. "But it looks familiar. Close to something I saw once in the Archives—years ago. Older than most relics they bother to catalogue."

He paused, lowering his voice. "Just be careful. If others are looking for it too… someone might already be watching you."

Clara hesitated, then asked, "If someone were to find a clue… where would it even be? The journals don't give much past the diagrams."

"Especially if the monocle was hidden after the Rebellion," Jasper added, trying for casual. "That kind of information wouldn't be in the regular archive."

Fennrick answered before he seemed to realize he'd spoken. "Well, no. Of course not."

He waved a hand vaguely. "Anything that sensitive would've been locked in one of the deep stacks… probably the restricted section beneath the east wing. You'd need clearance from at least—"

He stopped. Blinked once. Twice.

Clara raised an eyebrow.

Fennrick looked from one face to the next, then groaned. "Ah. No. Nope. That didn't happen. That conversation did not just leave my mouth."

"You definitely said east wing," Jasper said helpfully.

Fennrick glanced toward the greenhouse path, gave a small, weary shrug, and walked off muttering about needing to repot his thistleroot before it staged a rebellion.

****

That afternoon, the dormitory windows glowed gold with the last light of day. The room was filled with the soft clinks of tools, the occasional muttered curse from Jasper, and the tiny mechanical wheezes of a half-assembled rat.

Clara sat cross-legged on her bed, pages of Emberlain's journal spread around her like puzzle pieces. Sadie perched near the foot of the bed, fidgeting with a copper bookmark shaped like a sparrow, her brow furrowed.

"We're not going to find it in here," Sadie said suddenly.

Clara looked up. "The monocle?"

Sadie nodded. "If it's real—and I think it is—it won't be in the student archive. And it won't be in that journal either. Not unless we're missing a cipher."

Clara exhaled slowly, gaze drifting toward the shuttered window. "The restricted stacks."

Veilborne

"Exactly," Sadie said. "That lower level beneath the east wing. Fennrick mentioned it—said if anything was still on record, it'd be there."

Jasper added, "And, of course, they're patrolled by the archivist."

Clara frowned. "The archivist?"

Sadie smirked. "You haven't met him?"

Jasper leaned closer, voice low. "Moves like he hasn't slept in twenty years. Always shows up when you least expect it. Doesn't blink. Ever."

Sadie nodded. "He's got this way of staring at you."

"Rumor is," Jasper added, "the last students who tried to sneak down there were never seen again. No one knows if that's true, but no one's been brave enough to find out."

A silence followed.

Sadie raised an eyebrow. "That's comforting."

Clara didn't smile. "Then we'll just have to be the first ones to make it back."

Clara gave a dry smile. "So... not exactly on the student tour. Especially with enchanted doors that rearrange themselves if you take a wrong step."

"Which leaves us two problems," Sadie said. "Getting in and out... without getting caught."

From the floor across the room, Jasper cleared his throat loudly.

They both turned.

He was hunched over the cloth-covered box, tweezers in one hand, runeplate in the other. Percival's frame lay spread out before him—tiny gears aligned, eyes dim. Jasper leaned in close, muttered something under his breath, and with a delicate twist of his wrist—

click.

Percival blinked.

The rat twitched, sat up stiffly, and gave a tinny chirrup of surprise. Then it scampered in a tight figure-eight, stood on its hind legs, and bowed. The tiny clockwork rat was working even better than before.

"He lives," Jasper said, wonderstruck.

The girls stared.

Clara looked at Sadie.

Sadie looked at Clara.

They spoke at the same time.

"We have our distraction."

****

The plan wasn't complicated. It didn't need to be. Just clever enough, risky enough—and fast enough not to get them expelled. Or worse.

The restricted archives lay buried beneath the east wing of the library, hidden behind iron-bound doors that hadn't been opened freely since before the Silent Rebellion. They were guarded—not by Auricals, but by shifting wards, old enchantments that twisted the lower stacks' layout whenever they sensed intruders.

And by a single archivist: ancient, owl-eyed, patrolling the entry hall with the eerie silence of someone who'd made peace with never blinking again.

That evening, the Keep had fallen into hush—students tucked into study groups or drifting toward dinner, the halls lit only by torchlight and glimmering glyphs.

The trio crouched behind a row of towering shelves just beyond the library's second stairwell. Ahead stretched the hallway leading to the restricted archives, dim and quiet, save for the flicker of lamplight and the faint shuffle of parchment in the distance.

Jasper knelt, holding Percival like a precious gem.

"Ready, little knight?" he whispered.

Veilborne

The clockwork rat blinked twice, spun its gears, and scampered off down the hall—silent and sleek on the stone floor.

They waited, tense.

Percival weaved between the stacks, then veered sharply and knocked over a precariously balanced scroll tube with a crisp *clink-clack*. The noise echoed cleanly through the corridor as the archivist appeared almost instantly—tall, draped in dust-gray robes, moving with unsettling silence for someone so solid.

He narrowed his eyes at a fallen scroll.

Then he saw Percival.

The rat paused just long enough to make eye contact—if a machine could—and then darted off again, this time away from the trio's hiding spot.

The archivist gave an irritated grunt and followed.

Farther and farther they went—until Percival vanished around a corner. And from somewhere deep in the stacks, just loud enough to carry:

"I'm a distraction."

A beat of silence.

Then the archivist muttered:

"Bloody kids and their pranks…"

He turned down the hall, still grumbling under his breath.

Clara exhaled.

Now.

They moved together—fast, light-footed, silent.

The warded runes etched into the stone near the forbidden stairwell gave no resistance. They didn't flare. They didn't hum. They simply pulsed faintly, then dimmed as Clara passed.

Her fingers brushed the metal edge of the sealed door.

The locket warmed instantly.

There was a low click, and the heavy locking sigils dissolved into silver light.

The door swung open without a sound.

Sadie froze. "You just... opened it?"

"I didn't do anything," Clara said quietly. "It feels like it recognized me."

They exchanged a look.

Jasper nodded toward the stairwell. "Then let's not waste it."

Clara stepped through first. The others followed. The door creaked shut behind them, sealing them in darkness.

And the Keep, above, returned to stillness.

They were deep underground now, farther than any student was ever meant to go.

The air felt different—thicker, older. It tasted of parchment, rust, and ash. The shelves were iron-clad, sealed with arcane fastenings that flickered faintly as Clara passed, as though unsure whether to admit her.

Sadie ran her fingers along the stone wall. "These relics aren't just restricted... they're buried."

Clara's locket pulsed again.

A moment later, a nearby filing case gave a soft click.

A single drawer slid open—just a sliver.

Clara stepped closer.

Inside lay a long folio case of blackened wood, bound in tarnished brass. The nameplate was worn smooth, the letters erased by time. She reached for it, feeling heat bloom beneath her palm where the locket touched her skin.

The latch gave way with a soft sigh.

Veilborne

Inside lay a single aged file, its crisp pages scented faintly of ink and cedarwood.

At the top, handwritten in elegant script:

Aurical Containment Report: Emberlain Relic, Variant 03— Monocle.

Clara's heart skipped.

Sadie leaned over her shoulder. "You found it."

Jasper whispered, "No. She found where it went."

Clara flipped through the first few pages.

Diagrams. Aura frequencies. Use-case restrictions. And then—on the final page—a destination.

Sadie squinted. "That's not an Aurical site."

"It's not even in Eryndor," Jasper said.

A stunned silence fell between them.

Clara read the line again, her breath catching.

Relic recorded: Museum of Historical Science, Upper Manhattan. Labeled: Nikola Tesla Prototype—'Lens for harmonic wave isolation.'

Sadie blinked. "It's just... there?"

"In my world," Clara murmured. "On display."

Jasper leaned in. "No guards? No wards? No magical seals?"

"Just a plaque," Sadie murmured, reading over Clara's shoulder. "*'Believed to be one of Tesla's unfinished resonance experiments.'*"

Silence fell over the trio.

Then Jasper asked, "So... it's been sitting in a museum for nearly a century, and no one noticed?"

Sadie shook her head slowly. "Or they didn't know what they were looking at."

Clara stared down at the page. "It's been hiding in plain sight this whole time."

"Or waiting," Jasper said darkly.

A pause.

Then Jasper frowned. "Am I the only one who finds it completely bonkers that we're the ones piecing all this together?"

"No," Sadie said. "And it's starting to bother me."

"We're kids," Clara whispered. "We've been here for, what—weeks? And we've found a hidden lab, discovered a traitor, uncovered a relic, and now figured out where one of the most dangerous magical artifacts in history is hiding?"

"Meanwhile, the Auricals have had decades," Sadie added.

Jasper scowled. "Either they're very bad at their jobs… or they don't want anyone finding this stuff."

Clara hesitated, then said quietly, "Or maybe someone's helping us. Quietly. From the shadows."

Sadie turned toward her. "You think someone's guiding us?"

"I don't know," Clara said. "But this doesn't feel random. The journal. The mirror. Even Valen's lecture—it's like we're being… nudged."

Jasper scrubbed a hand over his face. "Okay, sure—but by who? And why?"

Clara ran her finger along the edge of the page, eyes distant. "Maybe because we're the only ones who could. The locket opens doors. The journal responds to me. And the relic… it's connected to my world."

She glanced at the name printed across the file's heading: Nikola Tesla.

Her brows drew together.

"Has anyone noticed how close that is to Nikolas Emberlain?"

Jasper's head snapped up. "You think that's a coincidence?"

Veilborne

Sadie's voice lowered. "You'd think someone would've caught that by now, if this were true…"

Clara stared at the faded ink, pulse quickening.

Sadie leaned closer, her brow furrowed. "Maybe the Auricals did go looking," she said. "But if the relic was in your world, Clara… maybe it didn't react. Maybe it just sat there, dead and ordinary. Without the journal—or without you—it might've looked like nothing."

Clara's voice was barely a breath. "What if it was waiting? Not hidden from them… just invisible to the wrong hands."

No one spoke.

Only the hush of the restricted archive answered them, broken by the faint, almost inaudible hum of something ancient finally stirring.

****

Clara slid the file into her satchel, wrapping it tightly in enchanted cloth.

They retraced their steps through the maze of wards and hidden stacks, each creak of old stone echoing like a scream. From somewhere above, the soft shuffle of the archivist's footsteps whispered down the stairwell.

"I think we're clear," Sadie whispered.

"Don't say that," Jasper hissed. "You never say that."

They turned a corner—

—and nearly screamed as something shot toward them out of the shadows.

Clara grabbed Sadie. Jasper ducked, arms flung over his head.

A gleaming metal tail, glowing eyes, and a familiar chirp—

"Percival!" Jasper hissed.

The rat gave a delighted squeak and spun in a tiny circle.

Sadie shoved him lightly. "You couldn't have announced yourself?"

"I think he just did," Clara said, heart still hammering.

They climbed the last stair, keeping low.

The runes didn't so much as flicker. Clara's locket glowed gently, letting them pass as silently as before. No alarms. No lights. The archivist didn't even glance in their direction as they slipped behind a support pillar and out into the main library.

Suddenly, the familiar sounds washed over them: whispering students, the scratch of quills, the soft rustle of turning pages.

It was as if nothing had happened.

As if they hadn't just changed everything.

Chapter 15
Threshold

The study room they'd claimed for the evening was quiet and mostly forgotten—a space of cracked stone and cobwebbed corners that guaranteed privacy. Outside, Calendor Keep was winding down: lanterns flickered behind tall windows, footsteps echoed in the upper halls, and the night carried on as though nothing had changed.

Clara sat cross-legged on the floor, fingers absently turning the locket at her neck, while Sadie and Jasper argued over logistics.

"Even if we figure out how to cross the Veil," Jasper said, gesturing toward Clara, "how are we supposed to find the monocle once we're there? Your world's a big place."

They fell silent.

Clara stared down at her boots for a moment, then spoke slowly.

"When Eldric brought me here… he didn't cast a spell. He had this device. It was round—like a disc. Flat, metal, with three rings that spun around each other. And there was light between them. It didn't look like magic. It looked… alive."

Jasper's head snapped up. "And that's what pulled you through the Veil?"

Clara nodded. "I believe so."

Sadie leaned forward, eyes narrowing. "Do you know what it was?"

"No," Clara admitted. "But Eldric called it a crossing wheel. Or something like that. He didn't explain much."

Jasper frowned, drumming his fingers on the table. "Spinning rings… light inside… That sounds like an Aether Ring. Maybe. I've only read about them in old case files. Devices calibrated to the Veil. Most of them were destroyed or hidden after the Resonance Crisis."

Clara arched an eyebrow. "You're making up words again."

Jasper blinked and tilted his head. "Aren't all words made up?"

Sadie snorted despite herself.

"So if it's real, and Eldric used one to bring Clara here… it could take us over and back," she said.

Jasper nodded. "If we can find one."

Clara sat up straighter. "He must've kept it. And if he did, it's probably in his chambers."

"Which is locked," Jasper said flatly. "And off-limits to students."

Sadie glanced toward the satchel where Percival lay sleeping soundly.

"Then we send in a professional."

Jasper groaned. "Why is my rat always the one getting us nearly expelled?"

"Because he's adorable," Clara said. "And you programmed him to pick locks."

"That was theoretical."

"So was this entire plan," Sadie said, already reaching for the satchel.

As she lifted it, Percival stirred, blinking open his little brass eyes with a slow, chattering yawn.

"Come on," Sadie whispered. "We need to borrow a relic from a very grumpy war mage. Quietly."

Percival chittered, sniffed the air, and darted out of the bag with the confidence of someone who'd done this before.

****

The hallway outside Eldric Ducart's chamber was silent—the kind of silence that pressed against the skin, making every breath feel too loud. Each footstep echoed in the dark. Even the creaks of the lanterns seemed suspicious.

The trio kept close to the wall, cloaked in shadow just across from the tall, rune-etched door.

Veilborne

"You're sure this is it?" Sadie whispered.

Clara nodded. "He brought me here after I first crossed over. I didn't see where he put the device, but... this is the room."

Jasper knelt, setting his satchel on the floor and unfastening the front clasp. Inside, curled beneath a folded rag that smelled faintly of engine oil and peppermint, Percival blinked open his brass eyes.

"Alright, champ," Jasper murmured. "Mission time."

Percival stretched with a soft metallic whirr.

"You're looking for something round," Jasper continued. "Three rings. Could be glowing. Might hum. Search the cabinet first, then the desk, then shelves. If you don't find it, try under the floorboards."

The rat squeaked, clicked, and gave his little mechanical tail a flick like a salute.

"Be subtle," Jasper added. "And if you see Eldric—play dead. Dramatically."

With a soft whir, Percival zipped toward the base of the door and disappeared under it.

****

They waited in breathless silence.

From inside the chamber came faint sounds—scratches, taps, the occasional soft metallic click.

"That's him," Jasper whispered. "He's moving."

Another pause. A gentle thunk.

"I think that's the desk," Jasper guessed. "Or... a wall. Hard to say."

Clara shot him a look. "You can't actually tell, can you?"

Jasper shrugged. "I like to think I can."

Then came a sharper noise—a quick mechanical whirr-click, followed by what sounded like a soft scrape.

Sadie frowned. "That didn't sound promising."

"Maybe he's just improvising," Jasper offered. "Like we usually do."

More silence. Then a faint clink near the door.

Moments later, Percival squeezed back under the doorframe, huffing softly. Flicking his tail with what could only be described as smug satisfaction, he dropped a scrap of parchment at Jasper's feet.

It was an old piece of vellum, scrawled with a quick sketch—three interlocking rings—and a note in tight handwriting:

Under floorboard. Center panel.

Jasper beamed. "Bingo. He found it."

Sadie muttered, "I'm still not convinced you knew what he was doing."

"I didn't," Jasper admitted. "But it worked, didn't it?"

Sadie was already moving. "I'll circle the corridor and watch for Eldric. If I whistle, run."

"Or yell?" Clara asked.

"Only if it's bad."

She disappeared silently down the hall.

Jasper nodded to Percival, who gave a proud chirp but stayed perched in his hand, whiskers twitching.

Clara touched the door handle.

"Locked?" she whispered.

"Not for Percival," Jasper said with a smirk.

The little rat clambered down Jasper's arm, gears whirring softly. He scurried to the doorframe, rose on his hind legs, and extended a tiny brass rod from his forepaw. With a few sharp clicks, he fiddled at the base of the handle.

Click.

Veilborne

The latch gave way.

The door creaked open.

****

Inside, Eldric's chambers were still and solemn. The scent of smoke and old parchment clung to the air, mingling with the sharper tang of steel oil and pine resin. The hearth burned low, casting restless shadows that shifted across walls and shelves.

Relic cases lined one side, their contents veiled behind glyph-sealed glass. Books and scroll tubes were stacked with careful order—not cluttered, but a controlled chaos that spoke of a mind always working, always preparing.

A heavy oak desk stood at the room's center, its surface unnervingly clear except for a single lantern and a closed folio. Even the worn leather chair beside it seemed to face the door with quiet judgment.

The only sounds were the faint tick of a wall-mounted chronometer and the occasional soft creak of the floor beneath their cautious steps.

Clara's breath caught. The room didn't feel empty. It felt like the space itself was holding its breath.

They shouldn't be here.

But they had no choice.

This wasn't betrayal. It was necessity. Eldric had protected her, guided her—but even he couldn't give them all the answers.

Jasper's hand hovered protectively near Percival, who shifted in his palm with a soft mechanical whirr. Sadie moved quietly at Clara's side, her posture tense but determined.

Clara swallowed the knot rising in her throat and took a slow, deliberate step forward. "It's beautiful," she whispered.

"It's a maze," Jasper muttered, scanning the floor.

He stepped to the center of the room and tapped his boot gently against the floorboards.

"Here. Just off-color. Newer wood."

Together, they pried the panel up with quiet effort.

Nestled beneath, resting on a cushion of folded cloth, lay the Aether Ring.

A disc of burnished silver, the size of a small plate. Three concentric rings locked within one another, each etched with runes that shimmered faintly even dormant. It pulsed with a gentle, quiet hum—like the ghost of a song long forgotten.

Clara stared down at it, breath caught.

"Is that—?"

"No doubt," Jasper said, already wrapping it in the velvet cloth. "It's humming."

As he closed the cloth over it, the locket at Clara's neck warmed—just slightly. Enough to notice.

Then—footsteps.

"He's coming!" Sadie's voice hissed down the corridor.

"Move!" Jasper snapped.

Clara grabbed the Aether Ring, and the three of them slipped back into the hallway just as Sadie rounded the corner.

"He's ten seconds behind me!" she gasped.

They bolted, ducking into an unused stairwell and flattening against the wall.

Footsteps grew louder, steadier, until Eldric himself passed, coat rustling as he approached the door. He paused, looked at the handle, and frowned.

Click.

He opened it slowly, peering inside.

"...I thought I locked this."

Veilborne

****

Back in the quiet of their borrowed study nook, they laid the Aether Ring on the table. It pulsed faintly beneath the cloth, as if aware of being found.

No one spoke for a long moment.

"So," Jasper finally said. "We have it."

"And no idea how to use it," Sadie added.

Clara looked down at the locket, still warm against her collarbone.

"Then we talk to someone who might."

"Fennrick," Jasper sighed.

"Fennrick," Sadie echoed, a faint grin tugging at her mouth.

"I just hope he'll help us again," Clara muttered. "Though he usually does. Whether he plans to or not."

****

Fennrick Bramble was elbow-deep in a tangle of rootvine when the trio found him.

The greenhouse was heavy with the scent of moss, sap, and something faintly reminiscent of burnt cinnamon. Bioluminescent spores drifted lazily through the air, and a leafy creature in the corner watched them with slow-blinking eyes.

Fennrick barely looked up as Clara stepped around a rack of vining thornfruit.

"If it's not bleeding or glowing uncontrollably, come back later," he said, yanking a knot of tangled roots free with a grunt.

"We found something," Clara said.

"That narrows it down."

She unwrapped the Aether Ring and laid it gently on the bench beside him.

Fennrick froze.

The rootvine hissed.

"Well," he said after a long pause, straightening. "I'll be."

He took a clean cloth from his apron, wiped his hands, and leaned closer. The Aether Ring gave a quiet, anticipatory hum.

"You're not supposed to have this," he said. "Which makes me very interested in how you do."

Jasper raised both hands innocently.

"It wasn't technically theft. More of a…" He hesitated, searching for a less damning word. "…loan."

A beat.

"From Eldric."

Fennrick didn't smile. Didn't move. For a long moment, he just stared at them—all traces of his usual levity gone.

"You borrowed a restricted Veil device from the High Aurical's personal quarters."

His voice was quiet. Too quiet.

Then his eyes narrowed.

"How in the depths did you even do that—?"

He stopped himself, exhaling sharply and raising both hands.

"No. Don't tell me. I don't want to know."

Neither Clara nor Jasper answered.

Fennrick raked a hand through his hair. "Of course you don't."

Finally, his gaze settled on Clara.

"And why have you brought it here?"

Clara gestured to the Aether Ring beside him. "We need to know how it works. It might be the only way across."

Veilborne

Fennrick exhaled, raking a hand through his hair again. "Of course you do."

He sat heavily on the nearest stool.

"Do you have any idea what kind of risk you're taking? What kind of risk I'm taking just by having it here?"

No one answered. The weight of it didn't need words.

Fennrick leaned forward, frowning at the device.

"You can't just turn this on anywhere. These things—Aether Rings—they were built to work at specific locations. Crossing points. Old places where the Veil is thin but stable."

His voice dropped. "If you try to force it somewhere else… you'll rip a hole. Like what happened at Glimmerden."

The memory hit like a stone between them.

Sadie's voice was quiet. "So where do we use it?"

"That's the real question," Fennrick said. "You'll need to find one of those sites. Ones that haven't collapsed or gone volatile."

Clara frowned. "When Eldric brought me here, we walked for ages. We had to stop along the way. He must've taken me to one."

Fennrick nodded. "Sounds like it. Probably one of the few left that's still stable."

"What about getting back?" Jasper asked.

Fennrick rubbed his jaw. "That'll depend on what's waiting for you on the other side. If there's a stable crossing point there, the Ring should attune itself and reopen the way. If not…" He hesitated. "You'll be stuck."

Jasper gave a thin, forced smile. "Good to know."

Fennrick stood and began to pace. "You don't understand what you're messing with. The Veil isn't just a doorway. It's a boundary. Two worlds balanced against each other. Crossing puts strain on that balance. The more it happens, the worse the damage."

Clara met his gaze. "If we don't do this, someone else will. Someone worse."

Fennrick sighed. "That's what I'm afraid of."

He paused, then nodded to himself. "I'll show you a crossing point. There's one not far from the Keep. Old. Predates the Auricals. It's held steady—so far."

Jasper blinked. "You're actually helping?"

"I'm not helping," Fennrick said. "I'm trying to keep you from turning yourselves—and the Veil—into a cautionary tale."

****

That night, under a high moon veiled by thin clouds, they followed Fennrick beyond the Keep's outer gardens.

The path wound past the old rookery and into a clearing ringed by ancient standing stones. Most were cracked or leaning, their carved glyphs worn nearly smooth.

"This was a Veil anchor once," Fennrick said. "The Council used it in the old days. For crossings. For sending things through. It's one of the few that hasn't collapsed."

Clara set the Aether Ring in the center of the circle. The air shifted instantly—cooler, heavier, charged.

Fennrick knelt to adjust the glyphs, fingers trailing through the damp earth.

"If you ever find yourselves trapped over there," he muttered, almost to himself, "follow the oldest bones of the city. They'll take you where the Veil still remembers."

Jasper blinked. "That's not ominous at all."

Fennrick didn't answer.

"These markings will stabilize the crossing," he said instead. "Long enough for the Ring to open and hold."

Veilborne

"And if it doesn't?" Jasper asked.

"Then you'd better be ready to run."

The Aether Ring stirred. The three metal rings began to rotate—slow at first, then faster, blurring into silver light.

Fennrick stepped back. "Last chance to turn back."

Clara didn't hesitate. "We're not turning back."

The glyphs flared. The air thickened.

The light sharpened. The Veil thinned.

The Aether Ring began to hum.

Jasper swallowed. "Here we go."

And the world began to change.

Clara looked at her friends. "Ready?"

"Nope," Jasper said.

"Let's go anyway," Sadie replied, gripping his sleeve.

Clara gripped the locket at her neck, feeling its familiar weight.

Miss Wren. Mum. Dad. Whoever you were... I'm going to find the truth.

Together, they stepped through.

The light rippled as each of them vanished—Clara first, clutching her locket. Sadie followed, steady and unflinching. Jasper hesitated just long enough to mutter something under his breath that Fennrick couldn't quite catch, then disappeared into the glow.

The portal flared one final time—then snapped shut with a sharp, breathless finality, taking the Aether Ring with it.

Fennrick stood alone in the circle. The chalk glyphs were already smudging, the damp air dissolving them into faint, broken lines.

He stared at the space where they'd vanished.

Ran a hand over his beard.

Mark Peters

"May the Nine watch over them."

The clearing fell silent.

Chapter 16
Veilbreak

The moment Clara crossed the threshold.

Gravity warped. Sound disappeared. Light became shape and memory and scent all at once. She was unspooled and rewoven, pulled through something vast and thin and very, very old.

And then—the world fell away and another took its place.

Her boots hit pavement.

She staggered. Sadie and Jasper quickly joined her.

Cold air.

The stink of engine oil.

Neon light flickering off nearby glass.

They were in an alley—narrow, empty, and silent.

Behind them, the Aether Ring sparked faintly once… then went dark.

The forest vanished.

The scent of damp earth and leaves was replaced by cold air tinged with exhaust. Beneath their feet, rough concrete stretched outward, cracked and faded. Somewhere nearby, a car horn blared. A dog barked. Streetlights flickered against the deep night.

The weight of the city closed in around them—familiar, sharp, and impossibly loud after the quiet of Eryndor.

They were now in Clara's world.

The alley was damp and narrow, lit by a flickering overhead lamp that painted long, twitching shadows on the rain-dark walls. The air reeked faintly of oil, metal, and something sour.

Clara staggered forward and caught her balance.

"Everyone all right?"

"Define 'all right'," Jasper groaned, leaning on a graffiti-tagged dumpster. "Did my spine survive the jump? I'm not sure."

Sadie didn't answer straight away. She was staring at the end of the alley, where red lights blinked on strange carriages and pale towers loomed like teeth against the clouds.

"Where... are we?" she whispered.

"My world," Clara said. "But I don't know where exactly. I never lived in the city. This isn't anywhere I've ever been."

Her voice was quiet. The reality of it was beginning to settle into her chest like a weight.

She turned to the ground, spotting the Aether Ring where it had landed—half-nestled in a puddle reflecting a flickering yellow light.

She knelt and picked it up carefully. The rings were still warm, trembling faintly beneath her fingers.

"It worked," she murmured. "Again."

The others gathered close.

Clara turned the device slowly in her hands.

"Maybe..." she began, thinking aloud, "maybe it exists in both places. At once. Or maybe just two versions of itself—one here, one in Eryndor—and when you activate it, it bridges the distance and collapses the space between. You're not really travelling. You're just... appearing where the other version is."

Jasper blinked. "So you're saying it doesn't move us... it moves itself. And we're just... passengers."

"Exactly," Clara said. "We just hitch a ride on the collapse."

Jasper stared at the Aether Ring. "That's... honestly unsettling. Cool. But unsettling."

The Aether Ring gave one final pulse and went still.

Clara tucked it into her coat.

Veilborne

The trio emerged from the alley and stepped onto a wide, unfamiliar street.

Cars whispered past on rubber wheels. Buildings loomed overhead—not enchanted spires or carved towers—just grey slabs of stone and glass, blinking with sterile light. Neon signs glowed from windows, and rubbish rustled in the wind like forgotten thoughts.

Sadie made a face.

"This... is it?"

"Apparently," Jasper said, turning in a slow circle. "Clara, are you sure this is the right world? I was expecting something a little more... inviting."

"Where I grew up looked nothing like this," Clara admitted quietly. "I don't even know where we are."

Sadie crouched to examine a parked car.

"They're like metal carriages. No horses. No enchantments."

"They use engines that require fuel," Clara said.

Jasper looked at a sewer grate with deep suspicion.

"This place doesn't hum with magic. It just hums."

They wandered along the street until a glowing red sign caught their eye.

OPEN 24/7, it read in big, bold letters above a dusty storefront with faded posters in the window.

"Maybe we can ask for directions," Clara said.

"To what, exactly?" Jasper asked.

"To the museum," Sadie said. "Assuming it's still here."

They pushed the door open. A bell jingled overhead.

The shop smelled like paper, gum, and cheap coffee. Fluorescent lights buzzed faintly above a narrow row of shelves stacked with glossy packages, bottles, and brightly coloured boxes.

Mark Peters

Sadie and Jasper froze just inside the doorway, eyes wide.

"What is this place?" Sadie whispered.

Jasper glanced at a rack near the entrance filled with crinkly bags in bold reds and yellows. "Food, I think? Possibly."

He reached out and touched one of the bags. It rustled sharply beneath his fingers. He yanked his hand back like it had bitten him. "Why does it make that noise?"

"It's just packaging," Clara said softly, though she couldn't stop staring at the rows of goods herself. She'd spent her childhood in a tiny village, not a city like this. These stores—with their fluorescent lights and endless choices—still felt alien to her.

Sadie drifted to a stand of small metal cans. She picked one up carefully, turning it over in her hands. "Why does it hiss?"

"It's sealed. For freshness," Clara explained, though she wasn't entirely sure herself.

Jasper peered at a rotating rack filled with glossy, brightly coloured papers. "Are these spell scrolls?" He pulled one out. "No... magazines?"

Sadie crinkled another packet cautiously. "Everything's so loud. Even the food."

In the corner, a dusty ceiling fan spun lazily, stirring the smell of gum, coffee, and something faintly sweet.

Clara wandered towards a counter lined with strange tubes and silver foil-wrapped bars. She picked one up, reading the bold, cheery letters across the front. *Chocolate.*

Miss Wren used to mention chocolate. She said it was a rare treat when she was young.

Behind the counter, a man looked up from his phone. He wore a faded denim jacket and thick glasses. For a moment, he didn't say anything—just watched the three of them wander cautiously through the store as if they'd stepped out of another century.

Veilborne

Sadie tapped the metal can gently against the shelf, listening to the hollow sound. Jasper poked at a touchscreen display near the counter and flinched when it beeped.

Finally, the man cleared his throat. "Can I help you?"

All three froze and turned at once, snapped back to the moment.

They glanced at one another. None of them knew what the appropriate etiquette was.

Clara cleared her throat.

"Um. We're looking for… the Museum of Historical Science?"

The man blinked. "Just down two blocks and hang a left. Can't miss it."

Then he paused. His eyes travelled over their boots, layered cloaks, and strange, slightly mismatched clothing.

"You guys doing cosplay or something?"

There was a long silence.

"Yes," Clara said quickly.

"Definitely cosplay," Sadie added, nodding.

"Naturally, we are doing… that…" Jasper finished, his tone strained as he tried to sound confident.

The man shrugged, mildly amused, and gestured with a pen.

"Cool. Watch out for the construction on Sixth. They're ripping up the footpath again."

"Thanks," Clara said, already backing out the door.

Once outside, they paused to breathe again.

"Cosplay?" Sadie whispered.

"I panicked," Jasper hissed. "Also, what is that?"

"I think it's like dressing up," Clara said. "Pretending to be from somewhere else."

"We *are* from somewhere else," Sadie muttered. "Not pretending."

"Then we nailed it," Jasper said.

****

Two blocks later, they rounded the corner and stopped cold.

There it stood: the Museum of Historical Science. A broad, pale building with stone pillars and a glass entry that shimmered beneath buzzing fluorescent lights. High above the door, carved in bronze, was a plaque that read:

Honouring the Visionaries: Nikola Tesla, Minds Beyond Time.

Clara's chest tightened.

Sadie stepped closer to the gate.

"You think it's really in there?"

"That's what the file said," Jasper replied.

Sadie frowned at the building's cold, modern face. "Why would they leave it out in the open?"

"Because we have no knowledge of relics in this world," Clara offered.

Jasper's gaze sharpened. "Well, that's lucky for us. Maybe it means this place won't implode like the last relic resting place."

The building loomed in silence before them, the air humming with electricity and possibility.

"So what now?" Sadie asked.

"Now," Clara said, stepping towards the shadowed entrance, "we figure out how to break into this place."

They circled the museum twice without speaking. Each pass only confirmed the same frustrating truth: the building was sealed tighter than a spell-locked vault.

Cameras perched on corners. Motion lights flared like electric sentries. Every door glared with reinforced hinges and steel locks, and the few windows still accessible were bolted from the inside.

Veilborne

"This place is obsessed with keeping people out," Sadie muttered, glancing up at a second-storey panel of frosted glass.

"For a public place, it feels awfully unwelcoming," Jasper said quietly.

Clara didn't answer. She studied the building in silence, brow furrowed, trying to figure out why something so public felt so heavily guarded.

They turned the final corner near the back of the museum, just beyond a row of rubbish bins and a cracked concrete loading dock. That's when Clara stopped short.

"Wait. Look at that wall."

The bricks were off. Slightly different in colour, too clean, too uniform—like a patch stitched over worn cloth.

Sadie stepped closer, crouching to examine the base. "You're right. It's been redone. Probably years ago, but still..."

"Why would they rebuild just one part?" Clara asked.

Sadie brushed away a line of moss and dirt with her sleeve.

"Back in the Gilded Quarter," she said, "we used to find things like this—old merchant tunnels, coal drops, cargo chutes, doorways. Buildings get renovated, sealed up, but they never erase everything."

"So... there might be something behind this wall?" Clara asked.

Sadie nodded. "If we're lucky."

Jasper, who'd been quietly pacing nearby, turned sharply and knelt beside the spot. He tapped at the bricks one by one.

On the third knock, a hollow thunk echoed back.

"Well, that's promising," he said. "Let's see what's underneath."

He pried at the edge of the bricks with his fingers, grunting against rusted metal and packed soil. Clara and Sadie joined him, and after a few minutes of digging, they uncovered the rim of a large iron hatch—circular, bolted, and sealed with age.

A faint emblem was engraved at the centre, worn smooth with time.

"What is it?" Clara asked.

"Old service entrance, probably," Sadie guessed. "Maybe for waste removal or deliveries."

Jasper leaned over it, brushing the grime aside. "The mechanism's jammed, but I think I can force it."

He rummaged through his satchel and pulled out a hooked brass rod capped with a gear-toothed dial—one of his lock tools. The moment he fitted it into the latch and turned, a low *clack* sounded beneath the hatch.

The seal broke with a hiss.

"That's either the sound of success," Jasper said, "or something very hungry waking up."

Clara grabbed the edge and pulled. With a groan of old hinges, the hatch lifted, releasing a breath of stale, dry air.

A narrow shaft led downward into the dark, lined with old stone and rusted pipes. A crumbling stairwell twisted along one side, barely wide enough for single file.

"We're going underground," Sadie sighed. "Of course we are."

"Could be worse," Jasper offered. "Could be raining."

"Don't tempt it," Clara said, already swinging her legs over the edge.

****

The tunnel was colder than expected.

Moisture clung to the air, heavy with the smell of mildew and dust. The walls were uneven brickwork, cracked in places, the floor gritty beneath their boots. Patches of black mould stretched like bruises across the ceiling.

They moved as quietly as they could, but every step echoed in the dark.

Veilborne

"Someone built this a long time ago," Sadie whispered. "It's older than the museum itself, I'd bet."

"It's still standing," Jasper added. "That's rare for anything built without wards."

The tunnel sloped upward again, eventually ending at a warped steel door half-hinged in its frame.

Jasper pressed his ear to it. "Quiet."

He took another tool from his coat—slimmer this time, made of etched copper—and slid it into the keyhole. A twist. A *tick*. The door creaked open.

Beyond it: a storage corridor deep in the bowels of the museum.

Low industrial lights glowed overhead. Crates lined the walls, labelled with exhibit numbers, and in the distance, an elevator shaft blinked on standby.

"We're in," Clara whispered.

Sadie nodded. "Let's move fast."

Jasper glanced back the way they'd come. "And quiet."

He reached for his satchel and tapped the side gently.

Percival's head popped up, whiskers twitching.

"Stay ready," Clara murmured. "We might need a distraction."

Percival gave a mechanical chirp and settled back, alert.

They slipped down the corridor, deeper into the museum's quiet heart.

Their prize was close.

The hallway ended at a solid staff door marked **Authorised Personnel Only**. A small keypad glowed beside the handle, the numbers worn from years of use.

"This must lead to the display," Clara whispered.

Jasper studied the keypad, frowning. "I've seen locks before… but not like this."

He pulled a flat brass disc from his kit—barely palm-sized, etched with simple runes. Pressing it to the panel, he muttered, "Let's see if old magic still has an opinion about new technology."

The disc sparked once. The keypad fizzled softly.

A sharp *click* sounded as the lock disengaged.

He looked at the girls, surprised it had worked. "Huh. I guess so."

The door creaked open.

They slipped inside, swallowed by the quiet of the darkened exhibits.

The Tesla exhibit was haunting in the dark.

Glass cases stretched down the hall like silent sentinels, filled with coiled wires, copper instruments, and spindly devices that looked part machine, part art. Diagrams lined the walls—Tesla's precise sketches blown up to life-sized panels, paired with photos of him standing beside strange machines.

The only light came from emergency wall strips, casting the room in muted blue.

"This place feels… empty," Sadie whispered. "Like all the life's been drained out of it."

Jasper stepped closer to the nearest photo—a black-and-white image of Tesla beside a towering coil wrapped in copper wire. He froze.

"That's him," Jasper breathed. "Nikolas Emberlain."

Clara frowned. "You mean Tesla."

Jasper nodded slowly. "Different name. Same man. I'd recognise him anywhere. The files, the diagrams, the journal we found… it's all the same face."

Sadie's gaze swept the room—the machines, the sketches, the strange electrical devices. "So this is where he ended up. After tearing the Veil

Veilborne

apart." Her voice dropped. "Look at what he built. Radios. Power relays. Those massive coils—like the old Aether conductors. He was trying to open the way again."

Jasper finished quietly. "But he couldn't. He didn't have the right relics."

The weight of it settled over them—the silent realisation that even in this world, Emberlain had kept searching for a way back.

Clara said nothing. Her eyes moved from case to case—until she saw it.

The monocle.

It rested inside a rectangular display near the centre of the room, mounted on a velvet stand behind glass.

It looked unremarkable. Ordinary. Because here, it was.

A single lens, brass-rimmed, with a fine etching of concentric circles across its surface. The chain curled beside it like a sleeping serpent.

"That's it," Clara said softly.

They approached the case. Her hand hovered just above the glass.

"It's so plain," Sadie whispered.

"Plain is easy to overlook," Jasper replied. "That's how it's stayed hidden."

Clara glanced around for sensors, lasers—anything suspicious. But this wasn't a vault, just a well-maintained display. No enchantments. No relic wards. Just locks and lights.

"Can you open it?" she asked.

"Of course I can," Jasper said. "With enough time and mild stress-related trauma."

He knelt at the corner of the case, quietly working the hinge latches. As he did, Clara stepped closer to the glass. The locket beneath her collar grew noticeably warm.

She frowned.

"It's reacting," she said.

Sadie tilted her head. "The monocle?"

"No—the locket. It's like when it woke up in the coal room."

Jasper popped the final latch. The glass shifted open with a whisper.

Clara reached out and, with careful fingers, took hold of the monocle.

It was heavier than expected.

And the moment her hand closed around it—the chain humming faintly against her skin—something shifted.

The lights in the room flickered. Just once.

A sound clicked through the air—subtle, sharp. Not a siren. Not a klaxon.

Something deeper.

They froze.

"That wasn't me," Jasper said quickly.

"Did we set something off?" Sadie asked.

"There was no pressure plate," he insisted. "I checked!"

Clara clutched the monocle. Her locket pulsed once. From inside the satchel, Percival stirred and gave a sharp squeak.

"I think we need to go," Clara said.

Then—

From the far end of the corridor came the quiet creak of a door opening.

Footsteps followed. Slow. Measured.

Jasper turned towards the sound, paling. "That's not a janitor."

The footsteps grew louder, steady against the tiled floor. A flashlight beam swept briefly across the far wall.

Veilborne

"We've got company," Sadie whispered.

Clara tightened her grip on the monocle. "Did we trigger something?"

Jasper shook his head. "No alarms. We were just... unlucky."

A radio crackled in the distance.

"Someone's doing rounds," Jasper added, voice low. "We need to move. Now."

The gallery lights flickered again. Not all of them—just a few. Enough to make the shadows twitch. Enough to set Clara's pulse racing.

"We can't go back the way we came," Sadie said, moving toward the exhibit entrance. "There's no time."

Clara held the monocle tight in one hand, the Aether Ring pressing cold and solid against her ribs beneath her coat. They couldn't afford to lose either. Not now.

A burst of static cut through the air. A walkie-talkie came to life somewhere down the corridor. A man's voice, low and distorted.

"Motion in West Gallery. Checking."

Footsteps followed.

"Percival," Clara whispered. "Now."

Jasper nodded, already unfastening the satchel. The little brass rat blinked to life, tail twitching. Without waiting, Percival leapt down and darted into the dark.

Seconds later, a crash echoed from a nearby wing—glass shattering, metal clattering to the ground. Another voice came through the radio:

"We've got movement in the Sound and Signal Room. Possible vandalism."

The footsteps shifted direction.

"He's gone," Sadie said, peering around the exhibit's edge. "We've got seconds."

They moved, fast and low, weaving between display cases and through silent hallways. The tile floor clicked beneath their boots, no matter how lightly they stepped.

They reached the service door—and stopped cold.

The door was shut. Jasper grabbed the handle and twisted.

It didn't budge.

"No," he muttered, trying again, harder. "It's locked."

Sadie's brow furrowed. "It wasn't when we came in."

"They must have sealed the staff areas for the night," Clara whispered, heart sinking. "Or someone noticed something."

Jasper cursed under his breath, fingers tracing along the frame for any catch or weak point. "We're cut off."

Behind them, the radio crackled again—closer now.

"North corridor clear. Moving to basement access."

Clara's grip tightened around the monocle.

"That's where we are."

Sadie's eyes darted to the shadows. "We need another way out. Fast."

Jasper's jaw clenched, knuckles white on his satchel strap.

Then Clara stilled.

A line flickered in her memory—Fennrick in the grove, muttering as he traced chalk symbols around the Aether Ring.

If you follow the city's oldest bones, they'll take you where the Veil still remembers.

"Wait," she said. "Follow me."

"Clara—what—"

"Just trust me!"

She turned on her heel and ran.

Veilborne

Back past the gallery, through the exhibit wings, into the dimly lit storage halls—until they reached the rusting service stairwell that led back underground.

They didn't hesitate.

They plunged into the dark.

****

The old tunnel felt tighter now. Like the air itself had closed in behind them.

"We're going back down?" Jasper hissed. "I thought escaping meant going up!"

"We're not escaping," Clara said. "We're following the old bones."

"She's quoting Fennrick," Sadie muttered. "Just go with it."

At the lowest level, where the walls turned to rougher stone and ancient bricks, Clara skidded to a halt. Jasper pulled a small light orb from his satchel. Its glow pushed back the dark—just enough to reveal something strange ahead.

A bricked archway. The mortar was cracked and old—older than anything else they'd seen here. In its centre: a rusted iron ring. The same pattern as the stone circle Eldric had used. The same symbols—not glowing, but there.

"There," Clara breathed. "That's it."

"You think this is a crossing point?" Jasper asked, panting.

"I think… I hope."

She pulled the Aether Ring from beneath her coat. The moment it cleared the fabric, it began to hum.

Not loud.

But steady. A deep, resonant vibration—like a string being plucked beneath their feet.

"That's good, right?" Sadie asked. "That's a good hum?"

Clara set it on the stone floor in the centre of the old bricks.

The rings began to turn.

Slow at first. Then faster.

The runes didn't light up like last time—but the air around them shimmered, distorting like heat off pavement. A wavering, fragile curtain of light built in the air.

"Come on," Clara whispered. "Come on…"

****

Footsteps above. Distant but growing louder. The guards had reached the stairwell.

A voice echoed faintly: "You hear that hum?"

"Hurry," Jasper hissed.

The Aether Ring spun faster. The shimmer thickened.

Then—

Snap.

A pulse of sound. The shimmer widened, forming a thin pane of rippling light.

The Veil opened.

Clara grabbed Sadie's hand. "Go!"

Sadie didn't hesitate. She stepped into the shimmer—and vanished.

Clara turned to Jasper. "Your turn. Go!"

But Jasper shook his head, eyes scanning the shadows. "Not without Percival."

"Jasper—"

"I'm not leaving him."

Above, footsteps pounded closer. The guards were descending fast.

"Jasper, we have to go!" Clara urged.

Veilborne

"I'm not leaving him behind!" Jasper's voice cracked—sharp, desperate.

The seconds stretched unbearably thin. The shimmer pulsed, already growing unstable.

Clara's heart slammed against her ribs. "Jasper—we *need* to go!"

"I said I'm not—"

A blur rounded the corner. Percival, metal gleaming, tail lashing as he sprinted toward them.

"There!" Jasper cried.

Clara grabbed his arm. "Now!"

Percival leapt. Jasper caught him as Clara hauled them both into the Veil.

The shimmer collapsed the instant they crossed through, the Aether Ring vanishing with them.

And then—

Silence.

The guard reached the corridor's end, flashlight beam cutting through dust and empty air.

"...What the hell?"

He stepped closer to the archway. Just old stone. No footprints. No sign of the trespassers.

Behind him, another guard called down.

"Nothing on the cameras. You?"

He frowned, tapping his radio. "Nothing. Just some old maintenance tunnel."

Chapter 17
The Unraveling Thread

The grass beneath Clara's boots was wet with dew.

She stumbled slightly as she emerged from the portal. Jasper landed beside her, clutching Percival against his chest. Sadie was already there, just a few steps ahead, turning back toward them.

Behind them, the Aether Ring rested where it had settled—half-sunken into the mossy ground, still faintly warm from use. The shimmer snapped shut with a crack of displaced air.

They were standing in the old stone glade. Moonlight spilled between the trees, silvering the circle where the Aether Ring had first spun them out of the world.

No alarms. No voices. Just wind.

"We made it," Clara whispered, hardly believing it.

Jasper knelt, setting Percival down carefully. The little brass rat shook himself off, gears clicking softly. Clara exhaled, then bent to retrieve the Aether Ring. The metal was cool now, no longer humming, but the faint echo of its power still tingled against her palms.

"I don't know if I want to throw up or sleep for a year," Jasper muttered, clutching his knees.

"That was…" Sadie paused, blinking at the stars overhead. "That was the most terrifying thing I've ever done."

"Same," Clara said, exhaling slowly. "But we have it."

She reached into her coat and drew out the monocle.

It didn't look any different. Just a lens, a chain, a curve of brass cooled by the night.

But everything was different now.

The three of them stood in the moonlit glade for a moment longer, catching their breath. No one spoke. The weight of what they had done—and what they still carried—settled between them like a silent pact.

Finally, Clara said,

"We need to get the Aether Ring back before Eldric realises it's missing."

They gathered themselves and began the quiet trek back toward the Keep.

****

By the time they reached the outer grounds, the Keep was asleep.

Its halls, usually alive with movement and magic, were hushed in the moonlight and the occasional flicker of rune stone lamps set to their nighttime dim. The air carried the scent of wildflowers and old wood, like the breath of a place gently reclaimed by nature.

Clara, Jasper, and Sadie moved like ghosts along the eastern wing.

They paused outside Eldric's chambers.

Clara, Jasper, and Sadie moved like ghosts along the eastern wing.

They paused outside Eldric's chambers.

"Percival?" Clara whispered.

The little brass rat twitched in her satchel, then leapt silently to the floor. He zipped down the hall, tail flicking in purposeful sweeps.

Moments later, he returned with a low chirp and a confident nod.

"Clear," Jasper whispered.

He pulled out the same lockpick relic he'd used once before, slipping it into the door's rune socket. It gave a satisfying click.

"He's not in," Sadie murmured, glancing at the dim, silent room beyond.

"No surprise," Jasper replied quietly. "Master Vaelryn's been having the senior Auricals check the outer wards every night since the last Veil tremor."

Clara nodded. "Good. That means no one's watching this hallway either."

He pulled out the same lockpick relic he'd used once before, but paused.

"Actually..." Jasper knelt beside Percival and gently tapped the brass rat. "Your turn."

Percival chirped softly, scampering to the rune socket. With a delicate flick of his tiny gear-tipped tail and a click of his forepaws against the mechanism, the lock disengaged.

The door eased open with barely a sound.

Inside, the study hadn't changed. Clara wondered if Eldric had returned at all—or if the survey had waited in silence since their last visit.

The fireplace was long and cold. Eldric's massive desk stood undisturbed, its surface clear save for a single ink bottle and the long-shadowed stem of a reading lamp. The quill floated gently over blank parchment, as though waiting for someone to gather their thoughts.

Clara dropped to one knee, pulling the rug aside beneath the desk.

"There," she said quietly.

She lifted the loose floorboard, revealing the narrow compartment hidden beneath. The space was shallow and cloth-lined, just as they had found it.

With careful hands, she placed the Aether Ring back inside. It settled into the groove with the weightless click of something returning home.

Jasper exhaled.

"Done. Let's get out of here while we still have the chance."

They slid the floorboard back into place, reset the rug, and moved toward the door.

Clara paused only to give the room one last glance, ensuring it remained untouched.

Veilborne

She stepped outside last, easing the door shut behind them.

Jasper gave Percival a slight nod. The little brass rat scurried up the doorframe, harness glinting faintly in the low light. He slipped the tiny lockpick tool into the rune socket and began working the mechanism with delicate, practiced motions.

As the gears inside the lock whispered into motion—

"I was under the impression students slept at night."

Clara's stomach plummeted.

They turned as one.

Eldric Ducart stood at the far end of the corridor.

Arms folded.

His long coat brushed the floor like a shadow with weight. His expression wasn't angry. Just unreadable. Calm. Alert.

Behind them, Percival clicked faintly, still locking the chamber door. He paused, as though even he sensed the danger.

"Professor," Clara began, trying to sound composed.

"We were just—" Jasper started.

Sadie stepped in quickly, voice steady. "We thought you might still be awake. We... needed to ask something."

Eldric's brow lifted, gaze sharp. "At this hour?"

Percival clicked once more. The lock sealed.

Without a sound, the brass rat slipped down the doorframe, darted behind Clara's boots, and climbed into Jasper's satchel.

"We didn't know when else to ask," Clara said. "It's important."

Eldric studied them for a long moment, eyes dark beneath the lamplight.

"What was so urgent it couldn't wait until morning?"

Jasper hesitated—but Sadie was ready.

"It's about the Veil," she said. "We—" She swallowed. "We've been having dreams. Strange ones. About crossings. We thought you might understand."

Clara felt a flash of admiration. Sadie's lie sounded almost true.

Eldric's expression didn't change, but his gaze sharpened, calculating.

"You should have come by daylight."

"We didn't want others overhearing," Clara said quickly. "Some of the younger students gossip."

"That they do." Eldric's voice remained level. But not warm.

He glanced at the door behind them. Then back.

"I'll consider your… curiosity. But whatever you came looking for tonight—leave it." His tone lowered. "The deeper you dig, the darker the roots."

Clara nodded. "Yes, Professor."

Eldric stepped aside, giving them just enough room to pass.

"Off to bed. All three of you. And try to keep your dreams your own."

They didn't wait.

They slipped past him and down the hall, not daring to speak until they rounded the next corner.

Only once they turned into the next corridor did Clara breathe.

"He doesn't know," Sadie whispered.

"I'm sure he knows something," Jasper said grimly.

"We need to move. Now."

They slipped into the outer passageways and descended toward the grounds, emerging into the cool night air where the grass still shimmered with dew.

They didn't speak until the Keep's towers were behind them, swallowed by trees and moonlight.

Veilborne

Their path curved through sleeping gardens and down a trail flanked by old stone walls, the air thick with dew and the scent of flowering vines. The weight of the monocle pressed against Clara's coat with every step—a quiet reminder that something world-changing rested just inches from her heart.

The glade opened like a secret remembered.

Silver mist curled low along the mossy floor, and the moon spilled its light across the clearing like a blessing. At its center, hunched on a lichen-covered stone, was Fennrick Bramble.

He looked up as they approached, not startled in the slightest. His coat was dusted with leaves, and his eyes gleamed in the dark.

"Evening," he said, as if they were simply late to a garden walk. "Judging by your faces, I take it that wasn't the smoothest retrieval—but the monocle's in hand?"

Clara drew it briefly from her coat, letting the brass rim catch the moonlight before tucking it away again.

"Good," he said. "One more thread tied… and one step closer to the knot."

He stood, his boots creaking.

"So," Jasper said, frowning, "we've got this monocle. A journal. We crossed into another realm, stole from a museum, nearly got caught—twice—and no one else managed this in… how long?"

"Decades," Sadie murmured.

"Right." Jasper turned to Fennrick. "So why us? Why now? Why were we the ones to figure it out?"

Clara folded her arms, silent. She'd been asking herself the same question for days.

Fennrick didn't answer immediately. His gaze dropped to the moss beneath his boots, as though the ground itself might offer a simpler truth than the one he held.

"Because," he said at last, "you weren't just following clues. You were following something's design. The locket, the journal, the monocle—they weren't just waiting to be found. They were moving. Shifting toward the right hands."

Jasper frowned. "So they chose us?"

"Or someone made them choose," Fennrick replied. "Not by chance. Not by blood. The relics… they've been guiding you. And maybe not entirely of their own will."

Clara swallowed. Her fingers found the locket at her collarbone, its weight cold and solid.

"Then what does it want from us?" Clara asked, voice barely above a whisper.

"Because someone—or something—set this in motion long before you ever crossed the Veil," Fennrick said. "You've been nudged, led. Every step. Whether by those who forged the relics—or by forces we don't fully understand."

Sadie's voice was barely above a whisper. "So all of this was deliberate."

"Deliberate—or desperate," Fennrick said grimly. "That's what troubles me."

Jasper scowled. "But who? Who started it? And why?"

Fennrick shook his head. "That's what we have to discover. The journal may hold some of the answers. Especially about the Veil itself."

Clara's breath caught. "There was a section in the diagrams. It wasn't just experiments—it looked like he was trying to map the Veil. And…" She paused. "I think there was a theory. About how to repair it. To stop the random breaches."

Fennrick's expression sharpened, tension flickering across his weatherworn face. "Repair it? Are you certain?"

Veilborne

"Not completely," Clara admitted. "But it looked like that's what he was working toward. And something else." She hesitated. "I didn't say this before but... Jasper and Sadie saw it too. Emberlain isn't just some ancient figure in this realm. In my world, he's known as Nikola Tesla."

Fennrick stiffened.

"He was a scientist. A brilliant one. Famous for creating things far beyond his time—radio, wireless electricity, things no one could explain. People thought he was just eccentric. But some believed he was working on something bigger. Experiments in... teleportation. He vanished. Without a trace."

Jasper chimed in, "It all fits. He wasn't just experimenting. He was trying to get back. Here."

Sadie's brow furrowed. "But if he made it back, wouldn't the Auricals have known?"

Fennrick's face darkened. "If he'd returned to Eryndor, he wouldn't have gone unnoticed. Unless..." His voice trailed off.

"Unless he didn't make it back here," Clara finished softly. "Maybe he ended up somewhere else."

"There are theories," Fennrick said slowly. "That there aren't just two realms. That there are thousands. Fractured worlds. Some are closer to ours than others. Some... so far removed they're practically unreachable." His eyes narrowed. "If he vanished between worlds, he might still be out there. Searching. Or trapped."

A heavy silence settled over them.

Jasper broke it. "So we're not just dealing with relics. Or lost history. We're dealing with someone—or something-that's been trying to stitch worlds together. And maybe still is."

Fennrick nodded. "And now you three have the pieces they need."

Clara closed her hand around the monocle. Its weight felt heavier than ever.

"What now?" she asked.

"Now," Fennrick said, his voice low, "we take this to the Council. Carefully. Not all truths should be told at once. Especially when we still don't know who might be working against us."

"You were the spark, Clara. The piece that fit a shape no one else could see. That's why everything changed the moment you crossed the Veil."

Clara didn't respond. She felt the weight of the monocle, of the journal, and her locket. All of it had led here. Not by accident. Not by chance.

Jasper stiffened. "You mean the actual Aurical Council?"

"The head of the Order and their circle," Fennrick said. "This doesn't belong in a classroom anymore. It belongs to the realm—and the storm that's coming."

"Won't they ask questions?" Sadie said. "About how we got it? Where have we been?"

"Let me worry about that," Fennrick said. "Just keep the relics safe. Tell them what they need to hear."

"And if they don't listen?" Clara asked.

Fennrick looked at her long and hard.

"Then we make them listen. And brace for what follows."

****

The Keep was asleep, but none of them could.

They sat huddled in their familiar hearth nook—just the three of them, shadows flickering across their faces as the last logs turned to embers. The fire crackled softly, but the warmth didn't reach the weight pressing in on all sides.

"Fennrick said the Council meeting will be first thing in the morning," Jasper murmured. "No more secrets after that."

"Maybe," Sadie said, hugging her knees to her chest. "But that doesn't mean everyone in the room is going to be on our side."

Veilborne

That hung there for a moment. No one named names. They didn't have to.

Clara reached into her coat and pulled the monocle free. It gleamed softly in the firelight—innocuous, almost dull, but the weight of it felt wrong in her palm.

"We can't bring it to the meeting," she said.

Jasper leaned forward. "Why not? Isn't that the point?"

"Because we don't know who we're showing it to, who to trust," Clara replied. "We can't risk losing it. Or the journal."

Sadie's eyes flicked to the satchel. "You think someone's... watching?"

Clara hesitated, then gave a slow nod.

"We've made too much noise. Since the museum, since the Veil jump. I don't know who's paying attention, but someone is. And we can't assume it's anyone we can trust."

"Then we stash them," Jasper said.

"Just until after the Council," Clara confirmed. "We need to see how they respond first, before we show our hand."

****

The three of them moved carefully through the quiet tower, climbing two floors to an abandoned storeroom tucked behind the astronomy wing—a room long out of use, where broken star-mapping tables gathered dust and parchment scraps littered the floor.

Jasper knelt behind an overturned cabinet and pried up a cracked floor tile, revealing a shallow, dry recess beneath.

"Found it the other day," he muttered. "Percival sniffed it out while chasing a moth."

Clara handed him the journal. Its aged leather cover was smooth and cold.

Sadie passed over the monocle, still wrapped in the same cloth they'd used to smuggle it back from the museum.

"They'll be safe here?" she asked quietly.

Jasper nodded. "Only we know where. And I'll have Percival check in tonight. If anyone else even breathes near it, he'll let us know."

He closed the tile and pressed it down firmly. The cracks sealed almost perfectly. Dust swept back across the stone like time reclaiming its place.

"If anything happens at the meeting…" Clara said softly, "We come back here. No matter what."

"Agreed," Jasper said.

"We don't say anything unless we know it's safe," Sadie added. "Not everything. Not yet."

"Right."

They looked at each other, tired, but resolute. Too far in to stop now. Too close to the truth to turn back.

They left the storeroom in silence.

Behind them, the shadows returned to stillness. And beneath the floor, the truth waited, unseen but no longer untouched.

Chapter 18
The Council

Dawn came like a held breath.

Mist clung to the outer windows of Calendor Keep, painting the stone in silver and hush. Even the morning bells seemed subdued—no longer summoning students, but echoing with the weight of something inevitable.

Clara stood at the arched window of the Starfire dormitory, hands curled around a mug of tea grown cold. She hadn't touched it. She hadn't slept.

Behind her, Jasper paced. Sadie sat at the edge of her bed, twisting the silver ring on her finger with quiet, unconscious intensity.

"Do we even know where we're supposed to go?" Jasper asked for what must have been the fifth time.

"Fennrick said someone would come," Clara murmured.

"That's comforting," Jasper muttered. "I'm sure they'll be thrilled we hid the only two things that might explain what's happening."

Sadie looked up. "Would you rather we brought them—and handed them to the wrong person?"

Jasper didn't answer.

A knock at the door startled them all.

Not loud. But deliberate.

The door eased open to reveal a tall woman in deep green Aurical robes. Her face was lined but elegant, eyes a piercing moss-grey. She carried no wand. No staff. Just the quiet weight of authority.

****

"You are summoned," she said. "Follow me."

They moved in silence through corridors most students never saw—passages where the walls bore runes older than the Keep itself. The air grew colder, the light dimmer, until breath fogged and stone seemed to pulse faintly beneath their feet.

At last, they entered the Hall of the Aurical Council.

The chamber was carved directly into the cliffside. Tall windows opened to the pale sea, mist curling into the space like silver threads. A wide circular floor spread out beneath them, etched with ancient script and silver inlay that glimmered like starlight trapped in stone.

Seven high-backed chairs curved along the far side, raised above the floor.

At the center sat Master Vaelryn.

Grave. Still. Her robes were the color of old vellum and deep, flame-touched stone. Her presence calmed the very air.

To the right stood Eldric Ducart, arms folded, face unreadable.

Beside him, sharp-eyed and silent, Mistress Lirah Valen.

And flanking the other Councilors sat Councilor Astrid Cale, her robes emerald with silver embroidery, the sigils of the Outer Wards at her collar. Eyes like flint.

"Clara Holloway. Jasper Thorn. Sadie Emmer," Vaelryn intoned.

"You have crossed lines few dare even approach."

Her voice carried effortlessly, soft but inescapable.

"You've acted without leave. Crossed realms. Entered forbidden places. You have disturbed powers sleeping longer than your lifetimes."

A pause.

"Now. Speak."

****

Clara stepped forward.

Her throat felt tight. But her voice came steady.

Veilborne

"We didn't mean to cause harm. But once we found the journal—once it started connecting to everything else—we couldn't stop."

Sadie moved beside her. "The locket led us. It... reacted. Not just to places but memories. And then we found the journal. We think it belonged to Nikolas Emberlain."

"We're sure of it," Jasper added.

One of the Councilors frowned. "The hidden study was destroyed. How do you know what you found was real?"

"Because we saw it," Clara said. "We read the journal. We found designs and references to another relic. A monocle."

Murmurs rippled through the Council.

"And where are these relics now?" asked a soft, dangerous voice. Astrid Cale.

Clara's pulse quickened.

"Safe," she said. "Hidden. Until we know who to trust."

"You do not trust this Council?" Astrid pressed, voice like cold metal.

Clara hesitated. Sadie spoke for her.

"We trust that not everyone in this room will agree on what should happen next."

The chamber stilled.

Eldric stepped forward, gaze steady.

"There's something else," he said. "They crossed the Veil."

His voice cut through the tension like a blade.

"We've reviewed all realm anchors, all sanctioned portals, and every possible breach. No One explains how they moved between worlds."

He looked directly at Clara. Then Jasper. Sadie.

"They are keeping something back. The question is whether they are hiding it—or protecting it."

Clara felt the heat of Sadie's hand brushing hers, grounding her.

Then Eldric's eyes narrowed, thoughtful. A slow crease formed between his brows.

His gaze flicked past them.

To the hallway door.

To the memory of a night not long ago.

The night he found them outside his chambers.

His expression changed. Subtle. Realization dawning.

"You found the Aether Ring," Eldric said softly.

Clara's breath caught.

"We—" She glanced at Jasper, who gave a resigned nod. "Yes. We used it."

Eldric's tone didn't rise. But his next words were quiet thunder.

"You unlocked a realm portal from my private study. And I never even noticed the Ring was missing."

Sadie muttered, "We put it back."

Eldric's mouth twitched. Not quite a smile. Not anger either.

"You did," he agreed. "Which suggests I've underestimated all three of you. I'll have to find a more secure location."

More murmurs broke across the Council—but Vaelryn lifted a hand. Silence returned.

"You trespassed," Astrid Cale said, voice sharpening.

"You crossed Veil boundaries. You concealed relics and withheld dangerous knowledge. You endangered yourselves—and others."

Her gaze grew colder.

"The Glimmerden breach. The destruction of the study. The creatures are drawn to you. Are we meant to believe all this was an accident?"

Veilborne

Clara felt her throat tighten—but this time she did not look down.

"No," she said clearly. "Not an accident. But not entirely our choice either."

Sadie nodded. "The relics weren't just waiting. They were... moving. Leading us."

"And guiding others to follow you?" Astrid pressed.

Jasper scowled. "We didn't summon the creatures."

"But they found you," Astrid said darkly. "Again. And again. The pattern cannot be ignored."

She turned to Master Vaelryn.

"The children acted alone. Without training. Without oversight. We cannot dismiss the recklessness simply because they returned alive."

But before Vaelryn could reply, Fennrick Bramble spoke.

He stepped out from the archway where he'd stood silent.

"Not entirely alone."

Heads turned.

"I watched," Fennrick said, "from a distance. I didn't interfere—but I didn't abandon them either."

Astrid's eyes narrowed. "So you encouraged their disobedience?"

"No," Fennrick replied calmly. "I ensured it didn't kill them."

A pause. Then he added, "And I would do so again."

Silence stretched. Even Astrid didn't immediately answer.

Eldric exhaled slowly, his posture easing.

"They showed poor judgment," he said at last. "But not malice. They discovered relics and patterns we missed. They navigated Veil tremors better than trained scholars."

Vaelryn rose.

"You did act recklessly," they said, looking to Clara, Sadie, and Jasper.

"You lied. You concealed. You crossed boundaries meant to safeguard lives and history."

Their voice deepened.

"But you also showed instincts no training can teach."

Vaelryn's gaze swept the chamber.

"They uncovered truths we buried in fear. Patterns we ignored out of convenience. They brought knowledge back, not power. Not conquest. Truth."

They paused.

"And truth… has always been the Auricals' highest calling."

"You will not be punished," Vaelryn declared.

"But you will be watched."

Astrid Cale's lips pressed thin.

"You endangered yourselves," another Councilor said. "And perhaps others. But you may have prevented a far greater disaster."

Vaelryn nodded.

"You may return to your dormitory. Rest. And prepare. For tomorrow, your truths will begin their journey into light."

"But know this," she added, her tone like stone striking flint. "The matter of the relics is far from settled. The Council will deliberate, and our judgment will follow."

****

As they turned to leave, Clara felt the weight of many eyes.

She glanced back.

Astrid Cale glared at her, lips tight with barely contained disapproval.

Another Councilor—an older woman wrapped in crimson—watched with an unreadable intensity. Not suspicion. Recognition.

And Eldric…

Veilborne

His brow furrowed slightly, as though more pieces were shifting into place.

But Lirah Valen…

Still. Silent. Watching. Not angry. Not questioning.

Waiting.

The doors closed behind them with the hush of old magic.

And for the first time, Clara felt it fully:

They were not outsiders anymore.

They were players on the board.

And the game was now in full effect.

****

They followed Fennrick down a lesser-used stairwell, beneath quiet arches, and out into the gardens.

Past the manicured grounds and under a low stone archway, they emerged into a hidden glade where the Keep's outer walls gave way to wild edge.

Here, the trees grew close but welcoming. Lantern-flies drifted like tiny constellations among the roots. The tall grasses bent with the sea breeze, silvered by the late morning light.

Fennrick dropped onto a fallen log, weathered smooth by years of rain and salt air. He gestured for them to sit.

"This place always helped me think," he said. "Back when the walls felt like they were closing in."

Clara sank beside him.

Jasper folded into the grass, elbows on his knees. Sadie leaned back against a moss-covered stone, arms wrapped around herself.

For a moment, none of them spoke.

"They don't trust us," Clara said quietly.

"No," Fennrick admitted. "But for the first time... they're listening."

"And if it's not enough?" she asked. "What if they bury this—again? What if none of it matters?"

Fennrick was quiet for a long breath. Then:

"Truth's like a wildflower. It gets trampled. Cut back. Burned, even. But give it the smallest crack of sunlight, and it finds a way to grow. Stronger. Wilder. Harder to root out the next time."

His gaze swept across the three of them—not as children, but as something else now. Something becoming.

"They'll try to put you back inside the lines. That's what institutions do. That's what they're built for.

But you've stepped beyond those lines now. And once you do... there's no going back."

Jasper frowned. "Is that supposed to be reassuring?"

Fennrick gave a faint, lopsided smile. "It's supposed to be true."

The wind stirred the grasses, lifting small silver seeds into the air and carrying them out toward the horizon.

"Get some rest," Fennrick said at last. His voice gentled, but the weight in it remained.

"Tomorrow, you won't just be witnesses to history." He looked at each of them in turn. "You'll be shaping it."

They didn't fully understand what he meant. Not yet.

But the weight of it settled over them like a tide turning.

The others stood, but Clara lingered.

Her gaze drifted to the silvered grass, the lantern-flies dancing above the roots.

Back at Morrowmere, she'd once stared through a rain-fogged window at a world she thought she'd never touch. A world full of questions no one would answer.

Veilborne

She had lost Miss Wren. Lost the only adult who had tried—however coldly—to prepare her for what was coming.

She had lost her parents long before that.

But she had not lost this.

Not this fight.

Not this chance.

"We're not just shaping history," Clara said quietly, more to herself than anyone else.

"We're giving it back to the people who deserve to remember it."

Fennrick's eyes warmed, the lines at their corners softening. "That's exactly it."

Jasper and Sadie fell into step beside Clara as they made their way back toward the Keep. Without a word, Jasper slung an arm around Clara's shoulder. Sadie did the same on her other side. The three of them moved as one, the grasses swaying behind them like a promise kept.

Fennrick watched them go, a faint, knowing smile touching the corner of his mouth.

They weren't three children anymore. Not separate pieces.

They were a single thread now—woven, tested, unbroken.

Chapter 19
The Gathering of Houses

It had rained the night before, leaving the courtyard stones slick and shining beneath the morning sun. The banners had been unfurled at dawn—rich velvets and embroidered silks catching the breeze from Calendor's highest towers. Crimson and brass for Starfire. Sapphire and silver for Dawnspire. Deep green with copper filigree for Stonehearth. Midnight blue edged in white for Frostmere.

They fluttered above the arches like the colours of gathered kingdoms.

And for once, the air felt normal.

No shadows lurking at the edges of conversation. No Council murmurs. No restless glances toward the horizon.

Just the sounds of a school alive again.

Clara, Jasper, and Sadie made their way through the outer courtyard, weaving between students clustered in lively knots. Robes were freshly pressed. Scarves and sashes in House colours brightened the morning mist. For the first time in what felt like months, voices spoke not of rifts or relics or responsibilities—but of ordinary things.

Assignments. Upcoming spellcraft lessons. Which House would take the lead in the games, now that they were finally returning. Whispers about new events being added to the roster—and whether the Sky Relay would be as dangerous as some older students claimed.

Clara did her best to follow the conversations swirling around her in the corridors, but most of it blurred together. The games, the Relay, team drafts—it all sounded like another language. She caught fragments but no full explanation, and after everything that had happened lately, it didn't seem urgent enough to ask.

Until she passed the poster.

It had been fastened to a notice pillar at the central crossing where the eastern and northern halls met. Bright banners curled at the edges—

crimson, indigo, emerald, gold—each House's colours threaded in a sweeping arc across the parchment.

THE GATHERING OF HOUSES

The Concordia Trials return after three years.

Unity. Skill. Legacy.

All students eligible.

Families and honoured guests welcome.

Join us at high sun in the Glade of Concord.

Festival Stalls | House Celebrations | Luminar Procession at dusk

Clara stared, reading it twice.

Beneath the bold script were smaller lines detailing team selections, event times, and a grand closing ceremony.

Clara paused, frowning.

"What's this?" she asked aloud, touching the parchment's edge.

Sadie and Jasper, walking just ahead, doubled back.

Sadie's face lit up. "Oh! Right—the Concordia Trials! I completely forgot they were this week."

Jasper groaned. "With everything else going on, it slipped my mind too. But this is good. We need this."

Clara blinked. "The what?"

Sadie bumped her shoulder gently. "It's the event of the season. House against House. Magic, strategy, games. Some wild traditions thrown in."

"And food," Jasper added, adopting a mock-serious tone. "Mountains of it."

Clara tilted her head. "Isn't that what the House Cup is for?"

"That's academics. Dry, dusty glory." Sadie swept a hand toward the poster. "This is for everything else. The Trials are about Houses working together. History, magic, cunning. Each Trial tests different skills. Starfire's usually best at the magical challenges. Frostmere dominates the relay and endurance. Stonehearth always surprises everyone in the strategy games."

"And Dawnspire cheats," Jasper muttered darkly. "Just quietly enough not to get caught."

Clara managed a small laugh.

Sadie leaned in, lowering her voice as if sharing a grand secret. "The Concordia Trials only happen once every three years. That's why it feels so huge."

"We were supposed to have one last year," Jasper added. "But with the Veil disturbances, the Council postponed it. This year's Trials are the first since the tremors began."

Clara traced the shifting ink with her eyes, heart tight.

Families and honoured guests welcome.

She felt the sharp, cold ache of absence press into her ribs.

Family. She had none. Not really. Miss Wren was gone. Her parents—ghosts without faces.

She glanced at Jasper, who was already talking excitedly about the Sky Relay and something called Crest Seize. He had family coming. His parents. A reminder of the life he'd lived before this—before relics and Veil crossings and danger wrapped in secrets.

Sadie noticed the change in Clara's face instantly. She didn't say a word. Just wrapped her arms around Clara's shoulders from behind, resting her chin lightly on Clara's shoulder.

"Hey," Sadie murmured, voice warm but steady. "Me too. No family. Not really."

She tightened her arms slightly. "We've got each other now. That's what counts."

Clara nodded, unable to speak for a moment.

Veilborne

Jasper looked back, sensing the tone. His usual grin softened. "My parents are reserving extra seats. They'll want to meet you both. Hope that's alright."

That startled a laugh out of Clara. A real one.

Sadie grinned. "Looks like you don't get a say, Holloway."

Clara shook her head. "Wasn't planning to argue."

****

As they moved on, the courtyard seemed brighter somehow. Tents were already rising along the outer lawns, vendors unpacking crates beneath colourful awnings. The scent of baking bread and sweet butter filled the air as food carts began to arrive. Clockwork creatures—small mechanical birds and messenger rats—whirred through the crowd, delivering schedules and team announcements.

The Glade of Concord awaited beyond the river bend, but even from the high terraces, Clara could see flashes of magical preparation underway. Trails of coloured light arced into the sky as students practised their opening displays.

Banners rippled like the wings of a thousand different birds taking flight.

For the first time in what felt like forever, the world wasn't closing in.

It was opening.

****

Three days later

The sun rose over Calendor Keep, scattering the last veils of mist like silk drawn aside from a window.

The entire campus had transformed.

The Glade of Concord—normally a quiet field wrapped in old forest and riverbend mist—had become a world unto itself. House banners lined the edges where the trees thinned, their colours blazing under the rising sun. Starfire's crimson and brass fluttered alongside

Dawnspire's silver and blue, Stonehearth's green and copper, and Frostmere's midnight blue edged in white. Smaller pennants crisscrossed above the pathways, enchanted to ripple even when the breeze stilled.

Students poured in from every wing of the Keep. Parents and family members gathered at the outer pavilions. Some wore their children's House colours; others arrived in formal Aurical robes, traders' cloaks, or the working leathers of the Gilded. The diversity of Eryndor stood on full display—mages, artisans, stewards, and even a few wild-clad envoys from distant covens.

Clara could barely take it all in.

"All right," Jasper said, adjusting the Starfire sash at his shoulder. "First rule of the Trials—try not to get trampled."

Sadie smirked. "Second rule—don't get outscored by Dawnspire."

"And third?" Clara asked, watching a flock of floating lanterns rise into the sky, each bearing a trailing ribbon of light.

"Have fun," Jasper said with a grin. "That's the part people forget."

Before Clara could respond, a voice called out from the edge of the gathering.

"Jasper!"

A woman and man were weaving through the crowd towards them. The woman wore a slate-blue cloak pinned with the Starfire crest. Her copper hair was streaked with early grey, but her smile was quick and familiar. The man beside her had the same sharp green eyes as Jasper, and a tinker's satchel slung at his hip.

"Mother! Father!" Jasper's face lit up. "You made it!"

"We wouldn't miss the Trials," his mother said, pulling him into a tight embrace. "Especially not with all the rumours about your... extracurricular adventures."

Veilborne

His father leaned in, lowering his voice conspiratorially. "I hope whatever you didn't tell us is at least as impressive as what we've heard."

Jasper coughed. "Long story."

Then, with an eager gesture, he pulled Clara and Sadie forward. "Mother, Father—this is Clara Holloway. And Sadie Thorne. My… teammates."

Sadie gave a small, shy wave. Clara tried to find words, but found herself blinking instead.

Jasper's mother didn't hesitate—she pulled both girls into a warm, no-nonsense hug. "If you're standing with my son, you're ours too. Simple as that."

His father nodded. "And you'll sit with us after the Trials. The family terrace has plenty of room."

Sadie's hand found Clara's. Neither spoke, but the lump in Clara's throat eased.

****

Across the glade, more families were arriving. The Aurical Council stood at the head platform, observing the preparations without interference. Eldric Ducart watched the crowd like a hawk—calm, but clearly alert. Mistress Valen stood near Master Vaelryn, her expression composed.

And to one side, a new figure approached.

Lady Selvara Draven, Varek's mother.

She stood tall, wrapped in Dawnspire blue trimmed with black and silver. Her dark hair was bound in intricate braids, her eyes sharp and assessing. Varek followed at her side, robes immaculate, face unreadable.

For a moment, Lady Selvara's gaze locked with Clara's.

It wasn't anger. Nor approval.

Just the cold recognition of a rival not of her choosing.

She nodded once, almost imperceptibly, then turned away.

****

As the sun climbed higher, a bell tolled—deep and resonant. The Concordia Herald stepped onto the central platform.

"By tradition, and by the threads of unity, the Concordia Trials return."

Cheers erupted from all four Houses.

The events were announced in turn:

1. Arcane Assemblage – Teams craft and enchant a device to navigate the shifting Trial Maze. Creativity and daring are tested.

2. Sky Relay – A high-speed aerial race above rivers and forest canopy. Precision and teamwork determine the victors.

3. Spellweave Confrontation – Team-based duels across adaptive terrain, judged by spell mastery and tactics.

4. Crest Seize – A final tactical challenge. One player becomes the Bearer; the rest defend against illusion, stealth, and relentless pursuit.

Clara's breath quickened. This wasn't just sport. It was history—living and breathing around them.

Sadie elbowed her lightly. "Ready to forget the end of the world for one day?"

Clara smiled. "More than ready."

The crowd roared. Flags lifted. And the Gathering of Houses surged into motion.

****

By the time the morning mist had burned away, Calendor Keep had transformed.

Veilborne

Students gathered on the lower terraces and meadow paths in waves of colour. Robes were exchanged for tunics, sashes, or sleeveless training gear, each House's colours worn boldly. Face paint and enchanted ribbons shimmered in the breeze. Banners lined the procession routes.

And beyond the eastern gates, across the river bend—the Glade of Concord had become a world of its own.

The wide clearing had been expanded by magic and careful landscaping. Rows of bright pavilions ringed the space: food stalls offering delicacies from each House's traditions, tents where students and families gathered, and elevated viewing platforms woven from living wood and silvered rope bridges. Clockwork lanterns, shaped like birds and beasts, hovered in the air, ready for the evening procession.

At the heart of the Glade stood a great open arena, marked by four towering plinths, each displaying a House crest in shifting light:

Starfire. Dawnspire. Frostmere. Stonehearth.

****

Clara paused at the threshold, Sadie and Jasper flanking her.

"Whoa," Jasper breathed. "They really went all out."

Sadie grinned, eyes sweeping the festive chaos. "First Trials in years. And after what this school's been through? I think they needed to."

Clara couldn't disagree.

Crowds were already assembling—students, professors, and beyond. Parents and family members filed into the guest pavilions. Jasper's mother and father were easy to spot, waving him over with wide smiles. His mother wore a deep blue cloak edged in brass, and his father had a Starfire medallion pinned to his lapel.

Jasper waved back but didn't approach yet.

Clara's gaze lingered. There were so many family groups scattered across the Glade—parents, siblings, even grandparents. Little clusters of excited conversation and reunion.

The ache returned, sharp and hollow.

No family.

But before the weight could settle, Sadie's arm hooked around her shoulders—no words needed this time.

Jasper joined them, giving Clara a sideways grin. "Come on. Starfire's banner won't raise itself."

Clara smiled, brushing the emotion away before it could grow too heavy. They didn't need to say it. She already knew where she belonged.

****

The Opening Ceremony

The Concordia Trials began as the midday bells rang out—twelve resonant tones that echoed across the Glade of Concord and out towards the riverbanks.

The clearing, once just a wild hollow embraced by forest, had become a grand amphitheatre of colour and sound. The four House banners rippled high above the assembly: Starfire's crimson and brass, Dawnspire's sapphire and silver, Stonehearth's deep green and copper, and Frostmere's midnight blue trimmed in white.

Below them, stands had been raised for spectators, woven with enchanted vines and gently glowing lanterns. Students, families, and honoured guests gathered in clusters beneath brilliant canopies, their voices threading together in waves of anticipation.

As the crowd quietened, a single figure stepped forward.

Master Vaelryn.

They stood at the central dais, the runes at their feet pulsing softly beneath the clear sky. Robes the colour of aged parchment and deep ironstone moved gently in the breeze. When they spoke, no amplification was needed—the air itself seemed to carry their voice.

"This is not merely a contest," Vaelryn declared.

"It is a tradition. A covenant. While we stand as four banners, we defend one realm.

We celebrate the strengths that set us apart—and the unity that holds us together.

Legacy is not forged alone. It is forged in concord."

A hush. Then the sound of applause built, wave after wave, until the whole Glade rang with approval.

At Vaelryn's signal, silver horns sounded from each of the four House towers, and enchantments swept the sky. Ribbons of light burst upward, weaving into shapes that drew gasps from the crowd—phoenixes, hounds, storm dragons, and winged stags racing one another above the trees before dissolving into starlit motes.

The Gathering of Houses had begun.

****

The Concordia Trials Roster

A large, rune-lit board unfolded beside the dais, silver script blooming as the crowd gathered closer:

1. Arcane Assemblage (Creativity & Craftsmanship)
2. → Teams craft an enchanted device to navigate a shifting maze.
3. Sky Relay (Speed & Agility)
4. → An aerial race over rivers and forest canopy, testing precision and teamwork.
5. Spellweave Confrontation (Dueling & Adaptability)
6. → Team duels across adaptive terrain, judged by spell mastery and tactics.

7. Crest Seize (Protection & Strategy)
8. → A final challenge. One player becomes the Bearer; the rest defend against illusion, stealth, and pursuit.

****

Trial One: Arcane Assemblage

The Starfire team gathered at the maze staging grounds, nerves high but spirits steady. Jasper quickly took the lead, sketching out a design based on his earlier work rebuilding Percival.

"Not his size—but his wheel-leg balance system," he explained, eyes bright. "This one won't fall apart."

In just under forty-five minutes, they constructed a swift, four-wheeled device enchanted for agility and glyph recognition. As the maze's shifting walls tested every design, Starfire's construct navigated with precision—outsmarting heavier and faster models alike.

Cheers erupted as their machine crossed the finish line first. For the first time in over a decade, Starfire claimed victory in Assemblage.

Sadie whooped, Jasper beamed, and even the usually reserved Elias grinned.

"That's one down."

****

Trial Two: The Sky Relay

By mid-afternoon, the Glade's aerial course had been raised above the river bend. Levitating platforms, enchanted rope bridges, and glowing waypoint rings floated between the trees.

Sadie captained Starfire's flight team, with Clara and Jasper in support. The course was brutal—requiring tight turns, sudden dives, and bursts of speed through magical currents.

Dawnspire took an early lead, but Starfire's teamwork proved unmatched. A daring mid-race manoeuvre by Sadie reclaimed the advantage. They crossed the final ring a breath ahead of Frostmere, securing second place overall behind Stonehearth.

"Not a win," Jasper said between deep breaths, "but no one fell into the river. I'll call that a success."

****

Trial Three: Spellweave Confrontation

The duelling grounds shimmered with adaptive terrain as the Spellweave teams assembled. Starfire's group faced off against Frostmere and Dawnspire in rotating bouts.

Clara's training in defensive casting came to the fore, while Sadie used clever illusions to disrupt opponents. Jasper's knack for counters and shields held their lines firm.

Though Dawnspire ultimately edged them out by a single victory, Starfire's adaptability earned high praise from the judges.

"Third place," Sadie sighed afterwards, "but no injuries and no humiliations." She grinned. "Which, at this point, feels like a win."

Students poured from the stands into the wide avenues where food stalls and family tents clustered beneath bright pennants.

The smell of fresh bread, spiced meats, and candied fruits filled the air. Copper kettles steamed beside vendor carts, pouring out fragrant herbal teas and sugared elixirs. The scents mingled with woodsmoke and the crisp, green edge of the river breeze.

The Glade felt alive.

Jasper was the first to break away, scanning the rows of tents like a hawk spotting prey. "Right. Victory feast."

Sadie laughed. "You just ate before the Trials."

"That was fuel. This is celebration."

Clara smiled, her heart still racing. "Alright. But nothing that makes us sick before the next event."

They wove through the vendor lanes, passing students from all four Houses. Starfire and Frostmere teams were congratulating each other. Stonehearth's team was already joking about their miscalculated shifting frame. Even Dawnspire's normally aloof group seemed less frosty—though Lira Calix gave Clara a narrow-eyed *we'll get you next time* look as they passed.

The Vendors and the Families

Jasper led them straight to a stall shaded by the Starfire banner. The canopy was deep crimson trimmed with brass, and beneath it, platters of Gilded-style pastries and savoury tarts gleamed.

The vendor—a short, round man with gears tattooed along his jaw—beamed. "Starfire's first Assemblage win in twelve years. First three are on the house."

Clara picked a sunberry tart. Sadie grabbed a peppered cheese roll. Jasper… chose both.

They leaned against a nearby table, the tension of the morning easing for the first time.

"See?" Jasper said between bites. "This is the true glory of the Trials."

Clara's gaze swept across the crowd again. Families had gathered at long tables beneath the trees—mothers, fathers, younger siblings with house-coloured ribbons in their hair.

Near the Frostmere tent, she spotted a boy from their History class laughing as his grandfather conjured harmless blue snowflakes to entertain a cluster of little cousins.

At Stonehearth's pavilion, students and parents alike shared platters of herb-laced bread, while a small clockwork badger—clearly a family heirloom—wandered between the tables.

The sights and sounds blurred for a moment. She could almost forget the weight of rifts, relics, and what lay beyond the Trials.

Almost.

And beyond them…

Veilborne

Varek Draven.

He stood beneath Dawnspire's deep blue pennant, sharp uniform immaculate as ever. Beside him stood Lady Selvara Draven—his mother. Silver-streaked dark hair coiled in intricate braids. A face carved in patience and power.

Her gaze swept the grounds like a predator taking measure of the herd.

Clara felt the chill before she even noticed it consciously. Selvara's eyes paused on her—just briefly—but the look was enough.

Not judgment. Not disdain.

Calculation.

Sadie noticed the shift in Clara's posture immediately. "Don't worry about her," she murmured. "Let her watch. She can't touch us today."

Clara nodded, though the weight in her chest didn't fully ease.

Then a warm, familiar voice cut through the moment.

"There you are!"

Jasper's parents emerged from the crowd. His father—tall, broad-shouldered, with grease-smudged hands even in his formal tunic. His mother—bright-eyed, wearing a shawl in Starfire colours and already holding out her arms.

"You three," she said, gathering them in. "Our champions."

Clara and Sadie barely had time to react before they were both swept into the hug alongside Jasper.

"You fought like legends," his father added, clapping Jasper's shoulder. "Your invention work paid off. I told you it would."

Jasper grinned. "You also told me it would fall apart in the first turn."

"I said it *might*. Builds character."

When they pulled back, Jasper's mother rested a hand briefly on Clara's shoulder, then Sadie's.

"You were brilliant out there. And I expect no less in the next Trial."

Clara swallowed hard, smiling despite herself.

Sadie cleared her throat and pretended to brush lint off her sleeve, though her eyes were still shining.

"We'll save seats for the evening's Procession," Jasper's mother continued. "And there's plenty of food if you're still hungry after the next Trials."

Jasper's father leaned in conspiratorially. "And don't let Dawnspire steal the final Trial. They tried to bribe the judges once. We never proved it—but I *know*." His grin was wicked.

A resonant chime, lifted by magic, rolled across the Glade.

"Competitors for Crest Seize—assemble for briefing!"

Sadie groaned softly. "Knew that peace was too good to last."

Clara looked towards the forest clearing, where the final arena was already being prepared. Magical wards glimmered at the perimeter. Teams gathered. Banners rippled.

Jasper tossed the last bite of his tart into his mouth. "Victory or valiant disaster—we're ready."

Clara took a slow breath. The day had been full of joy, teamwork, and family. But it wasn't over. Not yet.

She squared her shoulders. "Let's go."

The late afternoon sun gilded the Glade of Concord in molten light. Shadows stretched long beneath the towering House banners, which hung still in the heavy, expectant air.

The field had transformed since the morning Trials. No longer an arena of clever devices or swift races—now it resembled a battleground.

A sprawling maze of stone walls and shimmering barriers had been conjured across the open meadow. At the far end stood a raised plinth bearing the Trials' sigil, marking the finish.

Between here and there, the Bearer would have to survive.

Veilborne

Master Vaelryn stood alone at the central dais. The gathering quieted, thousands of eyes turning towards the figure in pale ironstone robes.

"The final Trial," Vaelryn intoned, their voice as deep as the river's own current, "tests more than magic. More than strength. It tests loyalty. Resolve. And the willingness to shield what cannot shield itself."

A ripple passed through the crowd.

"The four Houses will field their champions. At the Trial's commencement, one among them will be chosen as the Bearer. That House shall defend. The rest will become the hunters."

As the names of each House's team were called, cheers and whistles erupted from the pavilions. Clara stood alongside her team, still uncertain who their chosen Bearer would be.

Vaelryn lifted a hand. "The Bearer has been chosen."

A brief pause. A breath held by hundreds.

"Clara Holloway."

A ripple spread through the crowd like wind across tall grass.

"House Starfire will stand as her protectors. The other Houses shall be the hunters."

Clara blinked, stunned. "Wait. What?"

Sadie let out a whoop, grabbing Clara's hands and practically bouncing on her heels. "Clara—you've just been handed the biggest spotlight in the Trials! Do you know how many people would give anything to be named Bearer?" Her grin was wide, eyes shining. "You're not just playing. You *are* the prize."

Jasper gave a wide, lopsided grin. "Look at you. Making a name for yourself." He nudged her playfully. "Half the field's probably hoping to get on your good side now."

Clara frowned. "My good side?"

Sadie laughed. "Because you're the Bearer! Everyone's going to be watching you. And not just today." She waggled her eyebrows. "Might want to start working on a signature wave."

Clara opened her mouth to argue, but the roster board shimmered again, updating for the Trial. She scanned it quickly—then froze.

"Wait. You're not listed."

Sadie and Jasper followed her gaze. Their names were absent from Starfire's *Crest Seize* lineup.

Sadie's smile softened but didn't falter. "We can't fight beside you this time. I guess that's the point of this Trial."

Jasper shrugged, though there was a flicker of disappointment in his eyes. "Spectators this round. But we'll be the loudest ones out there."

Clara's stomach tightened. She felt suddenly small beneath the weight of so many watching eyes. And yet... strangely steady.

Vaelryn raised a hand, voice carrying once more. "Champions, take your places."

****

Clara was escorted to a central starting ring etched with protective glyphs. The silver Crest token—a circular medallion glowing with faint light—was fastened to a sash across her chest.

All four Houses positioned their teams at different entry points around the maze. She counted them. Fifteen competitors in total—her guardians, and her hunters.

Above the maze, translucent viewing platforms floated, where spectators gathered in tense silence. Jasper and Sadie were there, faces taut with worry.

A horn sounded.

The barriers dropped.

The Trial began.

Veilborne

****

Starfire's defenders moved swiftly, forming a protective arc around Clara. The maze walls loomed high—some stone, others flickering illusions masking danger.

For the first ten minutes, it unfolded like a deadly game of chess. Teams clashed in swift skirmishes, alliances shifting as quickly as the maze itself. Clara's defenders warded off Frostmere's swift-strike team but lost two in the process.

Through it all, Clara focused on keeping pace, watching the paths ahead, searching for safe passage.

She spotted Varek only once in those early minutes—moving like a shadow between the gaps of battle. Calculated. Patient.

He wasn't just fighting. He was hunting.

****

By the time they reached the maze's final quarter, only four of Clara's defenders remained.

Stonehearth and Frostmere's teams had all but fallen or withdrawn. Dawnspire alone retained strength, their warriors moving with ruthless efficiency.

Except they weren't attacking only Clara's protectors.

Varek had begun striking down members of the other teams as well—removing anyone who might slow his advance or block his prize.

Clara watched, breath ragged, as he felled a Frostmere defender with a stunning curse, then another from Stonehearth with a whip-fast gesture of his staff.

Even some in the crowd had begun to murmur uneasily.

****

The final turning point came swiftly.

Two of Clara's defenders broke formation, chasing a decoy illusion conjured by Dawnspire. In seconds, they vanished into a side corridor—sealed by shifting walls before they could return.

Only one remained at her side now.

A senior Starfire student named Corric. Broad-shouldered. Reliable.

They advanced cautiously down a narrow lane flanked by towering hedges and rune-laced stone. The finish arch shimmered ahead.

But the moment Clara set foot into the corridor, a trap triggered.

A surge of magic blasted the path behind them—collapsing the walls and cutting off all retreat.

Corric turned, raising a shield sigil. But from the shadows, Varek struck. Not with magic. With force.

A silent blow to the back of Corric's neck. The older student crumpled without a sound.

Clara staggered back, pulse hammering.

Varek emerged from the gloom.

No illusions now. No polite restraint.

Just raw, predatory focus.

****

This section of the maze was hidden from the viewing platforms—sealed by high walls and layered illusion screens.

No one could see.

Clara's breath caught. "The Trial forbids harm outside the bounds of the Crest challenge. You can't—"

"I can," Varek said calmly. "And I will."

He stepped closer, shadows curling beneath his boots where the warding glyphs failed to reach.

Veilborne

"You think you've won something here, Holloway?" His voice was low but sharp as a blade. "Stumbling into glory. Earning titles you never deserved. Disobedient. Reckless. Disrespectful."

Clara's breath hitched.

"This school coddles you," Varek continued, "as if you're some rare flower instead of what you are. A disgusting Veilborne stray who doesn't belong in our world. You've defied tradition. Mocked your betters." His eyes flashed. "And in the hall, you dared to speak to me— me—as though we were equals. As though filth can stand beside legacy."

Clara opened her mouth, but no sound came.

"You've poisoned others with that illusion too," he hissed. "Even students of my own House whisper your name with praise. That ends now."

Before she could react, he struck.

Not with a curse.

Not with a hex.

With the back of his hand.

The blow snapped across her cheekbone, sending her sprawling to the stone floor. The Crest sash dug sharply into her ribs. Cold grit bit at her palms.

The world spun.

Pain blossomed across her cheek and temple in a hot, blooming haze. Her lip split against her teeth, the sharp taste of blood filling her mouth. For a breath, all she could hear was the pounding in her ears.

Then—a low, steady pulse.

Her locket flared once, deep and slow. Like a heartbeat.

Marrowmere.

The faces of the bullies from the orphanage surged in her mind. The cold nights. The jeering voices. The days when she had hidden beneath stairs or wrapped herself in threadbare blankets, wishing for the strength to fight back.

Back then, she had been alone.

But not now.

Not here.

Thump. Thump.

In time with her heart.

Thump. Thump.

As Clara struggled to rise, vision swimming, Varek closed in—hand raised for another blow.

"You've disrespected me for the last time, Holloway," he hissed. "You need to know your place."

But before his strike could fall, a blur slammed into him.

Renhold.

The taller boy tackled Varek sideways, driving him back with a force that surprised even Clara. They crashed against the warded arena wall, the impact sending a pulse of light through the glyph work.

"Enough!" Renhold growled, pinning Varek's arm. "This isn't the Trial. This is assault."

Varek twisted furiously. "She's not a champion—she's a stain on our history! A filthy Veilborne upstart stealing glory she doesn't deserve!"

A second figure stepped between them and Clara. Lira Calix. Her expression was stone.

"Not like this. We were meant to test her. Outwit her. Prove Dawnspire's strength." She glared at Varek. "But this? This is cowardice."

Varek tried to shake Renhold off, but Lira didn't flinch. She planted herself between him and Clara like a shield.

Veilborne

"Stand down, Draven. Or it won't just be the judges you'll answer to."

And then came a third voice—cooler, sharper.

"Keep flailing, Varek, and I might assume you've lost your edge completely."

Neris Emmer stepped in beside Lira, her braid streaked with silver from enchantment ash, her staff angled low and ready. Her eyes never left Varek.

"You talk of history," she said evenly, "but history will remember who defended honor, not who tried to shatter it from behind."

Clara, dazed and breathless, felt the weight of their words more than the sting of the blow.

For the first time in years, it wasn't just her standing up to a bully.

Neris turned to her, and the fierce glint in her expression softened. She knelt and reached out a hand.

"Easy now. You're alright. Let's get you up."

Clara took it, fingers trembling slightly as Neris helped her to her feet with quiet strength.

"You've got more fight in you than he ever will," Neris said, low enough only Clara could hear. "Don't forget that."

Lira nodded once, approving. "Go. You've more than earned this. We'll take care of him."

Clara's lip was split. Her vision swam. But she nodded.

As she steadied herself toward the exit arch, the locket pulsed again. Thump. Thump. Just steady beats, in line with her own. Grounding her.

She touched the warm metal through her sash, feeling its quiet beat beneath her palm—and wondered why it hadn't saved her this time.

It had once. Back at Morrowmere, when she was small, alone, and cornered by cruelty. The locket had answered then. It had struck back. Protected her.

But not today.

This wasn't helplessness. This was a Trial—a crucible meant to forge more than just strength.

And maybe that was the point.

The Trial wasn't about standing alone. It was about learning when to let others stand with you.

Corric. Lira. Renhold. Neris. Even strangers had chosen to protect her.

The locket hadn't abandoned her.

It was teaching her. Still teaching.

Sometimes, power was knowing when not to fight alone.

The thought steadied her more than any magic could.

She took a breath, squared her shoulders, and stepped toward the arch—not defeated, but changed.

The final corridor unfolded before her—straight and empty. The finish crest shimmered like a promise.

Behind her, she heard the scuffle of boots.

Varek snarled through clenched teeth, "This isn't over."

Clara paused. Turned.

Varek was still struggling against Renhold, who held him firm. Lira stood between them and the rest of the field, her face grim with disgust.

Clara wiped the blood from her lip, gaze steady.

"It never is," she whispered. "Not with you."

Then she turned and walked toward the finish.

****

Veilborne

As Clara crossed the line, the Crest flared beneath her feet. A surge of silver light rippled outward—sweeping across the Glade like a tide set free.

Above, crimson and brass exploded across the sky. Starfire's colours took the shape of a soaring phoenix. Trails of golden light rained down like falling stars.

The bell tower rang, deep and triumphant.

The crowd erupted. Cheers thundered from every direction, shaking the air. Starfire students leapt to their feet. Parents and Auricals rose, applauding with pride. Jasper's mother wiped tears from her eyes. His father bellowed a cheer that echoed across the Glade.

Clara stood in the heart of the light, breathless. Not as prey. Not as a pawn. As a champion.

But then—

The celebration faltered.

Voices shifted from triumph to unease. Murmurs rippled through the stands.

"Where are her defenders?"

"Why is she alone?"

"Why didn't we see the final minutes?"

"Why is she bleeding?"

Students leaned forward. Parents exchanged uneasy glances. Even the Aurical Council began whispering.

Beyond the glowing crest, the maze was already dissolving—but the truth of what had happened inside remained hidden.

Clara lifted her chin. Let them wonder. Let them talk.

She had won. But more than that—

She had understood.

The last of the maze faded with a shimmering sigh. Tall hedgerows melted into silver mist.

And there—

Varek stood, still held in Renhold's grasp. Lira stood beside them, arms folded, her expression unreadable but severe. Corric hovered nearby, jaw tight, speaking low and sharp.

The crowd gasped.

Spectators fell silent, eyes flicking between Clara and the disgraced Dawnspire heir.

As the mist fully cleared, the four students seemed to realise they were now in full view. Renhold released Varek's arm. Lira stepped back, unapologetic. Corric crossed his arms, expression set and cold.

For a long moment, no one moved.

Then Lady Selvara Draven stood in the dignitaries' terrace, her silver-streaked hair catching the light. For the first time in Clara's memory, her expression cracked. Shock flickered across her features—quickly masked, but not before hundreds saw it.

Moments later, Eldric Ducart descended the steps from the Aurical dais, his cloak sweeping behind him. He strode across the field, eyes like flint.

"What happened in that maze?" His voice cut through the silence—low, but unmistakable.

No one answered. Not yet.

But the murmurs resumed. No longer confusion.

Judgement.

Clara barely heard them. Jasper and Sadie had already vaulted the rail, rushing to her. Jasper steadied her, hands firm on her shoulders, while Sadie pulled her into a tight embrace.

Veilborne

"You did it!" Sadie gasped—but the joy quickly gave way to concern. She stepped back, scanning Clara's bruised face. "Wait—you're bleeding. What happened?"

"I'll be fine," Clara murmured, though her cheek ached and her lip still throbbed in the cool air.

Above them, Master Vaelryn raised a hand. The crowd fell still, as if the air itself were holding its breath.

"The Bearer has prevailed. Starfire claims Crest Seize."

A second wave of applause rolled across the Glade, crashing like thunder against the hills.

Clara's heart still pounded—but it wasn't fear now. It was resolve. Strength. She stood between Jasper and Sadie, their hands still on her arms, as if refusing to let her go.

Vaelryn's voice rang out again, calm and firm.

"This concludes the Concordia Trials. Let all Houses stand in unity. Competitors and families—rest now. The evening festivities shall begin at moonrise."

The final cheer rose—louder, brighter than the one that had marked the Trials' beginning.

Clara felt Sadie's hand squeeze hers before letting go. "You did it. We did it."

Jasper grinned. "And I don't care what anyone says. You made your name today."

As the trio turned towards the exit, more students came forward—faces from every House.

First were Corric and Lira, their expressions warm and unguarded.

"Well done," Corric said simply.

Then others followed—Frostmere's relay captain, Stonehearth's duel tactician, even younger students who'd watched the Trial with wide eyes.

Mark Peters

They gathered around Clara, offering words of praise, congratulations—and, from some, quiet relief.

For the first time, she wasn't just the Veilborne.

She wasn't the mystery. She wasn't the outsider.

She was the Bearer.

The girl who had stood her ground.

And this time—she hadn't stood alone.

Chapter 20
Lanterns for the Lost

"…I hear what you're saying, but I'm telling you now. I'm gonna kill him myself," Sadie muttered, arms folded tight across her chest as they crossed the stone bridge toward the west terrace.

Clara didn't answer straight away. She was too busy trying not to smile, despite the seriousness of the words. Sadie's glare could've cracked glass, but her loyalty had never wavered.

"Let's not make murder our first solution," Jasper said dryly, trailing just behind. "Second or third, maybe. Besides—I heard the Aurical Council themselves have gotten involved. It's turned into a political nightmare for Varek's mother."

Sadie snorted. "Good."

"The Council's investigating what happened in the maze. Properly," Jasper added, lowering his voice. "Rumour is, Lady Selvara's been summoned twice already. And Varek? No one's seen him since the Trials ended."

"Good," Sadie repeated, sharper this time. "He *should* be hiding."

Clara walked in silence between them. She could still feel the echo of the locket's last pulse from the Trial, like a memory tucked just beneath her ribs. Varek's words—the anger, the disdain—no longer felt as heavy. Not because they'd faded. But because she'd survived them. Outgrown them.

Ahead, the wide river terrace was already glowing with soft, golden light. Dozens of lanterns sat on the water's edge, carefully balanced atop broad lily leaves. Their glass sides shimmered with intricate patterns—some etched with House crests, others with protective runes or family sigils. The candles inside flickered gently, casting ripples of light across the surface of the water.

Above the river, the mist curled in silver threads beneath a deepening sky. High overhead, ribbons of pale green and violet undulated slowly across the heavens—ethereal veils of colour that shifted like silk drawn through water. At times, the bands rippled into silver-white, casting soft waves of light down onto the river. Where the colours touched the clouds, they shimmered faintly, as though delicate enchantments had been woven into the very fabric of the night.

Sadie followed Clara's gaze upward. "They only ever appear on this night," she murmured. "As if the realm itself mourns alongside us. Like it knows."

The veils continued to ripple—silent, slow, and solemn—as though the sky itself stood in vigil.

As they approached the main gathering lawn, a familiar voice called out.

"Clara!"

She turned to see Renley—tall, still looking a little nervous even now—and beside him, Lira, Caz, and Neris. The four had clearly come straight from their House gatherings, scarves and ribbons in place, but their faces were open and warm.

"That was incredible," Renley said, his words tumbling over each other. "The way you held your ground in Crest Seize—none of us could believe it."

"You made House Starfire proud," Lira added, giving Clara's shoulder a gentle nudge.

"And not just Starfire," Caz grinned. "Even some of the Stoneheart students cheered for you."

Neris gave a sharp nod, arms crossed but eyes warm. "You earned every breath of that win. Varek looked like he wanted the ground to swallow him." She smirked. "Shame it didn't."

Behind them, a few others gathered—faces Clara recognized from classes and the common areas. For months, they'd hovered at the edges. Peers, but not yet friends. Now, the lines felt different. Softer.

Veilborne

More students offered congratulations as they passed. Frostmere's Sky Relay captain raised a hand in salute. Two of the first-years Clara had helped with glyph-channeling control gave her shy smiles. Even a pair of Dawnspire students offered polite nods before moving on.

The crowd's mood was solemn but gentle. The rivalries of the Trials had quieted, replaced by the shared purpose of the evening ahead.

Clara felt the comfort of it—not just the lantern light gathering around them, but the quiet understanding that they'd faced something together. That the divides between Houses weren't so sharp tonight.

Sadie, ever the watchful one, noticed too. "Your fan club's getting bold," she teased under her breath.

"Better than being glared at," Clara replied, smiling.

Jasper leaned over. "I'm just glad someone else will be dodging the professors' questions for once. You've officially become the school's most interesting mystery."

Clara laughed softly, shaking her head. She wasn't sure she liked being a mystery. But for now… the attention didn't feel like a weight.

It felt like *belonging*.

And for a brief, fragile moment, she let herself remember how it had felt in Morrowmere—cold nights wrapped in a threadbare blanket, the hush of the orphanage halls after dark, always on the outside looking in. Back then, the idea of anyone noticing her—let alone choosing her—had seemed as distant as the moons.

Now, faces turned toward her not with indifference or pity.

But with *respect*.

She wasn't just surviving anymore.

She was part of something.

A chime sounded from the riverside—clear, soft, and resonant. The first signal that the procession would soon begin.

The crowd shifted, students moving toward the broad stone steps leading down to the water. The lanterns on the lily leaves pulsed faintly in response, their lights syncing as if the ceremony itself had stirred them awake.

"Come on," Jasper said, lowering his voice. "My parents have seats waiting on the family terrace."

Sadie nodded, her earlier fire softening into something quieter. "Right. Let's go."

The trio moved with the gathering crowd, the lantern light reflecting softly in their eyes as they headed toward the upper terraces, where Jasper's family stood waiting.

****

The family terrace offered a clear view over the river, the gathering lawns, and the long, mist-veiled arches beyond. Jasper's parents had already staked out a spot near the balustrade, where the wide stone railing curved outward like a gentle amphitheatre. Clusters of other families filled the terraces around them—Auricals in formal robes, traders in well-worn leathers, and mages in deep blue cloaks lined with silver thread.

Jasper's mother waved them over at once. "There you are. We thought you might be off signing autographs."

Jasper grinned. "Don't give Sadie ideas."

His father clasped his shoulder with a warm squeeze. "One victory and fame's gone to your head."

Clara returned the woman's smile, then glanced out across the river. The lily-leaf lanterns still rested unlit upon the water, a silent flotilla waiting for dusk's final light to fade.

Above, the sky's ethereal veils—those soft green and violet bands—continued their slow, spectral dance. Light rippled like silk in water, casting gentle waves across the terrace stone and the river's surface.

Veilborne

The ribbons of colour bent low near the horizon, as though the realm itself leaned close to bear witness.

"It's beautiful," Clara whispered.

"It's always beautiful this night," Jasper's mother replied, following her gaze. "But there are more lanterns this year than I can ever remember."

Her voice softened. "Too many lost."

A hush settled over their little circle as the sun finally sank beyond the treetops. Shadows deepened across the water. Torches flared along the riverbanks, casting warm light into the approaching dusk.

Then, the chime sounded again—low and resonant.

At the riverside dais, Master Vaelryn stepped forward. Her parchment-grey robes moved like quiet waves in the evening breeze. The murmurs of the crowd faded as she raised one hand for silence.

"Students. Families. Auricals. People of Eryndor."

Vaelryn's voice was clear and calm, carrying easily over the gathering.

"We stand together tonight, not only in remembrance, but in celebration. The Concordia Trials, after years of absence, have returned stronger than ever."

A ripple of quiet applause stirred through the crowd.

"Our Houses met in the field of tradition and tested not only skill, but ingenuity, courage, and unity. To all competitors—you have honoured the legacy of those who came before you."

Vaelryn paused—then turned slightly toward the terrace.

"And to House Starfire… for claiming victory overall, and to Clara Holloway, this year's Bearer—you have done more than win. You have shown us resilience. Growth. And that even the newest among us may rise to the challenges of both past and present."

A louder wave of applause followed this time, punctuated by a few cheers from the lower terraces.

Clara felt her cheeks warm. She dipped her head slightly, trying to keep the attention from feeling overwhelming.

Sadie leaned close, stifling a grin. "Notice who didn't get mentioned?"

Jasper sniggered, keeping his voice just low enough not to carry. "Someone's in trouble."

Sadie's grin grew wide and sharp. "Good."

Vaelryn lifted her hand again, and the terrace quietened.

"But tonight is not only for champions."

Her gaze swept the crowd.

"Tonight, we honour those we've lost. And those whose names may have faded from history—but not from memory. For even as we celebrate what we have built, we must remember what was sacrificed along the way."

A breeze stirred—gentle and cool. The lily-leaf lanterns rippled softly where they waited near the water's edge.

"The Realm remembers," Vaelryn said quietly. "And so do we."

She inclined her head toward the line of Auricals gathered by the riverbank.

One by one, the Auricals touched the lanterns with delicate gestures—soft, guiding sparks of magic blooming from their fingertips. The candles inside the paper casings flickered to life, golden flames weaving into silver and blue at the edges.

The lanterns floated slowly from the reeds, drifting into the open current.

But they didn't stay on the water.

As each reached the centre of the river, the air shimmered. Enchantments stirred. The lanterns lifted—slowly, gracefully—rising from the water's surface in waves. First a few, then a dozen, then hundreds, ascending toward the sky, where the realm's luminous veils continued their silent dance.

Veilborne

The reflection of their light painted the river and terraces in warm, golden hues.

Families leaned together, heads bowed. Some whispered names as the lanterns rose. Some stood in silence.

Clara, Jasper, and Sadie stood in silence for a long moment, each lost in their own thoughts.

Jasper's mother gently pressed a folded piece of parchment into his hand. "Go on, then. You should light yours."

Sadie had already retrieved a small, neatly folded slip from her cloak. She didn't say anything, but her expression softened as she opened it.

Clara hesitated. Her fingers brushed the locket beneath her collar, its weight familiar and grounding.

Not just a relic. A memory.

Jasper leaned closer, his voice low. "There's paper up front—for anyone who didn't bring their own."

Clara gave a small nod and crossed to a nearby Aurical tending one of the lantern stations. They handed her a small parchment slip and a sharpened stylus. The page felt cool beneath her fingers.

She wrote slowly:

For Miss Wren.

For those who crossed the Veil and were lost.

For my parents—whoever they were. You are not forgotten.

When she returned, Sadie and Jasper had each chosen a lantern. The globes rested in carved wooden cradles shaped like lily petals, each base marked with small anchor glyphs. Their soft glow reflected on the dark river below.

Sadie's message was folded neatly beneath the glass. She didn't speak of it. She didn't need to.

Jasper held his lantern gently in both hands. "For my uncle. He always said I'd either make something of myself or blow up half the Keep trying." He smiled, faint. "I reckon he'd be proud either way."

Clara smiled back, though her throat tightened.

Together, they stepped forward, joining the slow-moving line at the water's edge.

One by one, they placed their lanterns into the river. The current carried them gently toward the centre, where others drifted in quiet procession. As each lantern reached the open flow, the air shimmered—the enchantments stirred once more.

Clara's lantern rose.

She tilted her head back, watching it lift. The flame inside glowed golden at first, then deepened into silver and blue as it joined the hundreds already ascending into the night.

Jasper's followed. Then Sadie's.

Three lights rising in a tide of remembrance.

Above them, the realm's luminous veils folded and unfolded like vast, silent wings.

Sadie stepped closer to Clara and Jasper. The three stood together, still and quiet, watching until the last of the lanterns floated free of the river and became part of the constellation above.

For once, the shadows felt far away. The crowd remained hushed, bound together in shared reverence.

And for a moment longer, the night seemed to hold its breath.

As the final lanterns disappeared into the sky, murmurs slowly returned. Quiet voices shared names, memories, and farewells. Robes rustled as families began to gather their things.

But Clara stood still, her gaze skyward.

The realm's veils shimmered on, and the lanterns drifted into their light until it was impossible to tell where candle ended and stars began.

Veilborne

Jasper and Sadie stayed close beside her. The warmth of the crowd lingered like a soft shield against the wider world.

Then, quietly, Sadie's breath caught.

Clara turned. "What is it?"

Sadie didn't answer straight away. Her eyes weren't on the sky—they were fixed on the river's far side, where lantern light faded into shadows.

"I thought…" Sadie began, then shook her head. "Never mind."

Clara followed her gaze. Beyond the southern terrace, the trees stood silent. Shadows pooled beneath the old oaks. Nothing moved.

Jasper leaned in gently. "What did you see?"

"Nothing," Sadie said quickly. "Just the light playing tricks. It's nothing."

But Clara noticed the tension in her shoulders, the tight crease between her brows that hadn't been there a moment ago.

Across the river, the Aurical Council remained gathered in quiet conversation. Master Vaelryn's expression was unreadable, hands folded before her. Eldric Ducart stood nearby—but he wasn't watching the lanterns. His sharp gaze lingered on the same treeline Sadie had been watching.

Clara's pulse ticked up. Before she could speak, Jasper nudged her shoulder gently.

"Come on. We should head back before the whole crowd starts moving."

Clara hesitated, then nodded. She cast one last glance into the shadows Sadie had noticed.

Still nothing.

The three turned and walked back, following the slow ripple of the dispersing crowd. Above them, the lanterns shimmered like promises carried into the sky.

The riverside was emptying now. Families spoke in hushed tones as they gathered their cloaks and turned toward home. Jasper's parents hugged them goodnight and reminded them to visit for breakfast.

Their path to the dormitory twisted beneath swaying lanterns, the breeze cool against their faces.

Students they passed offered quiet greetings—some even murmured congratulations.

"Well done today, Holloway."

"Starfire's proud of you."

"Good bearing out there."

Clara smiled, awkward but grateful, nodding in return. More than once, Sadie smirked and nudged her whenever someone called her name.

"They're hoping some of your luck rubs off," Sadie whispered.

"Not luck," Jasper said with a grin. "Skill. And a little reckless bravery."

As they neared the dormitory tower, Jasper's tone shifted.

"Word's still going around about the Trials. Master Vaelryn didn't say Varek's name for a reason."

Sadie's grin sharpened. "Didn't go unnoticed. I heard the Council's still figuring out how to deal with what happened." She glanced back toward the now-quiet river. "Varek's mother can't shield him forever."

Clara nodded, though her thoughts had drifted—to the unity they'd found, the strangeness in the trees, and the weight of the day.

They paused at the dormitory steps. The world felt quieter here.

Clara took a breath. "One night of peace. We should take it."

"For once," Jasper agreed.

Sadie tilted her head to the sky. "Let's hope it lasts."

Veilborne

They stepped inside. The heavy wooden door closed behind them, muting the world outside.

Chapter 21
The Watcher

The corridor was nearly empty at this hour.

Most students had retired to their towers, and the Keep's usual chorus—laughter echoing up staircases, hurried footsteps between curfew bells—had softened to a hush. Only the occasional groan of settling stone or the distant flutter of owl wings broke the silence.

Sadie moved alone, arms folded against the chill, her boots tapping softly as she left the Lorehall. She'd stayed late to return a borrowed text on elemental tracing—nothing exciting, just something to keep her hands busy. Her thoughts were elsewhere anyway.

The air was cool and slightly damp, laced with the scent of old candles and ink. Her breath fogged faintly in front of her.

Halfway down the hall, she paused.

The torchlight ahead had flickered. Just a little.

She turned, expecting to see someone behind her.

But the corridor was empty.

She frowned, eyes drifting to the tall archway that led to one of the upper terraces—an old battlement now used mostly for quiet study or late-night views. Beyond it, the sky was a soft, endless grey, the stars veiled behind drifting mist.

And standing at the edge of the terrace...

was a figure.

Tall. Still. Cloaked in shadow.

Too far to see clearly, but unmistakably there. Facing her.

Sadie froze. Her heart gave a small, confused stutter.

The torches flickered again. Just for a breath.

She blinked.

Veilborne

The figure was gone.

The terrace was empty—only stone, wind, and distance remained.

Sadie exhaled slowly. Her hand had drifted to the wall beside her without realising, fingers pressing against the cold stone as if for balance.

That wasn't real. I'm just tired, she told herself.

But even as she walked away, the chill at the base of her neck didn't leave her.

****

The next day dawned grey and bright, with thin sunlight pouring through the windows like melted silver. The Keep stirred back to life—less haunted, more mundane. Laughter rose from the dining hall, and robes rustled between classes. Light returned. But some shadows don't lift with the dawn.

Clara, Sadie, and Jasper sat in a small garden alcove tucked between two stone corridors, finishing a late morning break between lectures. The garden was overgrown in a way that made it beautiful—ivy scaling one wall, violet moss clinging to the stone bench, and tiny golden blooms curling between flagstones.

"So," Jasper said, munching on something flaky from a linen-wrapped parcel, "does this look infected?"

He held out his wrist, where a faint magical burn—earned from a misfired rune exercise two days ago—still glimmered faintly.

"Only if you're secretly part cinderdrake," Sadie replied, managing half a smile.

Jasper blinked. "Part what now?"

Clara tilted her head. "What's a cinderdrake?"

Sadie grinned. "Small fire-dwelling lizards. Live in the ash groves near Frostmere. Mages used to keep them as familiars—until they realised they molt sparks during spellcasting."

"What you're saying," Jasper said solemnly, "is that I'm dangerous and rare."

"More like flammable and prone to drama," Sadie corrected.

Jasper feigned a wounded look. "Big words from someone who considers anything before noon a personal attack."

Sadie shrugged without missing a beat. "Hey, sleep is sacred."

Clara tried—and failed—to suppress a grin.

For a moment, it was almost normal.

Then Sadie stilled.

Her head turned slightly, eyes catching movement just beyond the garden wall. She leaned forward, blinking towards the open archway that looked out over the east lawn.

A shape.

A figure, standing just beyond the tree line, half-shrouded in the morning mist.

Unmoving.

Watching.

Her breath caught.

"Sadie?" Clara asked, already alert. "What is it?"

But when Sadie looked again—the figure was gone.

Not walked away. Not hidden.

Gone.

She sat back slowly, brushing her hair behind her ear.

"It's nothing," she said. "Just... I thought I saw someone."

Jasper raised an eyebrow. "Someone suspicious or someone tall, dark, and broody?"

Veilborne

"I've seen him twice now," she murmured. "Last night, and just now. He doesn't move. Just... watches. And then disappears."

Clara leaned forward, voice soft. "Are you sure it's not just—?"

She stopped herself. She didn't know what it was. And neither did Sadie.

"You believe me?" Sadie asked.

"Yes," Clara said immediately.

"We both do," Jasper added, quieter this time.

From the archway behind them, footsteps approached softly along the stone path.

So absorbed were they in their conversation, none of them noticed until the figures were nearly passing by.

Mistress Lirah Valen walked alongside another Aurical, speaking in hushed tones. Her pale robes caught the breeze, trailing silver-edged patterns across the mossy stones.

She didn't stop—but as they neared, her gaze shifted towards the trio. Just for a second. A glance meant to seem casual.

But her eyes lingered a moment too long.

Then she and her companion continued on, their voices fading into the quiet.

The trio said nothing.

But the silence that followed carried a tension they all felt.

****

Evening fell like a slow breath through stone.

The Keep's outer corridors were damp with mist, torches flickering in their sconces, their flames dancing more wildly than usual. A light drizzle whispered against the high windows, blurring the moon into a smudge behind shifting clouds.

The trio stood by a stretch of corridor that overlooked the north gardens. No other students nearby. Only the low murmur of voices, close and quiet.

"We're not going back for the relics yet?" Jasper asked again, arms crossed, shoulders tense.

"Not with the Council watching us like hawks," Clara replied. "There's always someone in the corridor. Lirah passed by our door twice this morning and didn't even pretend to be subtle."

"We'd barely make it past the stairs before someone started asking questions," Sadie muttered. "They *want* to catch us trying something."

Clara's eyes narrowed. "Then we wait."

Sadie's gaze drifted towards a tall, rain-streaked window just beyond them. It overlooked the north lawn, where trees moved gently in the wind.

She froze.

He was there.

The same figure. Standing still in the mist. Watching. Waiting.

Her breath caught in her throat.

"Sadie?" Clara asked, already sensing the shift in her expression.

Sadie stepped forward slowly, her boots tapping against the stone as she neared the window.

The man was closer this time. His face was shadowed beneath the hood, but his stance—broad shoulders, head slightly tilted—was unmistakable.

"That's him," she said quietly. "That's the person I saw in Glimmerden. The one I followed… before the Veil tear."

"You're sure?" Jasper asked, stepping beside her.

Sadie didn't look away from the window. Her voice was low but steady.

Veilborne

"He was there when the Veil tore open. Just for a second. I saw him before the creatures came. Same cloak. Same stare."

"And now he's here?" Clara whispered.

Sadie nodded—then blinked.

The figure was gone.

Like fog in moonlight.

She pressed her hand gently to the cold glass, her breath fogging against it.

"He keeps watching me," she murmured. "I thought he wasn't dangerous before, but... now I'm not so sure."

Clara stepped closer, voice soft. "You think he's here *for* you?"

Sadie hesitated. "Maybe. But maybe not. After everything we've stirred up..." She shook her head. "It might not just be me."

Jasper's jaw tightened. "Or maybe it's not just *one* watcher. Maybe we all have someone keeping tabs. And we've only noticed yours."

The thought settled heavily between them.

Sadie turned from the window, eyes wide—not panicked, but shaken.

"Whoever he is... whatever he wants... I don't think he's going to stop."

****

The dining hall flickered with low candlelight, the chandeliers enchanted to mirror the storm clouds outside. A soft rumble of thunder vibrated the floor now and then, but inside it was warm—buzzing with quiet conversation, clinks of cutlery, and the rich aroma of roasted root vegetables glazed with herb butter.

The long tables were lined with platters of honey-baked bread, braided rolls dusted with sweet fennel, and steaming bowls of spiced lentil stew. Golden root crisps crackled beside wheels of soft white cheese drizzled with wildflower honey. Copper kettles of mulled apple tea sent curls of fragrant steam into the air, mingling with the sharper scent of roasting meats and the sweet undertone of baked pumpkin pasties.

All around them, students gathered in loose, relaxed clusters—robes rumpled, sashes loosened after a long day of lectures and spellwork. The heavy rain beyond the high windows made the warmth and bustle inside feel like a protective cocoon.

The trio sat near the back, tucked at one of the smaller round tables by the hearth. Jasper had stolen a second roll and was dramatically shielding it with his napkin.

"You know it's not illegal to take seconds," Sadie said, half-smiling as she passed him the butter anyway.

"Tell that to the House of Flame," Jasper muttered. "They glare like I just stole the last one."

Sadie raised an eyebrow. "Was it the last one?"

Jasper shrugged, not meeting her eyes. "Possibly."

Clara laughed quietly and shook her head. Her shoulders had relaxed since the corridor—the weight of Sadie's haunting felt distant now, like the edges of a fading nightmare.

"I wish it could stay like this," Clara said suddenly, surprising even herself. "Just... quiet. Normal."

Sadie looked at her for a long moment, then nodded.

"So do I."

The hearth crackled beside them. For a few brief minutes, the storm, the politics, the secrets—all of it fell away. They were just three friends, halfway through too many questions, sharing food and stories like any other students.

Then Sadie shifted, a small crease forming at her brow.

"I think I'm going to head back," she said. "Bit of a headache. I'll meet you in the dorm."

"You sure?" Clara asked.

Veilborne

Sadie nodded and stood, brushing crumbs from her lap.

"Yeah. Just tired."

Clara watched her go, the firelight catching briefly on her hair as she vanished into the hall beyond.

Jasper broke the silence.

"She's not okay, is she?"

"No. But we'll figure it out. We always do."

She didn't know then—

That it would be hours before they saw Sadie again.

And everything after that would change.

****

The rain had thickened by the time Clara and Jasper made their way back to the dormitory tower. The Keep's corridors had grown dim and echoing, lit only by low-hanging lanterns and the silver thread of lightning that flashed now and then through the tall windows.

Clara pushed open the door to their shared study space, already expecting to see Sadie curled in her usual spot with a book and a blanket.

But the room was empty.

The fire had burned low. Sadie's coat was missing. Her bed unslept in.

Only the faint scent of lavender tea lingered in the air.

"Sadie?" Clara called, stepping further in. "You okay?"

No reply.

Jasper frowned and moved through to the adjacent dorm room. Both beds untouched. No trace of her.

"She's not here," he said, voice tense now.

That pressure—subtle and growing—clamped tighter around Clara's chest.

Then she spotted it.

A single folded note, placed neatly on Sadie's pillow. Her name scrawled across the front.

Clara.

Her heart dropped.

She crossed the room, hands suddenly trembling, and unfolded the parchment.

The message inside was written in a sharp, uneven hand:

If you want your friend back,

bring the artefacts.

Frostmar Rise.

No signature. No threat. Just a demand.

Jasper read it over her shoulder.

He didn't speak. He didn't need to.

The locket beneath Clara's shirt began to warm—just slightly. As if it too sensed the shift.

Clara closed her eyes for a heartbeat.

When she opened them, they were hard with purpose.

"They've taken her," she breathed, fists clenching at her sides.

Chapter 22
The Exchange

The door clicked shut behind them, muffled by the sound of rain against the high windows.

Clara stood in the middle of the room, the note still clenched in her hand. The fire in the hearth had gone out. The quiet pressed in like a fog.

She didn't sit. She didn't speak. She just stared at the folded parchment, fingers shaking only slightly.

Jasper hovered a few feet away, watching her, waiting.

"They took her," Clara said again, her voice hoarse now.

Jasper nodded once. "Yeah. And they want the journal and the monocle."

She didn't answer. Her eyes drifted to the floorboards—the ones where they'd stashed the relics days ago, just in case. It felt like weeks ago now. A lifetime.

"We should tell someone," Jasper said, though even he didn't sound convinced. "Eldric. Or the Council. They'll know what to—"

"No," Clara cut in.

He blinked. "Clara—"

"We tell them, they'll lock it all down. Call in reinforcements, delay everything. And Sadie doesn't have time for them to talk about it."

She paced once, then stopped. Her boots scuffed softly on the stone.

"They'll want to take the artifacts, guard them, study them—like that's ever worked out before."

She didn't finish.

Jasper ran a hand through his hair, still wet from the walk back. "Then what are we doing?"

Clara looked at him. Not as the girl from the orphanage. Not as someone begging for answers.

But as someone choosing.

"We go. We take the journal. We take the monocle. We get her back. I am not losing her. If it was the other way around, she would do the same for me… for YOU!!"

The words dropped between them like iron.

For a moment, neither spoke.

Then Jasper said quietly, "You don't have to do this alone."

"I know," she replied. "But you don't have to come either."

Jasper gave a small, tired laugh. "You're really going to try that again?"

She almost smiled.

"Just offering."

"You should know by now," he said, already reaching for his satchel, "not coming was never an option."

The air in the dormitory felt suddenly heavier. They both knew what came next—and what risks they were taking just to prepare.

Without another word, they moved toward the door. Percival, who had been dozing near Jasper's bed, stirred at once. The little clockwork rat gave a soft, curious whirr and scuttled to Jasper's feet, head tilted.

Jasper crouched down briefly and gave the brass creature a gentle tap between the ears.

"Not this time, Percival. Stay here. Look after the place."

Percival clicked his gears softly, clearly displeased, but obeyed. His small, glowing eyes dimmed to a softer blue as he retreated toward Jasper's blanket nest.

Clara glanced back as Jasper straightened.

"He knows something's wrong."

Veilborne

Jasper nodded grimly. "And he's correct."

They slipped into the corridor. The dormitory door closed behind them with a quiet click.

The halls beyond felt different at night. Not just darker—but heavier, as though the Keep itself were keeping a secret.

They moved carefully, keeping to the lesser-used passages where the shadows pooled between lanterns. The hour was late enough that most students had retired, but scattered patrols of senior Auricals still made their rounds. Even at this hour, they could hear the occasional murmur of voices—or the softer tread of bootsteps on the higher landings.

At one junction, the glow of approaching lanternlight sent them pressing into the recess of an old alcove, where a dusty suit of ceremonial armour stood watch. The clinking steps passed—two Auricals in quiet conversation—unaware of the figures hidden just beyond the archway.

Jasper leaned close as the voices faded. "Maybe we're getting better at this."

Clara didn't answer. She wasn't sure if that was something to be proud of anymore.

They wound their way through the east wing, descending a narrow staircase where the walls grew damp and moss crept between the stone blocks. At last, they reached the old study room in the east tower—the place where they'd hidden the relics beneath the floorboards after the chamber collapse.

The door creaked softly as they slipped inside.

The space smelled faintly of old parchment and lingering enchantments. A single dusty window let in the pale wash of moonlight.

Jasper crouched beside the worn wooden floor. His fingers hesitated briefly at the seam, then worked the loose plank free with careful precision. The sound echoed louder than it should've in the stillness of the room. Clara stood behind him, arms folded tightly, her eyes never leaving the dark space beneath.

From inside, wrapped in a cloth the colour of soot, lay the two relics that could shape everything to come.

Jasper lifted the bundle and set it on the rug. The cloth parted, revealing the smooth curve of the journal's dark leather cover—and the cold glint of the monocle, its lens faintly fogged with age.

Neither object stirred. Still, Clara felt a faint pressure—like the moment before a storm.

Clara knelt and reached for the journal first, her fingers brushing the edges as if seeking reassurance. The locket pulsed beneath her shirt in response—subtle, but sure. As if confirming this was the right path.

Jasper glanced at the bundled relics as he tightened the cloth.

"If only we had more time... more of a chance to read it ourselves."

Clara's grip on the journal stiffened slightly.

"We'll figure the rest out later. Sadie's what matters now."

He nodded, already pulling the cloth tighter around the relics. The wrap felt ceremonial—like dressing a wound, or preparing a lantern before a long night's walk.

When she stood, Clara slipped the bundle into her satchel, securing the flap tightly. The weight of it settled against her side—not heavy in mass, but in meaning.

They didn't speak for a while.

The rain continued outside. The walls creaked softly.

The corridors of Calendor Keep felt different at night.

Not just darker—but quieter, in the way an audience holds its breath. Each flickering lantern along the stone walls cast long shadows that twitched with every movement. The storm had passed, but the air still carried a hush of tension, like the sky was waiting for something.

Veilborne

Clara and Jasper moved quickly but carefully, their steps echoing in practiced rhythm. The satchel hung at Clara's side, the weight of the relics steady against her hip. They were nearly to the eastern stairwell leading to the outer glade when a voice slipped from the shadows.

"Leaving so soon?"

Clara stopped.

Varek Draven stepped from the archway ahead, flanked by Callum Tren—lean and sharp-eyed—and Maeric Vaughn, who loomed silently beside him. Varek's arms were folded, that infuriating calm curling across his lips.

"No guards. No patrol. Just the two of you sneaking off in the dark?" He clicked his tongue. "Very suspicious."

"Move, Varek," Clara said.

Varek's smile didn't reach his eyes. "You really do think the rules don't apply to you, don't you?"

He stepped forward, his voice low. "Keep walking down this path, Holloway, and sooner or later, even your Aurical friends won't be able to protect you."

He moved again, eyes narrowing. "You never learn, do you?"

Before Clara could react, his hand shot out towards her satchel.

She twisted away, clutching it close.

Varek's calm mask cracked. His eyes flared with something colder—anger, or perhaps something worse.

He raised his arm—not with the measured restraint of a formal duel, but with the reckless force of a strike.

Clara didn't flinch.

The locket at her chest flared—brighter than ever. A sharp burst of golden light exploded between them, followed by a low whomp of pressure that rippled down the corridor like a heartbeat.

Varek was hurled backwards into the stone wall. The impact stole the breath from his lungs.

His two housemates rushed to him but kept their distance from Clara.

Jasper stood frozen beside her, stunned.

But Clara didn't move. She didn't stumble. The force had passed through her this time, not against her. As if, at last, the locket wasn't just protecting her... it was acting through her.

She stood tall, her eyes locked on Varek's as the glow faded, steady and sure.

For the first time, she hadn't been shielded by luck.

She had chosen to stand her ground.

Jasper's breath caught softly beside her.

Her eyes—just for a moment—glimmered with pale silver light. A curl of smoke threaded faintly from her lashes, too subtle for anyone but Jasper to notice.

He said nothing. But his gaze stayed on her, even as Varek struggled to his feet.

Behind them, the corridor was silent—save for the sound of Varek dragging himself upright, stunned and shaken for the first time in recent memory.

His voice followed, low and bitter.

"Just wait until my mother hears about this."

They didn't stop walking until they were deep into the Keep's outer grounds, far from torches, windows, or watchful eyes. The path through the eastern grove was slick with damp leaves, and the scent of moss clung to the mist that still curled between the trees.

Clara moved with purpose, shoulders squared, the relics secured beneath her coat. The locket had gone quiet again, but its presence buzzed faintly against her skin—like it was waiting for what came next.

Veilborne

They walked in silence for a long time, the night cool and heavy around them.

Eventually, Jasper muttered, "What in the Nine was that?"

Clara didn't answer at first. She glanced down at the locket beneath her collar, still warm against her skin.

"It's happened before," she said softly. "Back at Morrowmere. The basement. When—when the Revenants came for me. The locket reacted. Knocked them back. Knocked me back too."

Jasper nodded slowly, absorbing this. "But this time... you didn't get thrown."

She shook her head.

Jasper's voice lowered. "And your eyes. I saw it. That silver glow, and the smoke. I've only ever seen Auricals do that. Eldric, when he's—"

He stopped himself. "What does it mean?"

"I don't know," Clara admitted. "And now's not the time to figure it out."

Jasper exhaled, still a little awed. "Fine. Then where are we going?"

"Fennrick's," Clara said. "He's the only one who'll help. And if anyone knows where Frostmar Rise is—it's him."

"You know," Jasper said quietly, "if only Sadie could've seen that. She would've loved it."

They rounded a bend in the path, mist curling around their boots, the Keep vanishing behind them.

The woods thickened the further they went—tall, moss-covered trees crowding the narrow trail like silent sentinels. The air smelled of pine and damp stone, with the faintest hint of spice wafting on the wind. No torches lined the path now. Just moonlight, patchy through the canopy, and the soft flicker of bioluminescent moths drifting lazily above the undergrowth.

Then, without warning, the forest opened.

A gentle slope gave way to a wide hollow where the trees bowed outward, forming a natural amphitheatre. Nestled into the earth like something that had grown there was Fennrick's home.

It looked as though a root system had decided to become a cottage.

Thick, gnarled branches arched over the roof like a hunched back, sprouting leaves despite the dim chill of night. Stones jutted from the ground in uneven rows, forming walls that pulsed faintly with embedded runes. A chimney, stitched from bark and clay, puffed lazy spirals of pale smoke into the air.

Vines crept up the doorway, blooming with tiny luminous flowers—some blinking softly, others unfurling like they'd just woken.

The windows weren't glass but overlapping panes of coloured crystal, shaped like dragonfly wings. They shimmered faintly with the light inside, casting shifting patterns across the clearing like reflections on water.

Clara paused at the edge of the hollow.

"This is... not what I imagined," she said.

"It's exactly what I imagined," Jasper muttered. "Weird and perfect."

They approached the crooked door, and before they could knock, it creaked open with a groan that sounded almost theatrical.

Fennrick stood there barefoot, wearing a robe stitched from various animal pelts and tea-stained cloth. A feather was stuck in his hair like he'd forgotten it was there.

He blinked at them twice, then leaned on the doorframe.

"Well," he said, sighing deeply. "This can't be good..."

Fennrick stepped aside with a grunt, and Clara and Jasper entered without a word.

The warmth hit immediately—dry and herbal, like old spice cupboards cracked open all at once. The main room was round, with a floor of polished wood that curved like a tree's inner rings. The walls were part stone, part living bark, some of it pulsing faintly with light from embedded glyphs, as if breathing.

Every surface was cluttered, but in a curated, chaotic sort of way.

Teacups rested in bird nests. A coat rack wore a cape made of starlings' feathers. Shelves sagged under the weight of books with titles that rearranged themselves when you weren't looking. Tiny chimes jingled lazily from invisible strings as they walked past, and something beneath the floorboards gave a polite sneeze.

Dried herbs and colourful roots hung upside down from the ceiling, wrapped in string and copper wire. A terrarium glowed inside a hanging cage in the corner—housing what looked suspiciously like a family of beetles playing cards.

The fire already burned low in the hearth, casting greenish-blue flames that threw long shadows across the room and made the angles of the space seem to shift gently with the light.

"Sit. Don't touch anything that hums, glows, or winks at you," he said, bustling toward a squat cabinet shaped like a badger. "Tea?"

"She's gone," Clara said, standing still.

That stopped him.

"Sadie," she added. "They've taken her."

Fennrick's shoulders fell. He didn't turn around straight away. When he did, his usual irreverent expression was gone.

"Who?" he asked.

"We don't know," Jasper said. "We found a note. No name, just a place."

"Frostmar Rise," Clara added. "They want the journal and the monocle in exchange."

Fennrick set the teapot down a little too hard.

"And you're actually considering handing them over?"

Clara nodded grimly. "We don't have a choice."

Jasper added, "Sadie's life comes first. We can't risk waiting. We need to find Frostmar Rise."

Fennrick's jaw tightened. He studied them for a long, silent moment.

"Why have you come to me?"

Clara met his eyes. "We need directions."

The silence between them stretched. The chimes above the hearth gave a quiet flutter.

Fennrick knelt beside a drawer with a beak-shaped handle, rummaging until he pulled out a faded, hand-drawn map. He smoothed it across the table and weighed the corners with a cracked teacup and a lump of amber that glowed faintly.

"Follow the river north," he said. "When the trees thin out and the moss turns brittle with frost, you'll be close. Look for the lilies—pale blue, low to the ground. Their leaves sting if you touch them."

He tapped a crooked curve marked with faint symbols.

"The cliffs'll rise up fast. Wind plays tricks up there. Watch your footing. And be wary—sounds don't always come from where you expect."

Clara leaned in beside him, reading the path. She didn't speak. Neither did Jasper.

Fennrick stood and dusted his hands on his robes. For a long moment, he just watched them—eyes narrowed, like he was seeing something further than the room allowed.

His gaze shifted—scanning them from boots to collar. He grunted, half to himself.

"You're dressed for an evening stroll, not a snowbound ridge."

He vanished into the next room, clattering through shelves and muttering names that may or may not have belonged to objects. When he returned, he was dragging a thick woollen blanket—deep green with silver stitching that shimmered faintly in the firelight.

"Here," he said, dropping it onto the table. "Enchanted weave. Holds heat, resists frost. You'll need it. That place gets bone-biting cold, and the frost creeps in deeper than you'd expect."

Then he turned, rummaged through another cupboard shaped like an owl with missing feathers, and produced a small lantern. It was strange—elegant and mismatched anywhere else but here. The frame looked forged from copper and antler bone, its glass panels etched with swirling symbols that shifted when turned. A pale blue flame flickered inside without fuel.

"This'll help you find what you're looking for," Fennrick said, placing it gently between them. "Don't ask me how. It's a bit temperamental. Listens to the holder—sort of. Attunes to your intent, or your need, or… your nonsense. Hard to tell."

"Like a magical bloodhound?" Jasper asked.

"Like a very moody one," Fennrick replied. "But it glows brighter when you're near what you need most. Just don't lie to it. It hates that."

He turned away once more, this time toward the small iron kettle hanging above the fire.

"One more thing," he said, grabbing a handful of jars from a shelf that looked like it was made from reanimated driftwood.

He began mixing herbs into the kettle with surprising precision—pinches of dried red root, shavings of silver bark, a swirl of honey-thick sap from a glass vial sealed with wax. The mixture hissed faintly when it hit the water, and a heady scent rose—warmth, spice, and something sharp, like wild mint.

"This'll help," he muttered, stirring slowly with a spoon carved from bone. "Courage, warmth, a touch of clarity. Might even settle your stomach, depending on how fast you're planning to run."

Jasper raised a brow. "That's oddly specific."

"So's the trouble you're walking into," Fennrick said.

He poured the mixture into two mismatched mugs—one shaped like a curled-up badger, the other like a tulip trying to yawn.

"Tastes awful. Means it's working."

Clara took hers with both hands, the heat already soaking into her fingers. Jasper eyed his warily, gave it a sniff, and immediately winced.

"To warm feet and colder heads," he said.

Fennrick grinned—half-mad, all sincere.

"To not dying."

He poured the remainder of the mixture into a battered, rune-etched thermos and handed it over without a word. Jasper tucked it into his satchel.

Then, without another sound, Fennrick walked to the door and opened it wide.

Cold air spilled in, carrying frost and pine and the faint howl of wind far off through the trees.

Clara and Jasper stepped out into the dark.

Fennrick didn't call after them. Didn't say goodbye.

He just stood in the doorway, staring after them.

And once they were gone—once the last trace of their footprints blurred into snow—he muttered to himself:

"Heaven help whoever stands in their way."

Chapter 23
The Pale Edge

The forest fell quiet behind them.

As Clara and Jasper pressed deeper into the wilds beyond Calendor's borders, the light seemed to thin, not dim, exactly, but stretch itself too far, like a fire burning low on wood that had long since gone cold. The trees here were older, taller, bent from years of wind, their trunks wrapped in frost-threaded moss and the brittle skeletons of last season's leaves. Every branch was coated in ice so fine it looked like spun glass, and when the wind brushed them, they chimed softly, like a warning.

Snowflakes swirled in the frigid air, gathering in shallow drifts. Each step pressed a quiet crunch into the hardened snow below.

Clara carried the lantern ahead of them, its strange blue flame flickering low inside the rune-etched glass. It pulsed gently in response to her movement. Every time they veered off the path, it dimmed; when they corrected course, the flame brightened again, glowing just enough to cut through the steadily thickening curtain of snow flurries.

Neither of them spoke much.

The silence wasn't awkward, it was heavy with meaning. They were no longer students on an adventure. They were two souls pushing into something ancient, dangerous, and unknown.

Clara's cheeks stung from the cold. She pulled the enchanted blanket tighter around them both, tucking it over their shoulders like a shared cloak. Jasper walked beside her, one hand resting on the strap of the satchel, the other ready at his side.

The wind picked up as the terrain sloped upward. They walked single file for a time, the path narrowing between outcrops of jagged stone. Frost clung to the rocks in swirling patterns, as though the cold itself had tried to etch meaning into them. Clara felt the ground firm beneath her boots, then *crunch*. The frost was thickening.

And then the forest ended.

They emerged at the edge of a steep drop. A chasm yawned open before them, at least twenty feet across, its depths a violent rush of river, half-frozen but not still. The water surged with icy rage, crashing against the stone walls far below, sending up a mist that turned instantly to flurries in the wind.

Clara's breath caught in her throat.

Across the gap, on the other side, a fallen tree stretched from one ledge to the next, its bark slick with ice, its width barely more than a narrow beam. The trunk looked ancient, silvered with age and bleached by weather. Roots still clung to the far side, half-buried in the snow like desperate fingers.

Jasper edged forward, peering over her shoulder at the makeshift bridge. The flame in Clara's lantern pulsed brightly.

"Figures," he muttered. "Would've been too easy otherwise."

Clara stared at the narrow crossing. Her heart thudded. The wind screamed through the chasm like a warning.

"We'll go slow," she said. Her voice came out quieter than intended. "Carefully."

Jasper nodded. "Side by side. Just don't look down."

"I wasn't planning on it," Clara muttered, tightening her grip on the lantern. "Eyes forward. One step at a time."

She hesitated, then nodded again. Together it would be.

They stepped onto the tree.

It flexed beneath their weight, not much, but enough to make her stomach clench. The snow that had settled along the bark offered little traction. She placed each foot carefully, holding the lantern in front of her, its glow shimmering across the slick surface. Jasper moved beside her, steady and slow, his hand just behind her back like a safety tether.

Halfway across, her boot slid.

Veilborne

Clara's foot skated across the bark, her balance tipping back as her arms flailed to catch air that wasn't there. The river roared beneath her. One foot lost, the other slipping, and then,

Jasper caught her.

His arm looped around her waist, anchoring her in place. The blanket nearly dragged them both sideways, but he braced with one knee against the log and held firm.

"Got you," he breathed.

She didn't answer. Just nodded once, hard, and kept moving.

They crossed the rest of the way in silence.

When their boots hit solid snow, both of them sagged, breath visible in thick plumes. Clara hadn't realised she'd been shaking until Jasper placed a hand on her shoulder.

"I don't remember that part on Fennrick's map."

She almost laughed, but it didn't come.

"Remind me to have words with him when we get back."

Clara turned toward the trail ahead.

The snow deepened with every step.

By the time they'd climbed another slope, the world had gone quiet again. Trees stood like frozen statues. The wind whipped in quick bursts, enough to sting the skin and steal sound from the air. The blanket swirled behind them like a cloak. The lantern's flame bobbed in the dark like a star that had gotten lost and decided to follow them instead.

They didn't speak. There was nothing left to say.

Only to walk, and find what waited at the pale edge of the world.

With every step, the snow pressed deeper, clinging to branches, rocks, and the folds of their clothes.

It clung to everything now, branches, rocks, the folds of their clothes. The trees had grown sparse, their gnarled trunks twisted like skeletal fingers clawing toward a pale, clouded sky. Wind cut between them in short, sharp bursts, not constant, but enough to sting every time it came. It hissed through the higher limbs above them, carrying no birdsong, no whispers, only the hollow voice of winter.

Clara held the lantern out in front of her. Its glass glowed more brightly now, the blue flame inside responding with a steady, guiding pulse, as if it knew the path when they did not. Every time they strayed, it dulled. When they turned again toward the direction it seemed to favour, it flared, soft, unwavering.

The cold pressed at the edges of her senses, trying to slip past the warmth clinging to her chest and shoulders. She thought of Fennrick's brew, the one that still pulsed faintly in her veins like a shield. Without it, the cold would have sunk deep into her bones by now, slowing her, numbing her. Jasper, too.

We'd never make it without him, she thought.

The incline grew steeper. No path, no trail, just snow and rock and wind. The blanket wrapped around their shoulders had become their only shield, the wool now crusted with ice. They moved as one beneath its cover, huddled close, Clara leading with the lantern, Jasper steady beside her.

Neither of them spoke. Not when the cold sank into their boots, numbing their toes. Not when the world narrowed to breath and frost and the sound of their own heartbeat in their ears. Words would have fallen flat here, swallowed by the wind or scattered like snowflakes on stone.

The climb led them to a narrow ridge, bare rock veined with frozen moss and glittering frost. Beyond it, the slope levelled out, and a strange hush settled over the air.

Then the trees stopped.

They stood at the edge of something vast.

Veilborne

The ridge curved outward, forming a natural ledge that overlooked what looked, at first, like a valley, but no valley ran this perfect, this still. It was too circular. Too sunken. A basin of land carved from the mountain's bones, rimmed by dark pines like sentries. Snow drifted steadily across the hollow, untouched and smooth, save for one detail:

At its centre, dozens of lanterns hung from wooden poles, tall, slender, and arranged in a precise ring.

The fire in them burned orange.

The warm colour flickered like a living heartbeat in the cold, casting long shadows across the white ground. Around the lantern ring, the trees stood still as statues. No movement. No sign of life. Only wind above, and fire below.

Clara stopped.

The lantern in her hand flared once, brighter than before, then steadied into a calm, unwavering glow.

A knot tightened in her chest, not fear, exactly, but something heavier. A weight of what was coming. Of what she might have to trade.

"We're here," she said quietly.

Jasper nodded. His breath fogged the air in front of him.

"Looks like they're expecting us."

They stood in silence for a long moment, staring down at the hollow below.

Then Clara took the first step forward, down the slope, toward the flame-ringed heart of the Pale Edge.

Chapter 24
The Price of Loyalty

The snow fell softly, cloaking the clearing in a fresh, unbroken layer of white.

Clara and Jasper crested the final slope, hearts pounding, the lanterns below flickering like coals in a bed of frost. The clearing was wide and ringed with ancient trees, their branches hunched beneath the weight of snow.

And at the centre of it all,

Sadie.

Bound at the wrists, arms drawn behind her back, she was kneeling in the snow. Her hair was wind-tossed, her cheeks raw with cold, but her eyes were sharp. Alert. Alive.

And standing over her,

A cloaked figure, dagger in hand.

Clara didn't stop to think.

"Get away from her!"

She surged forward, boots slipping slightly in the snow. The blanket fell from her shoulders, landing silently behind her. The lantern dropped from her hand, its blue flame flickering wildly as it rolled to a stop.

The locket burned against her chest, hot, urgent, awake.

The stranger turned, but too late.

Clara raised her hand, the motion fuelled by instinct and fury. The locket pulsed, brighter than it ever had before.

"Leave her alone!"

A beam of searing gold erupted from her palm, fast and focused, a line of light that struck the figure square in the chest.

Veilborne

They were thrown back with a crack of force, tumbling through the snow and landing in a heap near the edge of the clearing. The dagger skittered off into the dark.

Everything stopped.

Clara stood panting, hand still raised, eyes burning bright gold. Faint tendrils of silver smoke curled from the corners, dissolving into the cold air.

Jasper caught up behind her, breathing hard.

"Clara, !"

But Sadie's voice cut through the silence.

"No!" she cried. "No, don't hurt him!"

Clara blinked.

Sadie was struggling against her bonds, her voice ragged. Her gaze wasn't on Clara, it was on the fallen figure in the snow, who now stirred weakly, groaning.

"Clara, stop, please!"

"That's my father!"

The words slammed into Clara harder than any spell could have.

Her hand dropped. The locket dimmed, flickering once, like it, too, was stunned.

She turned slowly toward the fallen man, his hood now half-slipped, revealing grey-flecked hair, a bruised jaw, and eyes that flickered open with pain.

Jasper came to a halt beside her, staring at the figure in the snow.

"That's her dad?"

His voice pitched higher than usual, edged with shock. The disbelief caught in his throat like a swallowed breath.

Clara didn't answer.

She couldn't.

Sadie was still kneeling, still bound, but her voice had gone quiet. Her eyes hadn't moved from the man groaning in the snow.

Clara's breath turned to mist before her. The cold pressed in. The snow kept falling.

And for a moment, all was still,

The man groaned softly, one arm cradling his ribs as he tried to sit up. His hood had fallen back, revealing grey-streaked hair and a face lined not just with age, but with exhaustion. Clara could see it in his eyes, even from where she stood.

Sadie was already moving.

"Jasper, "

He nodded and moved quickly to her side, whispering a soft incantation. The ropes at her wrists loosened and dropped into the snow.

She didn't hesitate.

She rushed across the clearing and fell to her knees beside the man.

"You're hurt," she said softly, reaching out to steady him.

He managed a faint smile.

"I've been worse."

His breath came shallow, each word edged with pain. He didn't look at Clara right away. He only looked at Sadie, like seeing her up close, alive, free, was the only thing he needed in that moment.

"I didn't think I'd ever get to see you again. Not like this."

Sadie said nothing. She simply held his arm gently and waited.

Then he looked past her, finally meeting Clara's eyes. And in that look was something Clara hadn't expected to see.

Recognition.

Veilborne

Not of her name. Not even of her face.

But of her place in all this.

"I'm sorry," Clara said softly. "I didn't know. I thought you were going to hurt her."

He gave a faint shake of the head, wincing slightly.

"You did what you had to," he said. "I would've done the same."

He drew a shallow breath.

"Everything I did… every lie I let them tell, every errand I ran, it always led to you," he said quietly. "The moment I heard you were here, really here, I knew it was ending."

"Then tell me why," Clara said. Her voice didn't rise. "What has this all been for?"

He looked down at the snow, as if it might offer a gentler answer than the one in his chest.

"They wanted the relics. The journal. The monocle. Pieces of a map no one else could read, not without bloodlines and keys long buried."

"Why?" Jasper asked, stepping closer. "What does it unlock?"

The man didn't speak for a long time.

Then:

"A door."

He met Clara's gaze again.

"Not just into this world, or yours. Into what lies beyond the Veil. Into what was left behind."

His hand trembled faintly.

"I thought I could outsmart them. That maybe if I helped, I could find your mother… bring her back. Or at least know what became of her. But all I did was lose myself."

Sadie's breath hitched. She leaned closer, her hand gripping his now.

"Is she alive?"

He didn't answer.

Just looked away.

Jasper said nothing. Clara's fingers hovered near her satchel, where the relics rested.

And the snow kept falling.

"It's too late now," the man murmured. "They have what they need. Or they will."

"They?" Clara asked.

His expression shifted, guilt tightening behind his eyes.

But before he could answer,

"Such touching loyalty."

The voice sliced through the clearing like a blade drawn from silk.

"And entirely wasted."

The three of them turned as one.

From behind a moss-covered boulder near the edge of the clearing, a figure stepped forward. Snow clung to the hem of their cloak. Their hood remained raised, face veiled in shadow.

But the voice was unmistakable.

"You never were good at following orders," the figure said, cool, calm, and cutting.

Sadie's father flinched.

"No…" Clara whispered.

The figure stepped into the ring of lantern light, slow and certain. Gloved hands reached up and pulled back the hood,

And there she was.

Professor Lirah Valen.

Veilborne

Her dark hair was twisted into a coiled braid. Her expression unreadable. Not gloating, just... certain. The flickering orange light caught the silver threading of her robes as she took a measured step forward.

Clara's stomach twisted.

"Why?" she asked, barely getting the word out.

"Because some truths are too large to stay buried," Lirah said. "And some doors are meant to be opened."

She looked directly at Clara.

"Your presence here confirms everything. The missing key has finally returned."

Sadie's father stirred beside her.

"You said she wouldn't be harmed."

"And she won't," Lirah replied smoothly. "Not if Clara gives me what we came for."

Her gaze shifted.

"The journal. The monocle. Place them on the snow. Now."

Clara's hand hovered near her satchel. The weight of the relics felt heavier than ever.

"Why do you want them?" she asked. "What does this have to do with Sadie? With me?"

Lirah raised an eyebrow, as if mildly amused she had to explain.

"MalVaran," she said.

The name dropped like a stone into silence.

Even the trees seemed to still.

"Or perhaps," she added, "you know him as Nikola Tesla. But that was only his borrowed name."

Jasper stiffened. Clara's breath caught.

Lirah stepped closer, her eyes aglow with something more than firelight.

"You already know he was Emberlain. But what you don't know is what he became. He wasn't born in your world. He was born here, in Eryndor. A prodigy of reliccraft, obsessed with what lay beyond. He uncovered forbidden texts, lost artifacts. And then… he found a way through."

Her voice took on a reverent hush.

"He was the first to cross the Veil willingly. Not by accident. Not by fate. By design."

She paused.

"Only, " her smile thinned ", he miscalculated."

The air grew colder.

"It was supposed to be a moment. A crossing. But instead, it became a prison. A one-way door slammed shut behind him. Stranded in a world with no magic, only machines."

She paced before them now, every step deliberate.

"So he adapted. Took on a name that would let him work unnoticed. Tesla. In your realm, he studied electricity, magnetism, vibration, matter displacement. He laid the foundation for ideas that world still doesn't understand."

"And again, he tried to return. Built machines to bend light, tear holes in space, move men from one point to another in a blink. But the Veil doesn't forgive easily. His second attempt failed, and cast him farther."

Her voice dropped again, as if even the forest should listen.

"World after world. Each attempt left scars, on his mind, his body, his soul. Always close, never quite enough. Until finally, he found one last place. A realm of distortion. And it… changed him."

"He became MalVaran. Not just a man. A force. One who has touched the edge of countless worlds and returned more than mortal."

Veilborne

She turned to Clara fully now.

"And he will come home. With the vessel awakened. With the artifacts in hand. We, his loyal subjects, will see it done."

"Home?" Clara said. "He'll tear the world apart."

"He'll tear many worlds apart," Lirah said, her voice reverent. "And rebuild them as they were always meant to be."

She stepped forward.

"The artifacts. Now."

Clara reached slowly into the satchel, her fingers closing around the two objects that had started all of this. The locket pulsed faintly against her chest, wanting to surge, to protect, but its light was dim, drained from its last discharge. It needed time. Time to recover.

She knelt, placing the journal and monocle gently in the snow between them and Lirah.

Then she stood again and backed away, one step, then two, returning to Sadie's side. Jasper moved with her, hands clenched at his sides, ready but uncertain.

The four of them stood there, facing the one who had betrayed them.

Clara didn't speak.

She wanted to act, to fight, to stop this, but she didn't know how. Not without risking Sadie. Not without making things worse. The feeling gripped her like it had that night in the orphanage. Powerless. Cornered. And she hated it.

Lirah moved forward with slow, deliberate grace, her eyes locked on the relics as though they were long-lost lovers finally returned. She crouched and swept them up, first the monocle, slipping it into a slender silver case at her belt, then the journal, which she cradled with both hands.

She rose, a silhouette of shadows and ambition, and turned her gaze on them.

"You've done well," she said. "None of this could have happened without you."

Her hand lifted.

Magic surged at her fingertips, glyphs blooming like razor-edged blossoms, glowing sickly green and veined with black. Her eyes gleamed the same poisoned green, black smoke curling from their corners like venomous mist. Even the snow trembled, caught in the gravity of what was coming.

She lifted her hand.

Clara's breath caught.

Lirah cast.

A flash of violent green shot toward them,

And then, out of nowhere,

"NO!"

A blur moved across Clara's vision.

Sadie's father, broken, bloodied, threw himself into the path of the spell.

The blast struck him square in the chest.

It knocked him clean off his feet and into the snow. Sadie screamed, dropping to her knees to catch him as he collapsed into her arms.

Smoke curled from the blackened scorch on his coat.

He didn't move.

Lirah advanced, magic building again, cold and merciless.

She raised her hand a second time.

"You've served your purpose," she said. "Now for the loose ends."

The glyphs began to spin faster.

Then,

Veilborne

A thunderous crack split the night.

A blinding surge of golden-white light exploded across the clearing.

Lirah screamed as it struck her, hurling her backwards into the snow. The journal flew from her grip, skidding to a stop between her and Clara.

A portal tore itself open in the air, roaring with heat and wind.

Eldric Ducart stepped through first, his cloak slicing the snow like a blade, eyes burning silver-blue, threads of light still crackling around his hands. The blast had come from him, precise, devastating, and unrelenting.

Beside him came Fennrick Bramble, robes flaring, staff glowing, his wild hair half-singed from the force of travel magic.

He did not look amused.

"All this… to harm children," Fennrick said softly, his staff glowing brighter. "You've lost your way, Lirah."

"You betrayed everything, and everyone, we swore to protect," Eldric added, his voice low and dangerous. "For a madman."

Lirah didn't respond.

She attacked.

What followed wasn't a fight, it was a storm.

****

Spells collided midair, bursting into cascades of light, blue flame, green sigils, bolts of gold and indigo screaming across the clearing. Glyphs flared to life and shattered like glass on impact. Trees bent under the pressure. The snow stopped falling. The world held its breath.

Fennrick's eyes blazed cobalt as he unleashed a column of fire that carved a smoking trench into the ice.

Lirah spun midair, eyes glowing with that noxious green, trailing smoke as she countered with a spiralling bolt of fire that crackled through the trees and obliterated a standing stone.

Eldric stepped forward, summoning shields of radiant silver that bloomed around them like armour, absorbing the next three blasts in brilliant bursts of light.

Magic collided and scattered like meteor trails through the clearing.

It was beautiful. Terrible. Ancient.

And in the middle of it,

The journal lay untouched in the snow.

Clara saw it.

So did Lirah.

Jasper started forward, just an inch, but Fennrick snapped a hand toward him.

"Don't move," he growled. "You're too close."

Clara didn't listen.

She ran.

Her boots slipped on the melting ice, her breath catching in her throat. She reached out, fingers stretched,

Lirah's eyes snapped to her.

Fury ignited.

She spun from Eldric and lunged toward the journal.

Eldric saw it.

"Clara, no!"

He stepped forward,

Paused.

He couldn't risk hitting her.

Veilborne

Neither could Fennrick.

That instant, that single breath, was all Lirah needed.

She dove.

Snatched the journal with one hand, yanked the monocle from its case with the other.

Clara skidded to a halt, teeth clenched in frustration.

Lirah turned toward the edge of the clearing, bleeding, hair half-loosened, eyes blazing with cold fire.

"You'll understand one day," she said, voice shaking but proud. "This is bigger than any of us."

She raised a final glyph, etched in flickering green, veined with dark, corrupted lines.

A seam of emerald light split open in the air behind her, not a portal, but a tear, ripping downwards like a dull blade slicing fabric. The air recoiled.

From within, black tendrils slithered out, thin, twitching coils of shadow that moved as if searching.

They coiled around her arms, her waist, her shoulders, not lifting her, but pulling her backwards into the wound, as though the spell itself were reclaiming one of its own.

Lirah didn't resist.

She looked at Clara one last time, her expression unreadable.

And then she was gone.

Drawn into the tear. Swallowed by the dark.

The tendrils snapped back with a wet hiss,

, And the wound in the world sealed shut behind her.

The snow began to fall again.

Softly. Slowly.

As if it had been waiting.

Behind Clara, Sadie was still kneeling, her father dying in her arms.

Clara turned.

Sadie held him close, arms wrapped around his shoulders, rocking gently as though the motion might somehow hold him here. His breath came in short, shallow bursts, each one a thread fraying in the cold.

Jasper dropped to his knees beside her, quiet, unsure where to put his hands.

Clara crouched down on Sadie's other side. The snow had soaked through their cloaks, but none of them noticed. Not now.

Sadie's father opened his eyes, just barely. Pale blue. Fading.

But they found Sadie's face.

"You look just like her," he whispered.

Sadie's lips parted, trembling.

"My mother?" she asked. "Is she... is she still alive?"

His eyes flickered.

A breath caught in his throat.

"She..."

His voice faltered.

He gave one last, shuddering breath.

Then went still.

Silence followed. Total. Complete.

Sadie leaned forward, pressing her forehead gently to his. Her shoulders curled inward, not sobbing, not yet. Just holding him. As if warmth could keep him here. As if that might change something.

Clara blinked hard, fighting the sting in her eyes.

Veilborne

Jasper stood slowly, brushing snow from his coat with hands that wouldn't stop shaking.

Soft footsteps approached from the trees.

Eldric and Fennrick emerged without urgency, no portal, no flare of magic. Just quiet steps on soft snow.

The wind had died. The storm, sensing the weight of what had passed, had gone still.

The snowfall returned, light, steady, mournful.

A hush settled over the clearing, as though the world itself mourned with them.

Fennrick didn't speak. He crouched near Clara and Jasper, his wild, silvering hair damp from snow, his eyes soft.

He reached into his coat, paused.

Then turned, walking to the edge of the clearing, to where Jasper and Clara had huddled hours earlier.

The blanket they'd shared still lay there, half-buried in frost.

Fennrick picked it up, shook it gently free of snow, and returned.

He knelt beside Sadie.

She didn't look at him.

He didn't ask her to.

Instead, he wrapped the blanket around her shoulders with the kind of care that speaks louder than words.

Sadie trembled once, then stilled.

Jasper moved closer, one hand resting gently on her back.

Clara rose slowly, her eyes burning.

Eldric stood near the treeline, arms crossed, gaze fixed not on them, but on the man lying in the snow. A soldier's silence. A mentor's sorrow. A weight he had carried before, too many times. A weight he would carry again.

None of them spoke.

There was nothing left to say.

The snow kept falling, quiet as breath, slow as memory.

They stood there together, in that clearing carved by truth and sacrifice, until the cold began to bite once more.

And then, at last,

They turned.

And walked into what remained of the night.

Chapter 25
The Weight of What Remains

The gates of Calendor Keep opened without ceremony.

No fanfare. No crowds.

Just footsteps, five slow, weary sets crunching through courtyard snow as dawn cast a pale wash over the ancient stones.

The lamps hadn't been relit. The towers still slept.

Clara walked between Eldric and Fennrick, her cloak torn and dusted with frost, the locket beneath it pulsing faintly against her chest. Beside her, Jasper's boots scuffed the flagstones, eyes down. Sadie trailed behind them, silent, wrapped in the thick woollen blanket. Her face was unreadable.

They didn't speak. Not even to each other.

At first, a few early risers paused as the group passed, students bundled in scarves on their way to lessons, two Lorehall attendants carrying a crate of scrolls.

One whispered, "What happened?"

The other said nothing, but their gaze lingered, wary, uncertain.

But the silence offered no answers.

Only stillness.

And the moment they saw the expression on Eldric's face, or the way Sadie's shoulders curled beneath the blanket, they understood:

Something enormous had happened.

And somehow, it would touch them all.

Clara barely registered them. Her hand hovered at the locket beneath her collar, as if afraid it might vanish… or roar back to life… or do something else she wasn't ready for.

But it didn't.

Its rhythm had slowed to a whisper. A heartbeat, half-remembered.

As they passed under the eastern arch and the shadows of the inner halls swallowed them whole, Clara glanced once over her shoulder.

The snow behind them had already melted, whether from the dawn or something older, she couldn't say.

****

The chamber was warm.

Firelight flickered in the sconces, casting soft gold against the deep stone walls.

Clara stood beside Jasper and Sadie before the curved arc of the Aurical Council table. The wood was ancient, grooved by time, polished by centuries of hands and hard decisions. Behind it sat Master Vaelryn, severe and shadowed by the tall back of her chair. To her right and left, the other Auricals took their places, six in all. Eldric and Fennrick remained standing near the far wall, silent, watching.

No one spoke at first.

Master Vaelryn was the one to break the silence.

Her voice was level, but it landed like iron.

"You left the Keep without leave. You brought ancient artifacts within reach of the very enemy we've long feared. And now, they are gone."

Her gaze swept over the trio, stern, calculating.

Then shifted, just slightly, to Fennrick.

"And we'll need to speak with you as well, Master Bramble."

Fennrick didn't flinch. He said nothing.

Clara stepped forward slowly, fingers tightening at her sides.

"I'm sorry we lost them," she said, voice barely more than a whisper. "I'm sorry. We tried. We did everything we could, but,"

Veilborne

"You are a child," Vaelryn said, gently cutting across the rising guilt in her voice. "And what you've done... no child should have had to do."

It wasn't an accusation.

Clara opened her mouth again, but for once, it was Jasper who stepped forward.

He told them what they needed to hear.

Not everything, but enough.

He spoke of Sadie's kidnapping, of the note left behind, of the desperate pursuit. Clara added details softly, the trek through snow and shadow. The stranger, and who he was in all of this.

Sadie remained silent, until her father was mentioned.

She lifted her head, eyes hollow but steady.

"He died saving us," she said softly. "Whatever came before... that's how it ended."

One of the Auricals, a silver-haired woman in blue-green robes, leaned forward slightly.

"And the artifacts? The journal? The monocle?"

Clara hesitated. Her hands curled into the folds of her robe.

"We lost them," she said. "Lirah escaped with both."

A silence followed. Heavy. Measured.

Clara stared down at the stone floor beneath her boots.

"I'm sorry. We did everything we could."

"And it was more than we had any right to expect," Master Vaelryn said.

She looked up, startled.

"You are still children," she went on, not unkindly. "But children who have stood where many grown Auricals would have fallen. Who faced betrayal and blood… and still returned."

She let the words settle before finishing:

"The artifacts may be gone. But the truth is not. A traitor revealed. A plan unearthed. And proof that the old war never ended."

She looked at each of them in turn, Clara, Jasper, Sadie.

"It only slept."

"This isn't over," Clara said, her voice barely above a whisper. "She has the artifacts. She'll use them."

Vaelryn didn't argue.

She simply said:

"Then we prepare. The vessel has awakened. The old war breathes again."

****

The sky above Calendor Keep had deepened to violet, the stars like pinpricks through velvet. The tower's outer rampart was quiet, wind slipping over stone and heather with the hush of a held breath.

Clara stood at the edge, gloved hands wrapped around the icy stone, her locket beating faintly beneath her coat. One pulse. Then another. Not afraid. Just… watchful.

Footsteps approached behind her. She didn't turn.

Sadie came to stand beside her, arms crossed against the cold. She didn't speak right away, just stared out across the forest, where the shadows were soft and the mountains distant.

A moment later, Jasper joined them, silent, for once.

The three of them stood there without speaking, backs to the Keep, faces to the wild.

Then, at last, a quiet cough.

Veilborne

Fennrick.

"Didn't mean to interrupt," he said, his voice unusually gentle. "Just... forgot something."

He stepped closer, holding something small in his hand. Not glowing. Not enchanted. Just simple and metal and worn.

A ring.

"He dropped it," Fennrick said, offering it to Sadie. "Back in the snow. Figured you ought to have it."

Sadie didn't take it at first.

When she did, it was with both hands. Like it might vanish otherwise.

She turned it over slowly in her fingers. No spellfire. No glyphs. Just a faint etching on the inner band. Her breath caught as she read it.

She didn't cry.

Not here. Not yet.

But she nodded. Just once.

"Thank you," she whispered.

Fennrick gave her a small, crooked smile, then stepped back, as if he knew the rest was theirs.

Clara looked down at her boots.

Jasper watched the stars.

The locket pulsed again at Clara's chest, gentle, like a heartbeat steady in the cold.

For the first time in days, she let her eyes close.

Just for a moment.

****

The dormitory was quiet.

Sadie lay curled beneath her blanket, turned toward the wall. A cup of untouched tea sat cooling by the hearth.

Clara lay beneath her own covers, eyes wide open in the dark. She didn't speak. Didn't move.

Jasper had finally fallen asleep across the room, his breathing even. The faint metallic wheeze of Percival resting on the shelf gave rhythm to the silence.

And then the locket pulsed.

Not a warning.

Not fear.

Just presence.

Clara's eyelids grew heavy.

Then heavier still.

And she fell…

****

The snow was gone.

Instead, endless twilight. A sky suspended in swirling greys and purples. A forest of dead trees reaching upward like hands too long unheld.

The world was silent.

Not still, silent.

At the far end of the glade, a figure stood.

Cloaked. Tall. Unmoving.

The wind bent around him.

She couldn't see his face. Only the sense of wrongness. Of something that had been a man once, and wasn't anymore.

He turned. Not fast. Not slow. Just certain.

And though he had no visible eyes, Clara knew he was looking straight at her.

Veilborne

Something ancient whispered beneath the wind:

"She's awake."

Clara tried to speak, but her voice had vanished.

Then another voice, soft, fierce, and familiar. A woman's voice, coming from within the locket.

"Clara, you need to move. He knows who you are now. Listen to your mother, run!"

She gasped, and sat up in bed, breath sharp in her chest.

The fire had long since died to embers.

Outside the window, the stars burned a little colder.

Clara clutched the locket at her throat, pulse thudding beneath her fingertips.

And all she could think was:

He's coming.

THE END

Mark Peters

About the Author

Mark Peters grew up in the quiet town of Boonah, Queensland, and now lives in Ipswich, where he balances writing with day-to-day life and a head full of stories. A lifelong lover of fantasy, his creative spark was first lit by the pages of The Lord of the Rings, the eerie pull of Stephen King novels, and countless Dungeons & Dragons rulebooks and novels.

Though Veilborne is his debut novel, Mark has long been drawn to coming-of-age tales like Harry Potter and Percy Jackson-stories where ordinary kids uncover extraordinary destinies. With The Holloway Chronicles, he set out to craft a fantasy adventure with heart, mystery, and a strong female lead at its center.

When not writing, Mark dreams up future stories-ranging from post-apocalyptic survival to full-blown horror -and hopes to one day write full time. He's currently at work on the next installment of Clara Holloway's journey, with plans for a multi-book arc that grows alongside its characters.

www.ingramcontent.com/pod-product-compliance
Lightning Source LLC
Chambersburg PA
CBHW052009070526
44584CB00016B/1673